A FAMOUS INDIAN REGIMENT THE KALI PANCHWIN

A FAMOUS INDIAN REGIMENT THE KALI PANCHWIN

REGINALD HENNELL

GYAN

Published by

Gyan Publishing House
5, Ansari Road
Daryaganj, New Delhi-110002
Phone: 011-47034999, 9811692060
E-mail: books@gyanbooks.com

Distribution Network
gyanbooks.com
India, USA, Canada, UK, Australia

ISBN: 978-93-7447-528-7 (PB)

First Published, 1927

2nd Impression 2026

Printed at: Gyan Press, Delhi.

A FAMOUS INDIAN REGIMENT THE KALI PANCHWIN
Author: REGINALD HENNELL

A FAMOUS INDIAN REGIMENT

THE KALI PANCHWIN

[*Dickinson*

COLONEL SIR REGINALD HENNELL, C.V.O., D.S.O., O.B.E., IN HIS UNIFORM AS LIEUTENANT OF THE KING'S BODY GUARD OF THE YEOMEN OF THE GUARD.

[Frontispiece

A FAMOUS INDIAN REGIMENT

THE KALI PANCHWIN

2/5TH [FORMERLY THE 105TH] MAHRATTA LIGHT INFANTRY

1768—1923

BY THE LATE
COLONEL SIR REGINALD HENNELL
C.V.O., D.S.O., O.B.E.

PREPARED FOR PRESS BY HIS SISTER-IN-LAW
MARY C. HENNELL

LONDON
JOHN MURRAY, ALBEMARLE STREET, W.
1927

DEDICATED

BY GRACIOUS PERMISSION

TO

H.R.H. THE DUKE OF CONNAUGHT, K.G.

FOREWORD

I HAVE long contemplated writing the history of this, my old Regiment—one of the oldest and most distinguished Corps in our glorious Indian Army, which, recruited from the martial races of India, have helped to win for us our great Asian Empire, so well called "The Star of the East."

For many years I have been collecting materials for this story, and therefore readily and gladly acceded to the wish of the past and present officers that I should complete it, so that it may be a permanent record of the Regiment for all those who have served, are still serving, and, more than all, for those who will serve in it in the future that they may be justly proud of their Regiment.

The writing of this story has been a labour of love, more than amply repaid by the gracious permission of H.R.H. the Duke of Connaught that it should be dedicated to him.

I should like to add how much I have appreciated the help I have received from the commanding and other officers who have placed at my disposal their letters and diaries bearing on the part taken by the Regiment in the late Great War, and especially to Major Houghton, who has devoted much time out of his furlough at home, in assisting me to arrange the latter.

I wish also to thank Colonel Delmé Radcliffe for permitting me to give some of his letters in full with their very interesting accounts and plans of certain operations in Mesopotamia and Palestine.

REGINALD HENNELL,

Colonel.

THE KALI PANCHWIN

(Black Fifth)

THE 2ND BATTALION 5TH MAHRATTA LIGHT INFANTRY REGIMENT

Raised in 1768 with the 2nd Battalion of Bombay Sepoys.

Became in—

1788 The 5th Battalion Bombay Sepoys.
1796 The 2nd/1st Regiment Bombay Native Infantry.
1798 The 1st Battalion, 3rd Regiment, of Bombay Native Infantry.
1824 The 5th Regiment Bombay Native Infantry.
1841 The 5th Regiment Bombay Native Light Infantry.
1885 The 5th Regiment Bombay Light Infantry.
1901 The 5th Bombay Light Infantry.
1903 The 105th Mahratta Light Infantry.
1922 The 2nd Battalion 5th Mahratta Light Infantry.

CONTENTS

APPENDICES

LIST OF ILLUSTRATIONS

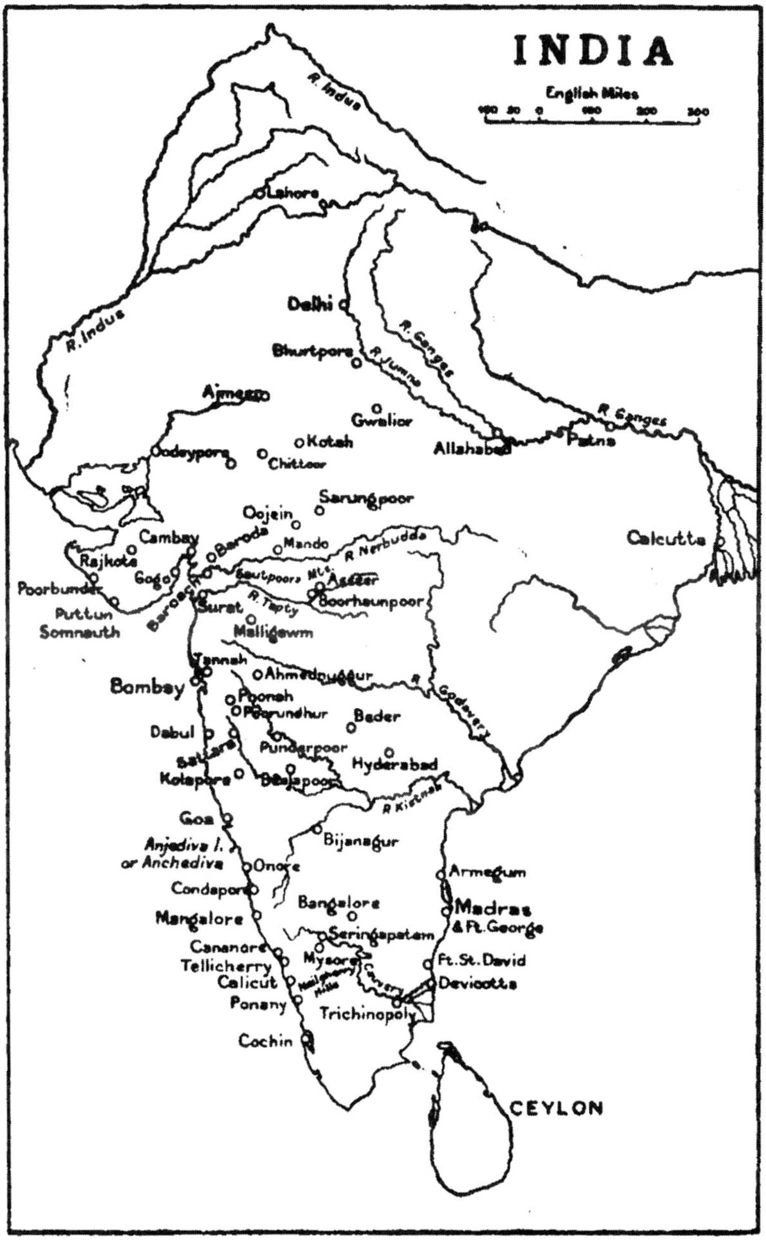
INDIA
English Miles
R. Indus
Lahore
R. Indus
Delhi
R. Ganges
Bhurtpore
R. Jumna
Gwalior
Kotah
Oodeypore
Chittoor
Allahabad
R. Ganges
Patna
Sarungpoor
Oojein
Calcutta
Cambay
Baroda
Mando
R. Nerbudda
Rajkote
Gogo
Sautpoora Mts.
Poorbunder
Baroach
Surat
R. Tapty
Boorhaunpoor
Puttun Somnauth
Tannah
Bombay
R. Godavery
Poonah
Poorundhur
Bader
Dabul
Sattara
Punderpoor
Hyderabad
Kolapore
R. Kistnah
Goa
Bijanagur
Anjediva I. or Anchediva
Onore
Armegum
Condapore
Bangalore
Madras & Ft. George
Mangalore
Seringapatam
Cananore
Mysore
Ft. St. David
Tellicherry
Calicut
Cavery
Devicotta
Ponany
Trichinopoly
Cochin
CEYLON

A FAMOUS INDIAN REGIMENT

THE KALI PANCHWIN

CHAPTER I

INDIAN RACES AND CASTES

THE vast continent of India has been, from earliest times, the envy of the nations beyond its borders. For three thousand years, at least, it has not only suffered invasion after invasion, from the north and west (rarely from the east), but has been the scene of perpetual internal warfare, King against King, race against race, tribe against tribe, religious fanaticism as well as plunder being the mainsprings of the strife, until at last it rests in peace and security under the beneficent rule of our King-Emperor George V and his Counsellors.

As Belgium has always been the cockpit of Europe, so India has been the cockpit of Asia. Other dynasties have ruled for longer periods than that of Great Britain, but not one of them has been able to confer so many benefits on the inhabitants in so short a time. None have rested on so secure a foundation, because they lacked "Command of the Sea."

A wonderful story it would make, with all its romantic tales of stirring adventure, perpetual warfare and intrigue, covering a period of thirty centuries, if we had time and space to tell it in full. But we can only give a bare outline of it, just sufficient to enable our readers to grasp our own part in its history.

Hindostan, or India, as it is more generally called,

means the Land of the Hindoos, and it is to this great race, a congeries of nations indeed, numbering at the present time nearly three hundred millions of our Indian fellow-subjects, that we owe the earliest written records of this vast peninsula.

The Hindoos were the first to open up the country. Coming from the north-west, and founding colonies as they pushed on, they gradually drove the original inhabitants before them into the mountain fastnesses. These—like the ancient "Bheels," are still to be found living their simple life, with their own primitive beliefs and languages, amongst the hills and forests of the inland districts. The Hindoos brought with them their ancient religion, with its four distinct divisions or castes, i.e.:

1. The highest and most powerful—the Brahmin, or Priestly Caste.
2. The second, and rival—the Kshatriya, or Military Caste.
3. The third—the Vaisya, or Merchant Caste.
4. The fourth—the Sudra, or Cultivator Caste.

Their religion gave them rules for living, based upon a wonderful set of laws which dealt with every phase and detail of human life. There is no other such code, detailing how a human being, male or female, should live from minute to minute, asleep or awake, as the "Laws of Manu."

We learn from them that India is the original home of the Races of the Sun and Moon, and they tell us that these two great Royal Races were in constant warfare with one another. The Brahmins espoused the cause of the Kings of the Sun, and the Kshatriya sided with the Kings of the Moon. We are given a wonderful description of these wars in that renowned epic poem, the *Mahâ-Bhârata*. If further proof of the existence of these myths relating to the Kings of the Sun and Moon, and of the Serpent Race, were needed, it has lately come to light in the recent discoveries in Mesopotamia, where the ancient city of Ur of the Chaldæans has been discovered, and monuments have been found bearing the names of the Kings of the Sun and Moon, and the insignia of the Serpent, as worshipped in the days of Nebuchadnezzar.

These mythical tribes have their survivors at the present day. The Brahmins still retain much of their old power, and those renowned soldiers, the Rajputs, of the important Province of Rajputana in Central India, claim to be direct descendants of the Kshatriya or military caste. Amongst these, we must ever hold in esteemed remembrance that grand old Rajput warrior, the Maharaja Sir Pertab Singh Bahadur, who old as he was, served as a Major-General in the British Army in the late Great War, his chief ambition being to lead into action the 34th Poona Horse, of which he was Honorary Colonel.

It may be centuries, it may be thousands of years ago—for, in the old accounts handed down to us, kings reigned thousands of years, and periods of time ran into hundreds of thousands of years—that the invasion of the Scythians, called "Takshuk," or Serpent Race, took place. They too came from the north—probably from what is known as Siberia—but of them and their conquests we know little or nothing, save that they also became absorbed in the inhabitants of India. The 4th Caste, the "Sudras," may be the descendants of the original inhabitants of India before the Aryan invasions, and were therefore treated by their conquerors as a servile race, and not entitled to be included amongst the *twice born* as the Brahmins, Kshatriya, and Vaisya were designated, and so named in the Books of the Laws of Manu. The designation "twice born" entitled them to wear the mysterious Holy Thread.

The mass of the population of the present day whom the Brahmins still call *pariahs*, or outcastes, are the descendants of the menials of the land when the Sudras were the masters.

CHAPTER II

THE LURE OF THE EAST

WITH the advent of Darius, King of Persia, we have before us the first trustworthy record of the many invasions of India from the north-west, and as this story develops we shall see how most of the great historical characters, in their ambitious projects of world conquest, have been dominated by the "lure of the East." Of this we have in Darius the first striking example, for though his main campaigns were towards the west, against the Greeks, he was not content with these conquests, but turned to the east to replenish his coffers with the riches of India. Darius, however, was to lose all when Alexander the Great, King of Macedonia, appeared on the scene.

What was the position, politically and geographically, when Alexander came to the throne?

It was no less than a struggle to the death between the Macedonians and the Persians for the dominion of the world. The contest had lasted for more than two centuries, from the rise of the Persian Empire under Cyrus, who overran Mesopotamia, Asia Minor, and Egypt, and even penetrated into Macedonia itself, to the final defeat of the Persians at the decisive battles of Marathon and Salamis. Beaten back, as we are told by Xenophon, in his story of the "Retreat of the Ten Thousand," almost to their own country, another century passed before the Persians, under Darius III, recommenced the great struggle with Philip of Macedon. Before his tragic death, Philip confided to his son Alexander all his schemes for the conquest of Asia, and imbued him with his own enthusiasm in their preparation.

Historians affirm, and the opinion is still maintained, that Alexander was the greatest soldier that ever lived, and that the invasion of India from Macedonia was one of the most marvellous military exploits the world has ever known. When we come to consider that Alexander was only twenty years of age when he succeeded his father Philip of Macedon, and took upon himself the avenging of his assassination, and the carrying out of the contemplated campaign against the Persians, as a preliminary to the conquest of India, we realise how wonderful was the undertaking so undauntedly faced by this youthful monarch. The task before him was gigantic, we may almost say unparalleled.

The route he took can be traced at the present day, not only by the cities he built, to which he gave his name, but also by the many well-known sites of his battles, on some of which the crumbling remains of monuments are still to be seen.

In order to understand the exact line of route that Alexander followed in his march, we must explain, in as few words as possible, that, his first object being to crush his father's enemies to the north of Macedon, he proceeded at once to march against them, crossed the Danube, and, after somewhat severe fighting, finally crushed them, thus securing his base at home. He then cleared his front, by suppressing the rebellious Greeks in Thessaly, who had taken advantage of his absence to rise against Macedonian rule. This accomplished, he marched to the Hellespont, embarked his army, and crossed into Asia Minor.

The whole of Asia Minor was at this time dominated by Persian rule, though nearly all the coast towns, and many of the inland cities as well, were in reality Greek Colonies, with Greek garrisons, under the control of Persian Governors. In fact the Persian Army was mainly composed of Greek mercenaries.

The moment Alexander set foot in Asia Minor he learnt that the Persian Army was awaiting him at Zeleia, prepared to bar his progress east. Zeleia lay on his direct route. Obviously he might have struck a blow at once, which would have cleared his path, but here comes in that masterly caution which he had shown on his father's death, in securing his base before setting out on his great expedition. Realising that the Persians, with their Greek mercenaries, hoped to entice him away from the coast, he determined to balk them. Instead of advancing to the attack, he halted, gathered supplies and recruits from the Greek Colonies long established on the southern coast, who were yearning to be freed from the Persian yoke, and thereby placed himself on a more equal footing with his formidable foe.

What was the result? The Persian Governors, against the advice of the Greek Memnon, the Commander-in-Chief, left their strong position at Zeleia and advanced to the River Granicus, on the farther side of which Alexander's force was drawn up. With a fiery daring, the historian tells us, Alexander threw his Macedonian Cavalry across the river, and, at their head, took the Persians in the rear. Darius, and the Persian Army with him, fled in confusion.

Why, it may be asked, did not Alexander pursue and complete the destruction of his foe? Why did he turn south as he did? Because he wished first to free the whole of the Greek Colonies on the coast from the dominion of the Persians.

This was part of the plan his father left him to carry out, and which he so successfully accomplished. First he marched south-east, through Lydia, and took Sardia (modern Alas Beha), its capital, which had risen into importance as the starting-point of Cyrus in his invasion of Macedonia. Then he turned back to the coast and marched down, taking Miletus and Halicarnassus. Gathering supplies and recruits from these colonies, he pursued his way to the coast with added prestige. On reaching Phaselis in the ancient province of Lycia (modern Ciladelh, near Adalia), he felt strong enough to move into the interior and consolidate his power. Turning north, he marched to Gordium, an important city in Asia Minor in these days, near the present town of Bebazar, where he struck the main line of his projected advance, on one of the great trade routes still existing. There he spent the winter, reorganising and increasing his army for the spring campaign. His first advance was to Aneyra, the modern Angora, now the Turkish Military and Political Head-quarters, and present terminus of a branch line of the Bagdad Railway. Thence he struck south, following the left bank of the great Kizil or Red River, which flows into the Gulf of Sinope on the Black Sea, to Mazaca (modern Kaisareyeh) between the mountain range and the little lake Tatta (modern Tozla).

From Mazaca, Alexander made for Tyana (modern Nigdeh) at the foot of the great Taurus range and at the mouth of the Cilician Gates, the celebrated Pass leading directly to the valley and plains of Ardana and the southern coast of Asia Minor. It was through these Gates that Alexander entered Cilicia. The Taurus range has proved to be one of the engineering obstacles on the Bagdad Railway. It has lately been tunnelled, but until the tunnel was finished the Cilician Gates or Pass had to be used for all traffic. It was here that Alexander struck the route of the present railway at or near the town of Adana. But instead of turning east at once, he followed the main route to the coast and reached Tarsus the capital, the Persian garrison evacuating it on his approach. Note again, that Alexander would never advance until his rear was cleared of his enemy, and he always kept near the seaboard as long as possible. In the descriptions of these marches we recognise the names of several towns of the present day.

At Tarsus, news reached him that his enemy Darius was encamped at Sochi on the far side of the Arnemus Mountains which divide Cilicia from Syria, the next obstacle in his route, and he at once marched along the coast through Issicus on the Gulf of Issicus—now known as Alexandretta—to meet him. Through the range are two Passes, one known as the Syrian Gates to the south, and the other the Armenian Gate to the north. Alexander chose the southern coast Pass, and was advancing through it when he found that Darius had himself advanced by the northern Pass to take him in rear. There was nothing for it but to double back. Again Darius committed the same fault as at the Granicus, leaving a well-chosen position where his vast armies could be advantageously deployed, for a narrow front where this was impossible. The two Emperors met on the River Pinarus (modern Jehun) just south of Issus, and with the same result. Darius was overwhelmed by Alexander, and fled in confusion, leaving the whole of his camp and family, troops and supplies, in the hands of the Macedonians.

Once again Alexander permitted his foe to escape. Instead of pursuing him, he turned south to conquer Syria and Phœnicia, and marched along the coast of Tyre (Sidonia) between the modern towns of Beyrout and Acre, down to Gaza, where he halted to prepare for his invasion of Egypt to free it also from Persian dominion.

All being ready, he marched to Memphis on the

western bank of the Nile, and following the river up to its mouth, he founded in honour of his conquest the city and seaport of Alexandria, which preserves his memory to the present day.

Being reinforced by the Greek colonists there, he marched through Syria, crossed the Euphrates at Thapsacus, traversed Mesopotamia, crossed the Tigris and again defeated Darius on the plain of Sangamad, fifty miles from Arbela (present Erbel), and advanced on Babylon, Susa, and Persepolis. The following year (330 B.C.) he turned north-west to Ecbatana, Media, and pursued Darius through Parthia, crossed the Oxus and Jaxartes, and laid siege to Maracanda in Sogdiana. Thence on to Scythia and Bactria. It was in Sogdiana that Alexander found his beautiful Eastern bride Roxana, the daughter of one of the principal chieftains. Drawn by the attractions of these countries of Turkestan, which were in a high state of culture and advanced in all the arts, Alexander and his army rested there for some months before going on to invade India. This also enabled him to cross the mountain passes of Afghanistan, after the winter snows were over.

On approaching the Indian Frontier, Alexander found his advance contested by Porus, the powerful Hindoo reigning monarch of Northern India; but crossing the Indus at Attock, he immediately attacked his foe, who had taken up a strong position commanding the River Hydaspes (modern Jhelum). Staunch as was the resistance Porus offered, Alexander defeated and scattered his army and took him prisoner. It is pleasant to read that when Porus surrendered, Alexander received him as an honoured guest, and when he left India, restored all his territory to his late antagonist and placed him again upon his throne, truly proving himself a generous foe and an example to all conquerors.

Continuing his advance, Alexander next took Sangla (modern Lahore). Here, however, owing to sickness and other causes, chief amongst them being that a large portion of his army had tired of their long marches and lengthy absence from their distant homes, Alexander decided to abandon for a time the further conquest of India, and turned his steps homeward. It was destined that he should never see his country again, for he died on the way back, at Babylon, at the early age of 32, leaving a son by his Eastern wife to succeed him and thus perpetuate the memory of his link with the East.

The unbroken success that had attended him throughout his glorious victories is rendered the more astounding when we grasp the fact that the conquest of all the countries lying between Greece and China was accomplished in the brief space of thirteen years—a wonderful achievement when we remember the difficulties of moving and provisioning a large army in those days, and take into account that the march was mostly through unknown lands, fraught with numerous obstacles and untried hazards. We must indeed be profoundly impressed with the extraordinary genius, personal bravery, and unbending will which rank this youthful leader amongst the great conquerors of the world.

A striking fact in his march for the invasion of India is that his route—except when it was diverted to Egypt, and later to the north, across the Jaxartes into the land of the Scythians (Siberia)—followed generally, in its most important features, the line of the present Bagdad Railway. It is therefore interesting to note that, after more than two thousand years, the project of the invasion of India by the ex-German Emperor would, if carried out, have been designed to follow the selfsame route as that taken by Alexander the Great. The lure of the East that first attracted Alexander, drew many imitators to follow in his steps: notably the insatiable conqueror Napoleon, in 1799; and lastly, the German Emperor William III. Both attempted to rival Alexander's successes, and failed—the last ignominiously. Napoleon never got beyond Egypt, and the Kaiser did not get farther than the Danube.

CHAPTER III

MAHOMEDAN INVASION

Though, after this, India was free from foreign invasion for nearly a thousand years, it was torn by continual internecine strife, the rival Hindoo kings and chieftains spending their lives in fighting one another. And then arose that mighty Turko-Arabian Power which was to press forward from the north with religious fanaticism, not only to dominate India for seven centuries, but to carry with fire and sword its growing strength through Arabia, Asia Minor, Africa, and Europe, even up to the gates of Vienna. It was in 1666 that the tide of Mahomedan invasion reached its most western point. Thence it began to ebb. The rise and spread of Mahomedanism is a truly wonderful story, only to be briefly referred to here, on account of its immense bearing upon the subsequent history of India, political, social, and religious. A slight account of its early growth may help the reader more fully to understand this little story of an Indian regiment. The Mahomedan religion, which was to rival and for a time retard the growth of Christianity, is now held by one-twelfth of the population of the world, and at least one-fifth of the people of India.

Mahomed, its founder, was born at Mecca in Arabia in A.D. 569, and at the age of 40 declared himself a prophet commissioned by God to convert the human race to the "True Faith," and if necessary, by the agency of the sword.

Having by his genius and the force of his eloquence gained many proselytes in his native land of Arabia, he raised an army of Arabs to subjugate the surrounding natives to his power and creed, and commenced that career of conquest which was pursued by his successors with unexampled vigour and rapidity. Province after province, kingdom after kingdom, submitted to his and their arms, and within the brief space of half a century they had converted or shaken the political and religious institutions of almost the entire Eastern world.

From the birth of Mahomedanism its votaries were animated by one great absorbing resolution, to establish by force of arms—peaceful means failing—a universal monarchy, under which there should be ONE Law, civil and religious, ONE People, ONE religion or creed. Every Mussulman or Mahomedan (these terms are identical, the former derived from "Islam," the creed of the Prophet, and the latter from his name) was promised that if he fell in any "jehad," or holy war, against an enemy of any other religion, he would enter into Paradise and enjoy the society of "Black-eyed Houris." This teaching holds good even now. It was not to be expected when "the Faithful," as they designated themselves, had conquered Africa and Spain, crushed the Persian Empire, and looked on all these as their own, that the rich provinces of India, which had so often been the prey of previous conquerors, should long escape their notice. The Caliphs who succeeded Mahomed, advancing from Bagdad down the Persian Gulf, struck the province of Scinde, on the north-west of India, and penetrated as far as the Ganges, and also in other directions. But these were, in a way, minor operations. The first serious invasion of India by the Mahomedans took place in A.D. 1000, under their well-known Mahomed of Guzni, one of the chieftains of Afghanistan.

For two centuries the struggle went on, until, under the sovereignty of the great Mahomed Ghori, Mahomedan supremacy was firmly established, with Delhi as its capital.

In 1219 another renowned historical figure, Jenghis Khan, stepped on to the stage of Central Asia. He was the real founder of the Mogul Empire in India, with its long list of Emperors at Delhi, who reigned from the thirteenth century until the Mogul Empire was finally broken and became extinct as the result of the suppression of the "Indian Mutiny" in 1857. Of these Emperors, the best known are: Tamarlane, who sacked Delhi in 1398; Baber, 1526; Akbar, the most enlightened of them all, 1567; Jehangeer, 1605; and Shah Jehan, 1627.

It was during the sway of the Mogul dynasty that the West came into more direct touch with the East. India had long been reached only by the land route, and it was not till Vasco da Gama made his famed voyage round the Cape of Good Hope (then known as the Cape of Storms), in 1497, that a sea route was discovered, and trade by water between Europe and Asia made possible. It is curious that so little was known of the world at this period, that Christopher Columbus, when deputed by the King of Spain to discover a sea route to India, sailed to the west, and it was on this voyage that he discovered America. King John of Portugal, who was vexed that he had not listened to Columbus and given him permission for this voyage of discovery, realising that the sea route to India must lie to the east, entrusted Vasco da Gama with the command of an expedition which was to sail by way of the Cape of Good Hope, already discovered by Bartholomew Diaz. Thus it came about that the Portuguese established direct sea communication with India and began to found trading ports on the Malabar and western coast of the Indian Peninsula. One of these, Goa, which Albuquerque, the Portuguese Viceroy and Admiral, built and fortified in 1511, as the capital of the Portuguese dominion in India, they hold to the present day. Calicut was the first port which Vasco da Gama reached on his voyage in 1498.

For nearly a century the Portuguese held in their hands the bulk of the sea trade to the East, for it was not till 1584 that any real attempt was made by the English to contest their supremacy. Fitch and other English merchant adventurers, who had penetrated to India by the old-established land route through Aleppo and Bagdad, brought back such glowing accounts of the wealth of the country, that during the reign of Queen Elizabeth the first East India Company was formed in 1600, and granted a charter to trade with India, with special privileges for fifteen years. To obtain confirmations and extension of these privileges which were about to expire, King James I despatched Sir Thomas Roe as Ambassador to the Emperor Jehangeer at Delhi in 1615.

We have now reached a date when the real history of British India may be said to commence, and we can start on the story of the "Kali Panchwin," the "Black Fifth," now the 2/5th Mahratta Light Infantry Regiment.

Like its partial namesake, the distinguished Scots Regiment, "The Black Watch," the Indian Regiment was in times past, and is still, more familiarly known by its nickname, the "Kali Panchwin," or the "Black Fifth." It is not certain how or when it first came by the name. It is supposed that in some campaign the native Regiment was brigaded with the English Regiment of the same number as itself, and was dubbed *black* fifth to distinguish it from "Ghori Panchwin," or *white* fifth. Some think that the name arose from the black leather facings on the uniform. Anyway, the "Kali Panchwin" is the familiar name by which the Regiment is known throughout its large recruiting area—practically the whole of the Deccan.

CHAPTER IV

SIVAJI

The Mahrattas were a warlike race who inhabited—as they still do—the mountainous districts north and south of Bombay. At the end of the sixteenth century they were coming greatly into prominence and steadily gaining influence.

The word Mahratta comes from two words, Maha Ratcha, meaning the Great Kingdom. Their territory was in fact a very extensive one, extending both inland and along the coast below and above Bombay.[1] The main portion of this extensive kingdom had for some time been ruled over by two rival kings. Bijapur held sway in the south, and Ahmednagar in the north. They were in perpetual strife one against the other and continually called for levies of men from the mountains to fight for them. The Mahratta Chiefs, whilst continuing to give assistance first to one ruler and then to the other, whichever bid the higher price, chafed against this servile position in a land which they claimed as their own. Why should they serve? they argued. Why should they not rather unite to select a leader of their own and proclaim him King over their country? This movement for political as well as military power first began in earnest under the guidance of a man named Malik Umbur, but at the time when our first British

[1] The proper limits of the Mahratta country were from the Satpura Mountains on the north, to Goa on south, Indian Ocean on west, and a line drawn through Goa, Bidar Chanda (on the River Warda), Nagpur, and the Nerbudda River gave the eastern boundary.

Ambassador landed at Surat, in 1615, Maloji Bhoslay, a powerful Mahratta Captain of Horse in the employ of Ahmednagar, was the leading spirit of this revolt.

It was the Mahratta Captain's son, Shahji, who finally carried out the latest design of welding together the elements of strength amongst the Mahratta races, to establish an independent Hindoo sovereignty. It remained, however, for his son, the renowned Sivaji, to crown his father's work and found the Mahratta Empire with which our history of the Regiment is bound up.

Sivaji was born in 1627, and was sent by his father to be educated at Poona. Whilst submitting to the religious teachings of his tutor and imbibing a profound veneration for his Brahminical tenets, Sivaji had no love of study. His heart was ever in outdoor pursuits. To these he turned whenever he could, and he became an expert in the use of the weapons of his nation, the bow and the sword. At the age of 16 he threw off all parental control and gathered around him youths of wild and lawless habits. With these boon companions he engaged in hunting and marauding expeditions, revelling in this exciting life of adventure which made him familiar with all the paths and defiles of the land of his birth. His father's death suddenly placed in his hands the means of further fostering this adventurous and warlike spirit. Sivaji utilised the treasure he inherited, by organising his followers into a fighting force. So strong was this, that, under his personal leadership, it was able to wrest a large slice of territory from the King of Bijapur.

Elated by this success, he secured the services of a considerable body of Mahomedan Cavalry which the King had foolishly dismissed. This became the nucleus of the Mahratta Light Cavalry which later on developed into the scourge of the surrounding country, eventually proving to be the most powerful factor in the spread of Mahratta power.

By the time Sivaji had reached his thirtieth year, his army had grown to 50,000 foot and 7,000 horse, a force out of all proportion to the territory he had conquered. This merely amounted to about 130 miles in length and 100 miles in breadth, including a valuable stretch of coast line, but he then proceeded to carry out a series of expeditions to extend these territories in every direction. Before long he began to build and organise a fleet, and by 1665 he had got one together consisting of 88 vessels. With this little fleet he set sail and laid siege to Bandore on the Malabar coast. Having taken it, he inflicted a heavy levy on some wealthy Mahomedan pilgrims assembled there *en route* to Mecca. This was the first and last sea voyage Sivaji took, for on his way back he was so violently sea-sick that his spiritual guides assured him that it was a punishment by the gods for his treatment of the pilgrims. This argument is readily understood, for up to only fifty years ago the Brahmins considered that anyone of their faith who crossed the seas, which they called the *Kala Pani*, i.e. *black water*, became an outcast, only to be readmitted after a long series of purifications.

Aurangzeb, the then reigning Mogul Emperor, was so enraged at these unprovoked attacks on his pilgrims, that he sent a large force to chastise Sivaji on his return. Realising that he was not in a position to resist, Sivaji at once submitted and placed the whole of his army at the Emperor's disposal, a submission the Emperor was only too glad to accept. Thus was a formidable enemy turned into an apparently zealous adherent. This friendship, however, did not last long. We read that for the next ten years there was continual warfare between the Mahomedans and the Mahrattas, until, at the climax of his successes, Sivaji announced his independence and assumed the insignia of Royalty.

After many and prolonged religious ceremonies, the Brahmins fixed on June 6th, 1674, as an auspicious day for Sivaji to be enthroned at Rajgadh. He then proclaimed himself "Rajah of the Mahrattas of Northern India," "Satrap of Ancient Persia," "Lord of the Royal Umbrella," etc. In accordance with oriental custom, he was weighed against gold, and the amount was distributed amongst the Brahmins who had placed him on the throne.

These ceremonies being over, Sivaji at once recommenced his expeditions north and south, capturing ports and cities as far as Madras on the far eastern coast, defying all attempts to stop his progress. But Sivaji's career was cut short by his sudden death on April 5th, 1680, and the expansion of the Mahratta power was checked for a time, as his son proved a weak and dissolute ruler, incapable of any action.

Sivaji had, however, laid the foundation of Mahratta power so firmly that even his son's weakness could not shake it.

Just as historians have pronounced Alexander to be the greatest of the world's soldiers, so do they distinguish Sivaji as the greatest and most striking figure in Indian history, greater even than Runjeet Singh, "The Lion of the Punjab." Both were adventurers. Both began life as such, and ended as mighty sovereigns. Sivaji's greatest foe, the Emperor Aurangzeb, who had held him in contempt during his life, said of him on hearing of his death, "Sivaji was a great chieftain, and the only one who has raised a new and powerful Hindoo Kingdom. Whilst I have been endeavouring to destroy the last of these, and my armies have been engaged in fighting him for nineteen years, his Kingdom and power have never ceased growing."

3

And so the contest went on for a hundred years, until it became the question which power was to predominate throughout India—Hindoo or Mahomedan? This was solved by a trial of strength for the supremacy on the field of "Panipat," January 7th, 1761, when Sadasnes Bhao, with a combined Mahratta army, which included 55,000 horse, and 300 guns, was utterly defeated by the Mogul Emperor Ahmed Shah, with a smaller but more highly disciplined force, which comprised 42,000 horse and 70 guns. The defeat was attributed to the dissensions among the many rival chiefs of the Mahratta Divisions, each playing for his own supremacy. Had the spirit of Sivaji lived amongst them, victory, not defeat, had been theirs.[1]

The victory of the Mogul Emperor, however, was short-lived, for it was only a few years later, on October 22nd, 1764, that Clive—then Governor of Bengal—annihilated the Mogul Army and laid the foundation of British Power on a firm basis throughout Bengal, and eventually the whole of India.

[1] Panipat has been the site of several decisive battles. In 1526, Bahar defeated the last of the Afghan Kings. In 1556, Akbar crushed the Afghans and entered Delhi. In 1761, the Mahrattas were defeated by Ahmed Shah the Mogul Emperor.

CHAPTER V

RIVAL MERCHANT SETTLERS

We must retrace our steps and glance for a moment at the growth of English commercial enterprise in the East, from the time when, in Henry VIII's reign, Robert Thorne, an English merchant residing in Spain, drew the attention of his sovereign to the great benefits which would arise to our trade by direct communication with China. It was apparent from the success of the Dutch adventurers, that a strenuous effort must be made by our country if it was to share in the rich trade opened up by the Portuguese. In 1600 Queen Elizabeth granted a charter under the title of "The Governor and Company of the Merchants of London trading to the East Indies." Their first voyage was undertaken the following year. Among many expeditions during the ensuing period, those of Sir Henry Middleton were the most famous. He found the hostility of the Dutch so strong that he determined to fight them, a resolve carried out with but varying success. All these, though in themselves only minor ventures, had the effect of showing that if English trade was to have a real chance, a big, well-manned fleet was a necessity. One was accordingly fitted out by the E.I.Co. in 1612, under Captain Best, who sailed to Surat, where the Portuguese ships lay. Captain Best attacked and destroyed them, thus raising the prestige of the English, who up to then had been looked upon as mere "traders," to such a degree that the Mogul

Emperor Jehangeer entered into a treaty with Captain Best, granted him many privileges and agreed to an English Ambassador residing at his court at Delhi. Sir Thomas Roe was selected for the post by King James I, and despatched in 1615. At the same time, a new East India Company was formed with a capital of a million pounds, a huge sum in those days. A fleet of thirty ships was likewise provided. During the reign of Charles I considerable friction arose out of the rival claims of these two East India Companies, both at home and in the East. It was at last arranged that the two should be amalgamated, and Surat should be the Presidency town with jurisdiction over the Persian Gulf and factories on the Malabar and western coasts, whilst Madras, or Fort St. George, should govern those of Hoogly and the east coast.

The progress of our commercial power in the East produced so great an impression in England that when, at the Restoration in 1660, an alliance was effected with Portugal, and Charles II was betrothed to the Infanta of Portugal, the most striking feature of the marriage settlement was the cession of the Island of Bombay. This was the turning-point in Anglo-Indian history, and in 1668 the island was taken possession of, fortified, and handed over to the East India Company. The forces of the latter made so stout a resistance to the all-powerful Sivaji as to win his respect and aid against other enemies. Bombay with its magnificent harbour became the chief capital of the East India Company, who set about fortifying it with 100 cannon and a regular garrison of European soldiers, as well as native levies.

The 1st Bombay European Regiment—now the 103rd (2nd Battalion Royal Dublin Fusiliers)—claim, and rightly so, to be descended from the one or two Companies of the oldest Regiment of the British Army, the Royal Scots, which formed the nucleus of the first garrison of Bombay when the Company received it from the British Government, and took formal possession in 1668.

Though frequently checked by expeditions against native forces and rivalry of other traders, Dutch, Danes, French and Portuguese, as well as of our own merchants, steady development of the trade of the Company continued, and we read of new factories being established, not only along the Malabar and western coast, but as far south as Calicut, and as far north in Persia as Ispahan and Shiraz. All of these came under the direct control of the Bombay Government, though, as already stated, Central Offices were founded on the eastern or Coromandel Coast with Madras—known then as Fort St. George, as the southern representative, and at Calcutta, Fort St. William, on the Hoogly, as the capital for the Bengal Presidency to the North.

It would be interesting to follow the rise and progress of the Presidencies of Madras and Bengal, and their amalgamation with Bombay in 1708, which are closely connected with the history of British India. We must, however, confine ourselves to the Bombay Presidency, and especially to the Mahratta country around Bombay, that being the birthplace of our Regiment's people, the Mahrattas.

Despite the efforts of the authorities in Bombay to maintain neutrality, the piracies of the Mahratta chieftains increased to such an extent that the Portuguese authorities at Goa, and ours at Bombay, combined to suppress them. The success of this policy was but slight, and for many years there was perpetual strife along the coast. The Mahratta Chief, Kamojee Angria, actually built a fort at Colaba, a tongue of the Bombay

Harbour itself, and defended it for a long time against any attempts at capture.

While the British were doing their utmost to maintain neutrality—for the trade of Bombay was increasing by leaps and bounds—the Portuguese were entering into negotiations with the Mahrattas. A curious situation resulted. There were at the moment two claimants for the Mahratta throne. The Portuguese helped the cause of the one while the Peshwa—the Mogul Emperor's Mahratta Viceroy in the Deccan—backed the other. The war between the two centred in and around Bombay and its defended harbour and the forts of Thanna, Salsette, and Bassein. These shores and inlets were continually attacked and fought for, during a struggle which lasted many years.

The Peshwa's forces eventually gained the upper hand, and the Portuguese were compelled to give up possession of all these forts, accusing the English, despite their announced neutrality, of having assisted the Mahrattas against them. The fact was that the English and Portuguese were rival competitors for the valuable trade of the Malabar coast, and the Mahrattas and the Peshwa were playing one against the other. In 1709 the war came to an end as between the Mahrattas and the Portuguese, but only between these two. At this period the Mahratta power was so great, under two powerful chiefs, founders of the well-known families of the present day—that is to say, Mulhar Rao Holkar and Ranajee Sindia—that they overcame the Mogul Emperor, who, after his armies had been continually defeated and his territories wrested from him, was forced to acknowledge their independence. Nothing could stem the advance of the Mahrattas. They not only penetrated up to the gates of Delhi—the capital—but invaded the Carnatic. This brought them into contact with another power, that of the

French, who had settled on the eastern coast at Pondicherry, in active rivalry with the English around Madras. Thus began a struggle for supremacy between them, the French, and the English.

As on the west coast we have seen both the English and the Portuguese competing with the Mahrattas for trade privileges and concessions, so we find the French pursuing the same course on the east coast, and offering their help to the growing Mahratta power against the English. This led ultimately up to the period when our story of the Regiment actually begins.

What was the position at this moment? The French Government, realising that war with England was inevitable, despatched Labourdonnais, the distinguished Governor of Mauritius, for the purpose of co-operating with Dupleix, the Governor of Pondicherry, to hold themselves in readiness, directly it broke out, to strike a blow against the English at Madras.

Dupleix refused. Labourdonnais, however, acting on his own responsibility, immediately declared war; attacked, captured and occupied Madras, agreeing with us that in return for a ransom it was to remain unmolested during the war. Dupleix repudiated the agreement after Labourdonnais' departure, and despatched all the English to Pondicherry, giving out to the Mahrattas that the English force was completely broken and prisoners taken. Meanwhile peace had been arranged between England and France, and all the operations in India were ordered to be suspended, and Madras given up.

Dupleix, however, had so firmly established his reputation and become so certain of the invincibility of the European soldier over the native, that he pursued his ambitious plans for final dominion in India. He trained his native levies as soldiers, put them under military discipline, and, with this reorganised little army, offered his services in the ever-prevailing rivalries between the native Powers on the coast and in the interior.

In his judgment, military power was of far higher value than any trade success. Apparently the English were beginning to realise this as well. Thus it came about that each was animated with the same object, the defeat of the other's military power in India.

CHAPTER VI

RAISING OF THE INDIAN ARMY

At this juncture a young English lieutenant, named Clive, serving with a small force on the Madras coast, began to make a name for himself by his daring spirit and skilful plans for safeguarding his position in the important town and fort of Arcot. He was here besieged by a large native force, but held it for seven weeks, until relieved by a detachment from Madras. The Siege of Arcot is one of the most splendid episodes in the military history of British India, and Clive's defence brought him so much to the fore that shortly afterwards he was despatched against the French at Trichinopoly, and later to the relief of the garrison in Bengal, after that horrible episode known as "The Black Hole of Calcutta." How Clive relieved it, and how he fought the battle of Plassey on June 23rd, 1757, and broke the power of the Moguls for good and all, is a matter of history that cannot come into this little regimental story. It must live in everyone's memory. Clive is a man who will never be forgotten.

Much as we should like to linger over these wonderful exploits in Bengal, we must turn again to Southern India—wherein our story lies.

In 1768 the Bombay Army—if so small a force could be called an Army—was reorganised and formed into Battalions and prepared for active service. A great change had gradually been coming over the relations between the English Government and the East India

Company, which necessitated this step. The expansion of the trade of this Company, together with the annexation of coastal territories and the spread of factories inland, and further, the growth of treaties with both the Mogul and the Hindoo Chiefs, had altogether produced a very changed aspect. The Company had assumed so important a position that the English Government awoke to the necessity of taking active measures to secure the protection of their merchants. This was rendered all the more needful in view of the formidable antagonism of the French. Fleets and troops were therefore despatched from England, and the East India Company's military forces were ordered to be consolidated on recognised military lines.

Between 1760 and 1800, the Nawabs of Oude and Carnatic were the allies of the English. Three other Princes, the Nizam, Scindia, Hyder Ali, and his son Tippoo Sultan, were their deadliest enemies.

In face of these conflicting powers, it became a vital necessity that the Company's garrisons in Bombay should be prepared, not only for the defence of the port and harbour against the Mahratta chiefs, but also to co-operate with Madras against the rising power of the Mahomedan freebooter Hyder Ali, who had treacherously entered into negotiations with the French.

The various more or less independent tribes of the Mahratta Confederacy acknowledged as their head at this period, the Rajah of Sattara, whose capital lay amongst the mountain ranges to the south-west of Bombay. Since Sivaji's death, his successors had become more and more incompetent. The real power of the Rajah rested with his chief Minister, the "Peshwa," who resided, and kept up all the pomp of sovereignty, at Poona, on the summit of the Ghauts, overlooking Bombay, at a distance of only about fifty miles.

These mountain ranges were crowned with many strong forts—Singhur, Sattara, Purandhur, etc., all of which had been founded by Sivaji, and were now held by Mahratta chiefs. They presented a formidable barrier to any western co-operation with Madras against Hyder Ali. Not only so, but under the cover of these, the Mahrattas were able to threaten the English position on the coast. At the same time, the French, on the eastern coast, were intriguing with the Peshwa at Poona for assistance against the English on the western coast of Bombay.

While events were thus developing, the position of the British in Bombay became more and more critical. Not only was it threatened by the French and Mahrattas, but also by the Portuguese. In addition to the occupation by the Mahrattas, of the promontory now called Colaba, the Portuguese held a fortified station at Tannah, on an arm of the harbour itself.

In face of the weakness of the garrison, and the success of the French in organising their own native troops into well-disciplined and equipped Battalions, the Directors of the Honourable East India Company decided that their native troops in Bombay must be placed on a sound military footing. These had hitherto consisted of separate Companies, unnumbered, and known only by the names of the English officers who had raised and commanded them. It was accordingly ordered on the 4th of August in the year 1768 that these Companies should be formed into two Battalions, each Battalion to consist of ten Companies, aggregating a thousand of all native ranks, with three European officers, a Captain, Lieutenant, and Ensign, and two European Sergeants, 1 Subadar, 2 Jemadars, 6 Havildars, 6 Naiks, 3 Drummers, 1 Trumpeter, 1 Waterman, and 80 privates in each, making a total strength for the Native Army of 2,026. This formed the nucleus of the Bombay Army, which rapidly grew into that grand Force which has such a glorious history.

This organisation being completed, the authorities turned their attention to introducing some uniformity in the dress of the officers and men, and on January 3rd, 1769, an order was issued as follows:

"That the Sepoy Battalions be furnished as soon as possible with short drawers the colour of their turbans. [It does not state what the colour of the turbans was.] The turbans to be constantly worn in a uniform manner. The native officers are to wear boots, and constantly appear on duty in them."

From this very meagre account, it is somewhat difficult to say what uniform was worn at this time, but from an old picture of a somewhat later date, it would appear that the coats issued were of the same colour and pattern as those worn by the European troops, then garrisoning Bombay.

The succeeding years saw a rapid development of this small force, and its better equipment, dress, and training; and in 1779 the strength, which had been gradually increased from two Battalions to eight (exclusive of a Marine Battalion permanently quartered in Bombay) was further raised by the addition of seven new Battalions, making fifteen in all. The whole was now remodelled, each Battalion consisting of 2 Grenadier and 8 ordinary Companies, with 1 Captain, 6 Lieutenants (English officers), and 1 Native Commandant, 11 Subadars, 1 Native Adjutant, 20 Jemadars, 11 Sergeants (European), 20 Drums and Fifes, 2 Trumpeters, 60 Havildars, 60 Naiks, and 680 Sepoys.

Thus we find the Bombay Army, which in 1768 only consisted of two Battalions with a total strength of

SEPOY UNIFORM, LATE EIGHTEENTH CENTURY.

2,000 of all ranks, increased in 1779 to 15 Battalions of 12,000 officers and men.

Another ten years bring still further reorganisation. Evidently the experience gained pointed to the former being faulty in design and unwieldy in bulk. A serious attempt was now made to render the Army, though reduced in strength, more efficient, better drilled, dressed, and trained. Thus in 1788 the new Army consisted of a Grenadier Battalion, a Marine Battalion, with permanent Head-quarters in Bombay, and twelve other Battalions, formed into two Brigades. New Arms were issued, and, with a view to improving the musketry efficiency of the Army, it was ordered that "every soldier should fire a ball at a mark once a week, without wasting ammunition." This, it further stated, "will keep them in constant habit and make it familiar to them."

The subject of dress was also taken up, and we have more detailed regulations as to the uniform to be worn by all ranks of the newly organised Native Army in Bombay. It was laid down that the officers of the First Brigade should wear gold, and the men yellow lace, while the officers of the 2nd Brigade wore silver, and the men white lace. Turbans were to be bound round the edge with yellow or white according to the Brigade, with bands and tassels of similar colour. Two stripes of lace to be worn round the front of the cummerbund, and the short drawers were to be edged with stripes of blue and yellow or blue and white. Turbans and cummerbunds were to be blue. Fronts of black leather were to be worn on the turbans with the number of the Battalion in yellow or white metal in Roman characters in the centre. The plumes authorised for the 5th Battalion[1] were blue, and the badge a crescent. The 9th Battalion (now 104 Rifles) wore the same

[1] The "Kali Panchwin."

plumes, and had the same badge on their appointments, being distinguished by their lace only. The Grenadier Companies wore white plumes. These badges were given as stated in the general order, "as honorary marks of distinction to the old Corps forming the peace establishment of the Presidency."

CHAPTER VII

WAR IN MYSORE

Having dealt with the Bombay Army Organisations as a whole during the first twenty years of its existence, we must now go back and follow the career of our own particular Regiment during its initial period. Its first existence as a special unit is a little confused owing to the incessant changes in the early history of the Indian Army. It is clear, however, that the "Kali Panchwin" sprang, with the rest of the small force, from the original unnumbered Companies of Sepoys. These, as we have seen, were formed into two Battalions, each consisting of ten Companies numbering 100 Natives—all ranks—and five European officers. The regimental Records of the Kali Panchwin start from this date, i.e. 1768, as the *2nd Battalion*. In 1778–9, when the two Battalions were increased first to eight, and then to fifteen, the Kali Panchwin became the 5th Battalion. At the next reorganisation in 1796, when the Battalions were transformed into four Regiments of two Battalions each, it became the 2nd Battalion of the 1st Regiment. Two years later, on the formation of a fifth Regiment, it became the 1st/3rd Regiment.

These constant changes naturally produced a good deal of confusion. Tradition had it that the Kali Panchwin and the old 13th Battalion—the "Travenore"—were the same Regiment. It arose from the fact that the latter took the former's place when they became the 1st/3rd, hence both were in succession the 2nd Battalion of the 1st Regiment.

To turn to the first records (in 1768) of the Kali Panchwin.

Just as the description of the original uniform was somewhat vague, so is the reference to the two Battalions into which the old Companies had been formed. We find the 2nd Battalion stationed at the Presidency and furnishing detachments to subordinate Stations. This Battalion also provided most of the detachments sent on expeditions against the Portuguese and Mahrattas holding positions threatening Bombay.

Up to the year 1772 we are left absolutely in the dark as to where and for what purpose these expeditions were sent, but in November of this year we find that our Battalion was present and took part in the capture of Broach, and received prize money; an important fact, for this is the first mention of the Regiment on active service.

Broach was, and is, an important trading station, with a fort at the mouth of the Nerbudda River, about one hundred miles north of Bombay, then held by the Portuguese or Mahrattas.

For a long time past the Portuguese had possession of a fort at Thana, on an arm of the magnificent harbour of Bombay, only twenty miles from our own fort to which it had long been a standing menace, and it was decided to take it. Knowing that the Portuguese would put up a stout resistance, a force of 800 European soldiers, Artillery and Infantry, with the 2nd and 3rd Sepoys, under the command of Brigadier-General Robert Gordon, was despatched on December 12, 1774. On the 20th our Battalion opened fire, and on the 28th the fort was carried by assault. Again a liberal grant of prize money was made in lieu of plunder, i.e. half a lac of rupees. A Colonel received 1,000 rupees, and the sepoys 5 rupees each.

The next year a more important undertaking was planned, with the aim of freeing the great province of Guzerat, with its settlements at Surat and Broach, from the Mahrattas, who dominated it. With a few months' rest, the Battalion was again selected for active service, and ordered on March 29th, 1775, to join Colonel Keating's force, then operating in Guzerat. In advance the Column was suddenly attacked by the Mahrattas in a narrow defile, on May 18th. For the moment there was confusion, but the superior discipline of Keating's force, of which our Battalion formed a part, carried the day, and the Mahrattas were badly beaten. The victory was so complete that the action is recorded as the Battle of Arass. Though the expedition had been such a success, on the cessation of hostilities the force was ordered to return to Bombay by the Governor-General, who maintained that the expedition ought never to have been sent without his permission, as it endangered the Treaty with the Peshwa Ragoonath Rao (the head of the Mahratta Confederacy) to whom the Province of Guzerat had been given as a reward for services rendered to the East India Company. Great resentment was felt by the Bombay Government at this, and a vigorous protest was sent. The Governor-General replied that he alone had the authority for ordering warlike expeditions, thus of course weakening the prestige of the Bombay Army.

For five years the Battalion was on garrison duty in Bombay and Tannah and we may pause for a while to give a description of the life there, culled from a most interesting little book entitled *The Diary of a Field Officer*, the author of which, after being quartered in Madras, was transferred to Bombay to join in the Expedition to the Southern Mahratta country in 1782.

On arrival he was at once struck with the robust and athletic forms of the Parsee, Marwari, and Bunniah population as compared with the slim and fragile figures found in Madras. "Garrison duty was neither severe nor troublesome," he says, and when on guard at the Bazaar gate he was much diverted by the handsome females, who in passing, "cast admiring glances at the soldiers." He remarked that apparently there was no uniformity in the equipment and dress of the officers of the Native troops, and he makes the astounding statement that the *Town Major* himself usually attended the guard mounting, "in shoes and silk stockings!" When quartered later in Surat, he says, "Garrison life here is also very pleasant; many social entertainments, and plenty of sport, the naked Bheels from the hills joining in the hunts with bows and arrows."[1]

In 1780 we are given, for the first time, the names of the English officers of the 5th Battalion on its reorganisation, and we must certainly record them here, especially as the Commanding Officer, Captain Daniel Carpenter, is spoken of by the Field Officer, in his Memoirs, as "a man of great character, commanding a force on the Malabar coast in 1782." The six lieutenants were Lieutenant John Young, Richardson, R. Read, Abraham Hammond, Charles Patrick, and Thomas Ringrove.

Whilst the Battalion was in Bombay an expedition was sent out towards Poona, which proved a complete failure, but it is noted that our Battalion was not part of the force, though shortly afterwards, in September, it was selected for more important operations and

[1] In marching across from Deesa to Mhow in 1884, through their country, the Bheels attacked our advance party with bows and arrows.

joined Lieut.-Colonel Hartley's force with which it was engaged in the capture of Mullungurh during October, and shared in the subsequent campaign in which the Mahrattas under Ramchander Ganesh were driven out of the Konkan. Regarding the latter, we are told of the splendid support given by Hartley in covering the operations of General Goddard, who was besieging Bassein, a strongly fortified island near Bombay, then held by the Portuguese. It reads like an epic. Goddard was threatened by an attack of 20,000 Mahrattas under the celebrated Nana Furnawees, who was endeavouring to raise the siege, when General Hartley with only his 2,000 troops—and those suffering from sickness and lack of food—left his strong position on the Bhor Ghaut, advanced, and resisting the attacks of this apparently overwhelming force, for three days, counter-attacked, and defeated it at Doogaur, and thus enabled Goddard to capture Bassein on December 10th, 1781. This action is well described as a splendid victory, and General Goddard, on joining Colonel Hartley, expressed his high appreciation of the judicious dispositions which he had made, and the fortitude and gallantry of the troops which had enabled him to capture Bassein: a great tribute to a force mostly composed of Bombay Sepoys, of which our Battalion formed a part. When Colonel Hartley shortly afterwards gave up his command, it remained with General Goddard's forces and took part in the subsequent operations in the vicinity of Bhor Ghaut, returning to the Presidency before the breaking of the monsoon. There, the Battalion was given a short rest, and on December 14th, being ordered to hold itself in readiness for active service again, it proceeded to Tellicherry, a port on the Malabar coast near Cannanore, to support Major Abingdon, who with other Regiments of Sepoys from Bombay, was besieged by a detachment of Hyder Ali's Army. Again we see what a reputation our Battalion had won for itself, for it is recorded that Major Abingdon, who through weakness of his forces had been obliged to confine himself to purely defensive tactics, immediately on the arrival of our Battalion and one other, commenced active operations. He attacked Hyder's camp, drove his troops into confusion and demolished their works. After repairing the defences of Tellicherry, Major Abingdon advanced on Calicut—another port and settlement on the Malabar coast—which he captured on February 13, 1782.

We now come to the first serious operations against Hyder Ali and Tippoo Sahib's territories in Mysore, which lasted throughout the next three years.

It must be remembered that the successes gained in the north by Warren Hastings had driven the Mahrattas and Tippoo into forming a grand confederacy, with the object of driving the English out of India. The plans were that whilst Holkar, Sindia, and the Peshwa should attack Bombay, Hyder Ali should march on Madras, and Madaji Bhonslay, with the Rajah of Nagpur, should threaten Calcutta. These worked on what is in military language called "interior lines," well known as the strongest position for forces in co-operation. The English, on the other hand, were divided by hostile territories from these three capitals. They were thus at the serious disadvantage of being unable to effect combined movements.

A few days after Major Abingdon had captured Calicut, Colonel Humberstone Mackenzie joined him with about 1,000 European Infantry recently arrived from the Cape. He assumed command, and took the field in Hyder Ali's territories, driving before him the forces which had been left there to oppose his advance. He took several forts—Baja-Mandroog and Oronore amongst them—and only returned to Calcutta on the approach of the monsoon. No sooner were the rains over in September than active operations recommenced. Ramgworee was taken on October 6th, the garrison deserting it at night. Palacutcherry was next besieged, but for want of Artillery could not be captured, and what was worse, our troops, being in a very disadvantageous position, were forced to retire, before a relieving force with difficulty reached Pamiani on November 20th. Tippoo followed and started to besiege our encampment in retaliation, but news reaching him of the sudden death of his aged father Hyder Ali at his camp (the old warrior was 81 years of age), Tippoo abandoned the siege and retired to Mysore.

The Sepoy Battalions now marched back to Tellicherry, where they remained till the arrival of General Mathews from Bombay with fresh troops, i.e. the 7th, 8th, and 11th Native Battalions, and the 1st, 3rd, 5th, and 15th, from Surat and Broach. The whole force being concentrated at Merjee in January 1783, operations commenced at once. We have it on record that our Battalion was present at the storming of Hydergurh on the 25th, the capture of Bednore on the 26th, and later on at the taking of Ananpore and Mangalore, all of which were on the table-land of Mysore. After these successes, we learn that General Mathew's forces were dispersed in detachments, occupying almost every town and mud fort in the country, even along the Malabar coast, amongst others, Ancola, Raja-Mundroog, Karwar, and Seedaseer. We are told, alas, that all military precautions were neglected in the lust for plunder.

This was Tippoo's opportunity, nor was he slow to avail himself of it, with results truly disastrous to the British operations. On April 9th, 1783, he suddenly reappeared on the scene of action, besieged Bednore, and took most of the garrison prisoners. Mangalore, garrisoned by the 8th Regiment (now the 1st Grenadiers) and a few detachments which had succeeded in making their escape from Bednore, held on till February 23rd, 1784, when the garrison were allowed to march out with the honours of war. The main body of the 2nd Regiment fell into the hands of Tippoo, but a very small number eventually reached Tellicherry, where they remained until the peace of March 11th. Of the number of prisoners taken by Tippoo at Bednore, but few returned. "Field Officer," in his Memoirs, says that Generals Mathews and Goddard, and many of their officers and men were foully murdered. Of the survivors, 180 officers, 900 Europeans, and 1,600 Native soldiers were eventually released, but he adds, by Tippoo's orders all were cruelly treated. A sad picture indeed. The blame for this terrible disaster was largely thrown on the Madras Government for not supporting the Bombay force as they were asked to do, but we must not overlook the enormous difficulties which prevented them from doing so. We may sum it up as a heavy blow to the Bombay Army, which hitherto had had an unblemished record of successes and victories.

The next five years were spent in bringing it up to a higher state of efficiency. The 5th Battalion, which had behaved so gallantly but suffered so severely in the last disastrous campaign, was brought up to its former strength by drafts from disbanded regiments, and stationed in Bombay.

CHAPTER VIII

HYDER ALI, TIPPOO INTRIGUES

THE Hyder Ali, Tippoo Campaigns of 1782–3–4 were nothing short of disastrous in their results. The East India Company were faced with the necessity of so dealing with the situation as to guard against any recurrence. The consequent measures so intimately affected the future of the Bombay Army, that it is desirable to describe them somewhat fully before continuing the purely Regimental history

One of the first acts of Lord Cornwallis when he was appointed Governor-General in 1786 was to urge upon the Directors the absolute necessity of reorganising their forces, both Native and European, and placing them on a proper footing. He insisted most strongly on the importance of remodelling the Army on a regular system, breaking up the old irregular Battalions and re-forming them into regiments, numbered and officered as Corps belonging to the King's Royal Army. These measures were generally accepted, and two years later, 1788, we find the first record of a Commander-in-Chief's Staff in the Bombay Presidency, with the following appointments: Major-General W. Meadows, C.-in-C.; Major George Hart, 77th Inf., Deputy Adjutant-General; Lieut.-Colonel Hartley, Deputy Quartermaster-General.

The new Army was formed into Brigades of native troops. First Brigade, 1st Grenadiers, 2nd, 3rd, 4th, 5th, and 6th Battalions; Second Brigade, 7th, 8th, 10th, 11th, and 12th Battalions. The changes brought about by the re-forming of the Army produced a good deal of dissatisfaction, and "Field Officer," in his Memoirs (it must be remembered he was serving out there at the time), makes weighty comments on these changes, showing how bitter was the feeling raised by the redistribution of officers and the consequent breaking of the ties of loyalty between officers and men who had long served together. All who have spent their lives in our Native Army in India know how numerous are the occasions, both in peace and war, which have proved the strength of these bonds. Whether this reshuffling could have been avoided, however, is not the point here. Coming events soon showed how wise was the forethought that had urged the reorganising and strengthening of the East India forces.

At this time the great Province of Mysore, inhabited by Hindoos from remote antiquity, and ruled by a succession of Hindoo Rulers, made a strong appeal to the English for assistance. Their Ruler, anxious to raise a strong cavalry force to oppose the French who were threatening them, had most unwisely engaged the services of the Mahomedan freebooter Hyder Ali, to assist him in reorganising his army. No sooner had Hyder secured full control, which he speedily contrived to do, than he deposed his master the Hindoo King, and proclaimed himself Governor of Mysore. It was not long before he and his son Tippoo, in pursuance of the custom of those times, commenced a frightful persecution of all who would not accept their Islamic faith, and drove out and butchered nearly 30,000 Hindoo inhabitants, thus bringing on themselves the hatred of the Mysoreans, who appealed to the British to free them from this awful tyranny.

In response to this appeal, a large force consisting of eight Companies of various Battalions, the 5th being one of them, was sent to Tellicherry with a view to operations against Tippoo Sultan in Mysore. The first phase of these operations fell to the lot of the Madras troops, two detachments of the Bombay Army co-operating. One, under Colonel Hartley, consisted of the 75th Regt., the 1st Grenadiers, a Company of Artillery, 7th Sepoys, and two Companies of Lascars. The other detachment, under Captain Little, was composed of the 8th, 9th, and 11th Sepoys in concert with the Mahratta Army under Pureshram Bhao, the Peshwa, he, as well as the Nizam (or Subadar of the Deccan), though the most unreliable of Allies, being bound by treaties to assist us.

"Field Officer," in his Memoirs, gives a most interesting account of these operations and describes in detail the siege of Dharwar which was held by Tippoo's Chief Killadar Badroden-as-Zaman.[1] The Mahomedan garrison gallantly defended it for 209 days and then surrendered to Captain Little's force, the original garrison of 10,000 being reduced to 3,000. "Field Officer" mentions that while the old Killadar hated the Mahrattas, he and his men respected the English.

On December 14th the main Army advanced from Tellicherry and encamped in front of Avery Redoubt, which was taken and occupied the next morning. On the 19th, Cannanore was surrendered. In January 1791, the Army marched to Betiapatam, where a halt was made to allow of a reconnaissance of the formidable Pondicherrim Ghauts. The ascent proved most arduous. Roads had to be constructed and the batteries transported gun by gun, with ropes and tackles, over a succession of rugged mountainous ascents. It was not till March that the whole force was concentrated for

[1] The European soldiers, puzzled by his name, called him "Bothering Jimmy," much as they still coin amusing epithets for names they cannot pronounce.

the advance on Seringapatam, the capital of Mysore, now Tippoo Sultan's head-quarters. To the intense disappointment of all, the advance was countermanded and the force ordered to return to Tellicherry. The reason given was that Lord Cornwallis was unable to co-operate. This was owing to his Army being greatly reduced through lack of transport, food, and equipment of all kinds, and also by disease which had broken out amongst the troops as the natural result of bad food, heavy rain, and incessant hardships and fatigue.

The Battalion remained in Tellicherry until it returned to Bombay in 1794.

There is little more to record of the years 1792–3–4, save the curious order that the officers of the Grenadier and Light Infantry Companies should in future make use of their swords instead of fusils as heretofore. Also, that the cost of colours was fixed at 450 Rs. including tassels, pikes, spears, and staves.

In December 1796 our Regiment—just renumbered 2nd/1st., Bo. N.I.—was ordered to embark for active service in Ceylon. The force, under Major Petrie, joined the Madras Army at Negambo, thirty miles north of Colombo, and advanced to attack. There was little show of resistance and Colombo was surrendered. The Regiment then returned to Cochin. It is somewhat difficult to trace the causes which led to this expedition to Ceylon. All we know is that there had been great rivalry for many years between the Dutch and the English, who both had settlements there. The former especially had large establishments in the island, and the English had endeavoured to get the upper hand—in other words, they aimed at driving the Dutch out of Ceylon. As was invariably the case in all dissensions during these turbulent years in India, other countries and powers, ever on the alert to check any infringement of their rights, sprang jealously to the fore ready to take part in the quarrel. In this instance the French, who at the time were on the verge of war with England, came forward to support the Dutch. This brought about an open rupture in 1796, when the English came out as conquerors. Eventually the island of Ceylon was ceded to England at the Peace of Amiens, in 1803.

The Battalion was next engaged in operations under Colonel Dow, at Koliked (Calicut). These continued throughout the whole of the year 1797. Colonel Dow was Military Commissioner of the Province of Malabar, and under the pressure of his supporters was induced to send a detachment, in the command of Major Cameron, into the Wainad, then held by troops of Tippoo Sultan. This was resented by Tippoo's Commander, with the result that Major Cameron had to retreat in order to avoid serious defeat. There can be no doubt that this helped matters to a climax, though the latter was approaching in any case.

It had come to the knowledge of the new Governor-General, Lord Mornington, that Tippoo Sultan was in league with the French to drive the English out of India. A letter from Napoleon Bonaparte—who had just landed in Egypt—had in fact been intercepted, confirming these negotiations. It was realised that the state of affairs had become extremely serious and that no time must be lost in frustrating Tippoo's aims. The combined forces of Bombay and Madras were ordered to join hands for an immediate attack on Seringapatam. At the same time the Governor-General called upon the Nizam and the Peshwa to give their assistance in accordance with the terms of the Tripartite Treaty of 1790. Sindia and the Rajah of Nagpur were invited to join, but refused.

The Mysore capital could only be attacked when the River Cauvery was low. Tippoo's policy was to endeavour to retard the English advance until the rainy season, when the fording of the river would be impossible. He hastened therefore to meet his enemy's forces, devastating the country on his way so as to prevent them from reprovisioning on their march.

CHAPTER IX

BATTLE OF SEEDASEER

EARLY in 1799 our Battalion—now the 1st/3rd Bo. N.I. —moved to Cannanore and joined the Division which was assembling there under General Stuart, to co-operate with the Madras troops under General Harris. General Stuart's force totalled 6,420, all ranks—i.e. 166 European Artillery, 344 Native ditto. Right Brigade, Lieut.-Colonel Montresor—1/2 Regt., 1/3rd (our Battalion), 1/4th, 653, 663, 672 Sepoys. Centre Brigade, Lieut.-Colonel Dunlop—77th Bombay, 77th European Regiment. Left Brigade, Lieut.-Colonel Wiseman—2/3rd, 1/5th, 2/2nd, Pioneers, European Engineers.

Instructions having been received from General Harris to ascend the Ghauts and there await orders, the above force left Cannanore on February 21st, and arrived at the top of Pondicherrim Ghaut on the 25th. On March 2nd the Right Brigade advanced to Seedaseer on the boundary of Coorg, seven miles distant from Seringapatam, the main body of the army remaining at Seedapore and Almootenaar. About 10 a.m. on March 5th a large encampment was observed in process of formation in the vicinity, on the Seedaseer side, composed of upwards of 300 tents, many of large size, and there were indications of the presence of the Sultan Tippoo himself. A reinforcement of an additional Battalion of Sepoys was despatched by General Stuart to the 1st Brigade under Colonel Montresor. On the morning of the 6th, between 9 and 10 a.m., the enemy commenced the attack. Favoured by thick jungle and morning mist, they fell on the front and rear of the line simultaneously. The strength of the enemy was about 12,000. To oppose this, Colonel Montresor had only three Battalions, totalling 2,000 of all ranks. The additional Battalion (1/3rd), sent up by General Stuart, was posted some two and a half miles in rear, and, being cut off by the enemy 5,000 strong, was unable to effect a junction till later. The three Battalions held their ground magnificently, repulsing every attack of the enemy until nearly 3 p.m., when General Stuart arrived with two flank Companies of the 75th and the whole of the 77th. This reinforcement arrived none too soon, as the men of the Right Brigade were well-nigh exhausted. The 75th and 77th attacked with vigour and the enemy were driven off in confusion.

Such are the rough and bare outlines of this historic battle as recorded in the printed records of the Regiment, but we feel they hardly do credit to an action which Lord Mornington described, in a despatch to the Directors of the East India Company, as one which in conduct and success has seldom been equalled and never surpassed. We turn with pleasure to the "Diary of a Field Officer," who was present, and records in it what he actually saw of the attack on the position at Seedaseer by Tippoo Sultan's army, and its defence by the Right Brigade of General Stuart's force, reinforced by the 1st/3rd. He opens his account with these striking words: "This day must ever continue to be remembered with pride and satisfaction by all who feel an interest in the well-established renown of the Bombay Army."

The attack, opening as usual with a discharge of rockets along the front of the post, advanced within twenty or thirty yards of our bayonets. At this critical stage it was found that the muzzle-loading 12-pounder gun had been loaded shot first. The Lascars were drawn up in front of the gun whilst this was being remedied. The enemy continued the attack with great obstinacy, for they were under the eye of their master, Tippoo Sultan, but were foiled by the resolution and steadiness of our brave Sepoys (there were no Europeans present, officers excepted).[1] Whilst this frontal attack was being carried out, a far more dangerous operation was effected against the rear of the post, where a dense column of the enemy—said to be 7,000 strong—emerged from the woods behind.

It was not till 12 o'clock that the critical state of the post was reported at Head-quarters, when General Stuart marched, with the 97th and the flank Company of the 75th King's Regiment, to its relief. About 2 o'clock, after enduring almost suffocating heat through the jungle, they reached the rear post. Without a moment's delay, the European soldiers threw off their knapsacks, and rushed to the attack. They drove the enemy off, cleared the rear, reached our harassed brigade at the advanced post, and recovered the guns lost in the attack.

The Rajah of Coorg, our ally, who was present, is said to have exclaimed when he saw the splendid attack of the 77th and the 75th who drove the enemy pell-mell down the ravines, "These men ought to have been carried to battle in palanquins." Tippoo Sultan was present in the woods below, but, seeing the defeat of his force, withdrew quietly to his camp. The green tent proclaiming his presence showed the powerful force surrounding him. It is reported to have been 20,000 to 25,000 Infantry, 1,600 Cavalry, and over

[1] The special part taken by the 1st/3rd in withstanding this attack is not defined in this description.

100 guns, commanded by most of his distinguished generals.

"Field Officer" sums up:

"It must be borne in mind that the post at Seedaseer Hill, open as it was on all sides, with the exception of here and there a trifling abattis, was maintained against tremendous odds, composed of the Sultan's best-disciplined troops who were acting under the immediate eye of their despotic master. For ninety-five hours two Battalions of Bombay Sepoys with no other Europeans than the scanty complement of Officers and a few Artillery-men held out against them. The advanced post at Seedaseer hill was established to watch the Sultan's Army and cover the main force of the Bombay advance. Had it failed, it is probable there would have been a great defeat and an enforced retreat. It may well be said, 'The Bombay Sepoys saved the situation. They deserved all that has been said of them.'"

CHAPTER X

TAKING OF SERINGAPATAM

DISMAYED at his reverses, Tippoo hastened back to his capital, leaving a large portion of his Army behind to harass the enemy and keep watch on their movements. The post at Seedaseer was withdrawn shortly after the battle, and on April 9th the whole of the British force advanced in single column from Seedapoor, where they had been encamped, to march on Seringapatam. They reached Periapatam on the 11th, Campessor 12th, Kuttamalwar 13th, Bilwhooly 14th. During these marches they had several skirmishes with the enemy and the rear and baggage columns were continually attacked by Tippoo's troops. The ford of the River Cauvery being reported practicable, General Lloyd with most of the Cavalry and part of the Bengal Brigade crossed over on the 16th and marched to Mysore, to divert attention.

In order to clear the ground for our breaching batteries the Mill Work post on south of the river was carried by assault by European and Bengal Sepoys on the 20th.

On the 21st and 22nd the enemy maintained a heavy cannonade on our camp from the batteries of Seringapatam. On the 23rd the enlarged batteries of both attacks opened with great effect, our guns silenced every one opposed to them and had so perfect an enfilade that it appeared impossible, without some new means of protection, for any of Tippoo's troops to remain for the defence of their foremost position.

Our approaches were gradually advanced until the 26th, when it became imperative to dislodge the enemy from their last exterior entrenchment, distant only 380 yards from the fort, and covered on the right by a redoubt, and on the left by a small circular work, open in the rear. The Hon. Colonel Wellesley (afterwards the great Duke of Wellington), who commanded in the trenches, was charged with the direction of the attacks for dislodging the enemy.

A little after sunset the attack was made by two columns under Colonel Moneypenny and Major Skelly, on the enemy's right and centre. Both attacks were successful and the united columns pursued until the fire from the fort compelled them to take up a post in an aqueduct which had formed the ditch of the entrenchment and was now destined to be the third parallel of the besiegers. The circular work was still in the hands of Tippoo's forces and commanded the aqueduct. The enemy now collected there in great numbers. The position of the assailants was fast becoming untenable, when Lieut.-Colonel Campbell of the 74th Regiment, arriving with the relief for the trenches, charged with only 120 men, and dislodged the enemy from the circular work. Then, favoured by night, he pursued them across the Seringapatam bridge, entered the right of their camp, spiked some of their guns, and effected an orderly retreat amid the confusion into which they had been thrown. The enemy, however, managed to reoccupy the circular work that night, and it was not until the 27th that it was finally taken and included in the siege work of our troops.

On the 28th a small body of cavalry appeared in the rear of our camp. To counteract this we established a breaching battery of six 18-pounders, 450 yards from the fort, but the guns, being swamped, delayed fire.

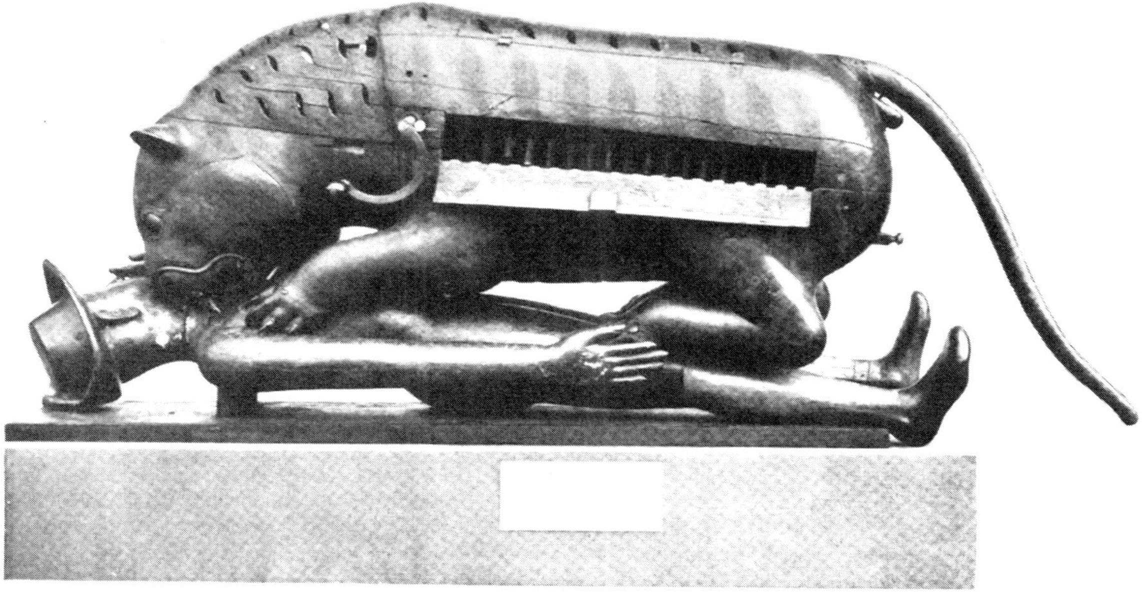

[*Victoria and Albert Museum Photo.* *Crown Copyright.*

TIPPOO'S TIGER.

This emblematic organ, in the form of a British (East India Company) officer, recumbent, being mauled by an Indian tiger, was made for the amusement of Tippu Sultan ("Tippoo Sahib"), ruler of Mysore, about 1790. It was found in the Palace after the storming of Seringapatam, by the British troops under General Harris in 1799.

Although the painted wood model is of Indian design and workmanship, the contained mechanical parts were probably made by a French craftsman.

On the 30th the fire of five guns opened, but was not very effective. The second breaching battery of two 24-pounders and three 18-pounders opened on the 2nd, with all other batteries. On May 3rd, two large Divisions of Tippoo's cavalry, led by their Commander with a large scarlet umbrella over him, threatened the rear of our camp whilst the bombardment continued, but they drew off from the fire of our 6-pounders.

The breach of the main ramparts, which had been continually enlarged, was now reported practicable for the assault, and arrangements were at once made for carrying it out the next day. The troops detailed to storm the great fort of Seringapatam are given in our regimental records as follows:

The flank Companies of the 75th, 77th, Bombay European Regiments under Colonel Dunlop, 77th Regiment, four Companies of the Scottish Brigade, and the Regiment de Meuron under Colonel Sherbrooke, ten Companies of the Bengal Regiment of Grenadier Sepoys, eight Companies of Grenadier Sepoys from Madras under Colonel Dalrymple; six Companies of Bombay Grenadier Sepoys, one from each Battalion as follows:

First and second Battalions of 2nd, 3rd, 4th, and 5th Regiments. As these Companies were weak they were made up to strength from other Grenadier Companies, so that practically both flank Companies of these Regiments were also engaged.

His Majesty's 12th, 33rd, 73rd and 74th Regiments, and 100 Artillery, under Major Robert Bell of the Madras Artillery. There were also 200 of the Nizam's Infantry, and the corps of Native and European Pioneers under Captain Dowse, in all about 2,500 European and Native troops.

The time for the storming of the breach was fixed for 1 p.m. on May 4th. It was thought that the Sultan's troops would be taking their midday siesta at that hour as usual, and at a quarter past 1 o'clock General Baird, with the assaulting force, passed over the rocky bed of the Cauvery—two miles from the fort—under heavy fire, crossed the ditch and ascended the breach, in spite of the violent opposition of the enemy, many of whom rushed down the slope to meet them. Our troops divided at the summit of the breach, the right attack under Colonel Sherbrooke proceeding to clear the ramparts to the right, the left attack, under Colonel Dunlop, going round to the left. The Bombay native troops were with the right attack. After an hour's heavy firing and great resistance, led by Tippoo himself though seriously wounded, the great fort of Seringapatam was captured and the British flag was hoisted on the flag-staff of the southern Bastion, displacing that of the Sultan over his once invincible capital.

After the capture of the fort, Wellesley rode to the Palace to confer with Tippoo. He was nowhere to be found, and it was not till evening that his body was discovered shot through the head and wounded by sword-cuts in many places. He received honourable burial the following day in his father's mausoleum. We are told that a violent storm was raging at the time, and that crashing peals of thunder mingled with the British cannons in a parting salute to the dead Ruler. A fitting requiem for this turbulent fighter.

After marching back to the Malabar coast with the rest of the Division when General Stuart broke camp before Seringapatam, our Battalion was ordered to garrison Kundapur. It remained there throughout the following year, being frequently engaged in expeditions against robber chiefs in the surrounding country. On one of these occasions, in an attack on a pagoda near Karwar, Subadar Ibrahim Khan and a small detachment distinguished themselves by such conspicuous bravery that the Bombay Government directed that a gold badge should be presented to the Subadar, and a silver one to each of the Havildars of the detachment, in commemoration of their gallant conduct.

More serious fighting, however, was soon again to fall to the lot of the Battalion, together with the whole of the British Indian Army.

CHAPTER XI

MAHRATTA WAR

AFTER the fall of Seringapatam, the capital of Mysore, and the death of its formidable ruler, Tippoo Sultan, the immense territory and revenues annexed by him and his father, Hyder Ali, were divided up by the conquerors. The real heir, a boy of five years old, who was the direct descendant of Sivaji, was proclaimed Rajah, and the ancient kingdom of Mysore made over to him. English Commissioners were appointed, with the assistance of its former able Finance Minister, Poorneah, to carry on the administration of the country during the young Rajah's minority. Tippoo Sultan's family was removed to Vellore and an ample allowance assigned to its members. The Peshwa and the Nizam, our allies in the war against Tippoo, were each allotted territories and revenues from the Mysorean kingdom, and the English took their share, claiming certain portions that adjoined their frontiers.

Thus at the beginning of the nineteenth century the political condition of India had undergone considerable change, and the English possessions and power were greatly increased. The strong rule of Hyder Ali and Tippoo being smashed by Wellesley, the only other great Power now beside the English in India was that of the Mahrattas, who were divided into five political parties more or less on bad terms with one another. There were:

1. The Peshwa—the treacherous Baji Rao—nomi-

nally the supreme Governor, reigning at Poona, and secretly a bitter enemy of the English.

2. Daulat Rao Sindia, at Gwalior—in reality the strongest of the Mahratta Chiefs, unreliable, and greedy for fresh power.

3. Eshwant Rao Holkar, at Indore, utterly lawless and rapacious, bearing deadly hatred towards Sindia, with whom he was constantly at war.

4. Madoji Bhonslay, Rajah of Nagpur, hating nobody in particular but willing to fight against anybody for a consideration.

5. Futteh Singh, Gaikwar of Guzerat, who never joined much in Mahratta politics unless called upon to aid in some grand *coup*.

There were other smaller States, half independent though nominally in feudal submission to their hereditary Sovereign the Peshwa.

Though the state of affairs was apparently tranquil, in reality it was full of a simmering disturbance. It became evident that the strong elements of jealousy, greed, and hatred amongst the Mahratta Powers must soon break out into open hostility, and a great struggle ensue between the Mahrattas and the English for the Empire of India. There could be little cessation of warfare in the country until all contentions and differences were settled and the actual rulers' ascendancy made manifest through the power of might.

Disorders in 1800 became rapidly more and more prevalent. The Peshwa, constantly engaged in petty intrigue, entangled himself in a war with the Rajah of Kolapur. Eshwant Rao Holkar, out on a pillaging enterprise, invaded and ravaged Sindia's territory in Malwah, resulting in deadly fighting between them which continued with unabated fury. Finally both appealed to the Peshwa for assistance, but he refused to be drawn into siding with one or the other. Apart from having enough on his hands at the moment, he had secret views of his own for not wishing to offend either of these Mahratta Princes. Ever at heart in bitter enmity to England, he was scheming in his mind to obtain these two powerful chieftains as allies in warring against the increasing British power. His refusal to take part in the two rivals' quarrel resulted, however, in both turning against him. They advanced in fact to Poona with their large armies, each yet hoping to enlist his sympathy and help, but the Peshwa took fright and fled to Bassein—then occupied by British troops—and appealed to Lord Wellesley for assistance. The result of this overture on the part of the Peshwa brought about a treaty, signed at Bassein, under which the Peshwa undertook to maintain 6,000 British troops with guns, and assigned large districts in the Deccan for their maintenance. This doubly infuriated Sindia and Holkar, and led to a confederation of all the Mahratta Chiefs against the Peshwa, for they considered that his treaty with the English was both threatening and derogatory to Mahratta independence.

They marched in a body to dominate the Peshwa. Wellesley, being bound to protect him, at once ordered out troops, and taking command himself, advanced to Poona with combined forces from Bombay and Madras. The celebrated battle of Assaye was fought on September 3rd, 1803, when, with a small force of only 4,000 British and Native troops, Wellesley obtained a complete victory over 50,000 Mahrattas. The fight was so hotly contested, however, that the Mahratta casualties were said to be 2,000 killed and 6,000 wounded, whilst nearly half of the small British force was placed *hors de combat*. Wellesley looked upon the battle of Assaye as his greatest military triumph in India. General Lake followed this up by driving the enemy's forces to the north, besieging and taking the strong fortress of

THE FORT AT DELHI.

Bhurtpoor, and after another successful victory at Alighur, he marched on Delhi where Sindia was waiting to oppose him with a large army. After a severe battle the latter was defeated, and the English flag waved on the walls of the ancient Citadel. The aged Emperor Shah Alum, dethroned and imprisoned there by Sindia, was then replaced in power under British protection. Sindia was again defeated at another big battle at Laswaree, and compelled to submit to the terms of a hard treaty.

The British were victorious at all points. The Rajahs of Bhurtpoor, Jodhpur, and Jeypoor, and the Ranee of Gohud were all in turn obliged to submit to English Generals and sign treaties.

Meanwhile Eshwant Rao Holkar, taking advantage of Sindia's absence, had evaded the British troops and returned with his army of over 60,000 men, to plunder his rival's territory. This accomplished, he turned back to confront the English, imagining himself capable, single-handed, of regaining the lost power of the Mahrattas. He did in fact meet with success at the onset. In an action with Colonel Monson near Agra, he came out conqueror and caused the English their only disaster in this Mahratta campaign. The elated Holkar then boldly advanced on Delhi. General Lake met his army at Deeg on November 13th, 1804, when Holkar was completely beaten, and fled. He joined Sindia, and the former rivals now joined hands, in conjunction with the Rohilla robber chieftain, Amir Khan, who was at the head of one of the finest armies in India. But after a time, during which some hard fighting took place, this combination was reduced to quiescence, and forced to submit to terms. Thus the first Mahratta War was quelled by our forces after severe struggles in four widely spread districts situated many hundreds of miles apart.

We find the Kali Panchwin with General Lake's force when he pursued the Mahrattas from Simla, besides taking part in the siege of the Fort of Bhurtpoor. The Battalion afterwards joined Colonel Murray's force and was present at attacks on Dewas in Guzerat, Ujjain, Indore, and Kotah, also at the second assaults on Bhurtpoor, when the English lost 3,100 men and 103 officers. It is not stated how many men the Battalion itself lost, but it is recorded that two officers, Captain Kemp and Lieutenant Lowry, were wounded. On the surrender of the fortress, the Battalion marched to Tonk and on to Bombay, arriving there in April 1806, and remaining till March 1807, when it went into cantonment at Sirur.

Throughout the year 1809 the Battalion was engaged in field service in the Khandeish against Mulhar Rao Holkar (Eshwant's successor). This irrepressible Mahratta Prince had renewed hostilities, treaties with the Houses of Holkar and Sindia apparently being regarded merely as truces, to be brushed contemptuously aside at will. On the successful termination of these operations, the Battalion returned to Sirur, where it remained till the end of the year, when it moved to Surat and was quartered at this port for the next three years.

In 1813 the Regiment was called upon to take part in the operations against the Pindharees. Before recording its share in these long-continued actions, it will be of interest to quote from what the historian of the period says of these warlike tribes.

"The Pindharees, a nation of freebooters, were in reality nothing but mounted robbers, divided into Clans under their separate Chiefs, who owed allegiance to no central authority but, like the Mahrattas, were each perfectly prepared to sell their military services to the highest bidder. One of them, by name Chitoo, was proclaimed Chief and Rajah over all the Pindharees. He took upon himself to offer assistance to Sindia in some of his enterprises. In return, Sindia rewarded Chitoo and other Pindharee leaders with small 'jagirs' or grants, of land. Becoming more independent, Chitoo joined the renowned Rohilla freebooter Amir Khan, and together, with an army 60,000 strong, these desperate robbers proceeded to plunder and devastate central India, amassing enormous booty. Their cruelties and destructions were as great as their greed. They ravaged as far south as the dominions of the Nizam at Hyderabad, and even to Mysore, and plundered English districts in Behar."

Returning to our records, we find the Regiment kept continually on the move during the next few years against this wholesale devastation and larceny. Leaving Surat on April 10th, 1813, the Regiment was at Sirur on and off between its marches in pursuit of the robbers. In November 1814 it joined Colonel Lionel Smith's force and was in the vicinity of Jafferabad for about six months, after which the troops marched into Jalna Cantonment for the rainy season.

Meanwhile the Peshwa was causing trouble. Gangadar Shastree, an able and trusted political agent of the Gaikwar, and held in high esteem by the English, was brutally assassinated by orders of the Peshwa's confidential adviser and favourite, Trimbukji Danglia. The Chief Commissioner, the Honourable Mountstuart Elphinstone, on hearing of this dastardly crime, commanded a rigid inquiry to be made, and ordered Danglia's arrest. The 1st/3rd Bo. N.I. (Kali Panchwin) was sent by forced marches to Poona to fetch him. The Peshwa refused to surrender his favourite to justice. Pressure being brought to bear, he was made to understand that stringent measures would be taken against him if he persisted in his refusal, and very reluctantly he consented to hand the criminal over to the English. Accordingly, after some weeks of stubborn wavering, the Peshwa allowed Trimbukji Danglia to be given over to the troops and taken away for imprisonment. Two years later, Danglia managed to effect his escape from prison and secretly returned to Poona, at once using his influence to stir up the Peshwa into open rebellion against the British. He helped his master to raise huge levies of troops and horsemen, which the Peshwa gave out were for protection against the Pindharees. The Rajah of Nagpur followed his example and also increased his army, alleging that it was as a safeguard against the country's common enemies the Pindharee robbers.

Lord Hastings,[1] having ample proof from a reliable source of the treachery behind these pretensions, knew that both the Peshwa and the Rajah had been receiving emissaries from the Pindharees and Rohillas, and realised that matters were becoming serious and that vigorous measures must be taken in hand without delay. He therefore at once made preparations for placing a large army in the field composed of the combined forces of Bombay and Madras.

[1] Lord Mornington, the late Governor-General, as well as his brother General Wellesley, had now left India.

CHAPTER XII

DEFEAT OF MAHRATTAS

THE situation rapidly became extremely threatening. Evidence came to light that the Pindharee and Rohilla combination had established an understanding with the entire Mahratta Confederation, and that the latter was preparing to join with them in an attack on English factories and military cantonments, as well as upon our forts on the coast. The position was so critical that the Governor-General, Lord Hastings, took the field in person with an army of about 120,000 men.

Ascertaining first that the Pindharee and Rohilla tribes were concentrating in their strongholds in Malwah for the purpose of an immediate attack, Lord Hastings ordered the Presidential Armies to close round them, forming a cordon so that none could escape. They were attacked in detail and so completely beaten that never again did they become a serious danger to our power. The gangs were not, however, entirely dispersed until after the death of Chitoo and other leaders, in the spring of the following year, and General Lionel Smith's force—our Regiment still forming part of it—continued to be employed in keeping watch over these robber tribes, and preventing their penetrating farther south. The regimental records mention Ensign Mathews, with 100 rank and file, being stationed for this latter purpose at Manniah Poonj, Lieutenant Michel, with 130 men, at Wakla, and Lieutenant Spar, with a detachment of 100 bayonets, at Lassoor, during the first three months of 1817.

In March of this year the Head-quarters of the Regiment and the Grenadier Company were detached towards Nagar.

On June 20th a Brigade composed of 100 of H.M.'s 65th Regiment, 2nd/9th Bo.I., and 1st/3rd, under Lieut.-Colonel Milne of the 65th, was told off to remain at Toka, the remainder of the force marched towards Jam, arriving there on March 30th. After four days' halt the force resumed its march in a southerly direction, arriving at Karkaira on April 12th. Immediately after reaching the camping-ground, a morning order was issued to the following effect: "A detachment of 200 men from each native corps with a proportion of European officers, the whole under command of Major Smith, to march this afternoon."

Accordingly, a force of 600 men—composed of 200 from each of the following regiments, 1st/2nd, 1st/3rd, Bo.I., and the flank Companies of the 1st/14th Mad.I. marched that evening. The officers of the 1st/3rd were Captain Deschamps and Ensigns Forster and Mathers. After a pursuit of 150 miles, covered in four successive days and nights, the party came up with the Pindharee force they were pursuing, which consisted of about 4,000 Horse. Our troops at once attacked and dispersed them, inflicting a loss of seventy killed and several prisoners taken.

A laudatory Order was issued by Colonel Smith applauding the cool judgment and military skill of Major Smith, and the conspicuous exertions of the officers and soldiers under him. "The result both in execution and success has been truly honourable," he states, "and both officers and men have all zealously upheld the character of the excellent Regiments to which they belong." (See Appendix.)

The force remained in the neighbourhood of Pargoan and Karkaira till April 23rd, when the Head-quarters of the Light Division moved towards Poona. The remainder of the force (styled the Reserve), under Lieut.-Colonel Fitz Simon, remained at Pargoan till May, when ordered to move on Koregaon, where it remained till July, after which it marched to Sirur.

On October 10th the 1st/3rd again joined the Headquarters of General Smith's force, and marched with it to Poona, war having been declared against the Peshwa.

As the British Army was gradually converging upon the Pindharees in the south-east of Malwah, the Peshwa had begun openly to show his hand, depending upon Sindia, Holkar, and other principal Mahratta Chiefs, to follow his lead, all combining together with the help of the Pindharee and Rohilla tribes to crush the English.

Taking advantage of the annual Festival of the Dussera, on October 19th, which commemorated the taking of Ceylon by Rama, the Peshwa held a grand military display and paraded his new army. News of this reaching Mr. Elphinstone, a force was sent out from Bombay and Sirur, and by forced marches arrived so unexpectedly upon the scene, that the Peshwa's plans to cut off any advance of English troops were frustrated. His hostile intentions were at once made apparent and an engagement was fought on November 17th, in which the half-disciplined army of the Peshwa, in spite of its great superiority in numbers, was defeated by General Smith's Division. Poona surrendered, and the Peshwa became a fugitive. The Regiment took part in the battle, and also formed part of General Smith's Light Division which started in pursuit of the broken forces of the Peshwa. The pursuing forces followed the enemy into the Ghauts. On November 30th, the 1st/3rd was rear-guard to the force. This was attacked by the enemy, who showed themselves in great numbers on the jungle-covered hills at the flank of the rear-guard, firing with gingals and match-locks and throwing rockets. The enemy's strong force was, however, driven off with but slight loss to our men.

On December 30th the Regiment was ordered to proceed to Sirur with the 9th B.N.I., and the 15th Madras Infantry, in charge of ammunition and stores. On completion of this duty, the Regiment marched to rejoin General Smith's force, and was present at the capture of Sattara on February 10th, 1818.

On February 15th the battle of Gopal-Ashti was fought, against the Peshwa's Cavalry, under his best General, Bapu Gokhle. The Infantry arrived too late to take part in this action, though they exerted themselves to the utmost to keep up with the Cavalry. Their zeal on this occasion led to a favourable mention of them in the Orders of the Day. They had arrived in time to turn the defeat into a rout, in which the Peshwa's army was dissolved, never to take the field again. General Bapu Gokhle was killed in the action. The historian Blackie calls this battle of Gopal-Ashti "a most brilliant affair; few similar actions being met with in Indian warfare."

The following extract from Divisional Orders by Brigadier-General Smith, dated Camp Sirur, January 27th, 1819, shows how the Kali Panchwin's good services were recognised and appreciated. It states:

"The Commanding Officer has the painful occasion of recording his regret upon losing the services of that excellent Battalion the 1/3rd Regiment Bombay Infantry, which has now been under his personal observation for nearly five years. In Lieutenant-Colonel Stuart, the Brigadier-General will gratefully remember that he found a Commanding Officer of a Battalion in whom he could always rely to support his authority and execute his orders."

He goes on to say that the 1st/3rd had upheld

its reputation in the Bombay Army and that it was entitled to all the praise of those qualities by which a brave Infantry can run down Horse, and its exertions in that trying service for seven months deserved the most grateful applause. The Brigadier-General conveyed his best thanks and desired that they should be delivered to all ranks of the Corps, together with his assurance that it carried with it to its new destination his confidence and admiration, with his ardent wishes for its future fame and welfare.

The following Memorandum, recording recognition of individual good work by the Kali Panchwin in these actions, must be also inserted here.

Private Bhowani Singh, acting Lance-Naik of the Light Company, was promoted to Havildar on March 3rd, 1818, for bravery and fidelity in defending the village of Sylapur against a large body of the Peshwa's army, until the whole of the ammunition of his party was expended, when they were made prisoners. Further, for subsequently refusing an offer to enter the Peshwa's service and taking the first opportunity to escape and rejoin his colours, which he did on February 27th, 1818.

Private Esnak Balnak was also promoted to Havildar for distinguished conduct. He attracted the universal notice of all the Officers of Colonel Kennedy's force, by his unremitting zeal and bravery. His intelligence respecting the nature of the country and its hill forts, was of real service, and at the storming of Mandangarh, he was the second man to mount the ladder, and materially assisted in clearing the gateway tower which was escaladed.

To go back to the events recorded during the last three months of the preceding year. At the time that the Peshwa took up arms against the English, Appa Sahib, the Rajah of Nagpur, acted in a similar manner, having also—as we have stated—increased his army for the same purpose. Gaining at first in some of his attacks upon us in which his forces numbered ten to one against ours, the tide was very soon turned against him. His citadel of Nagpur was taken and he found himself beaten and deposed soon after the Peshwa met with the same fate.

At Indore, matters were also at a crisis during these months and engaging the attention of our Generals, but after some severe fighting, Mulhar Rao Holkar's army was finally defeated at the decisive battle of Medipore, on December 21st. Mulhar was deposed and his son acknowledged Rajah, with curtailed power and reduced territory.

Sindia was the last important Mahratta Chief left with an army of any pretence to independence, and seeing the defeat of all his allies, he decided once again to submit to the English conqueror's terms.

Thus fell the sovereignty of the Mahrattas, and the great robber combination was now subdued and under British rule. The Peshwa and the Rajah of Nagpur were both fugitives, the former's kingdom in a state of anarchy. A proclamation was issued by the English Governor-General announcing that the authority of the Peshwa had ceased to exist.

The effect of these wars was immense. When they commenced, the Princes, Rajahs, and other Chiefs of India were ready, and in most instances eager, to combine to crush our power and with the aid of the French to drive us out of India. At their close, the British had so crushed them that we remained supreme, and British authority was established from henceforth on a firm basis.

CHAPTER XIII

PERSIAN GULF CAMPAIGN

THOUGH these three great wars had come to a successful conclusion, affairs throughout India and its neighbouring countries were still very unsettled. In Goldsmid's Biography of Sir James Outram we read: "Amongst other *Outer* Barbarians who gave trouble, the Joasnic pirates in the Persian Gulf were conspicuous. An attempt had been made in 1809 to coerce them, but no real stop was put to their misdoings. They scared our fort at Bu-sharh (Bushire), threatened Basrah (mouth of the Euphrates), plundered ships from British India and butchered their crews."

Major-General Sir William Keir, who had just done such good service in Sawant Wari, and Bhuj, was sent in command of troops against them, and once again our Regiment was selected to form part of an Expeditionary Force. Having unfortunately suffered greatly from fever during the rains at Parli, in S. Konkon—where the Regiment had been from February 1818 till the following September when it was ordered to Bombay—it was reduced to such a feeble condition that there was scarcely a man who had not been in hospital. The flank Light Companies, having been despatched to Bombay immediately on the arrival of the Regiment at Parli, had escaped the sickness which struck down the other Companies, therefore they were the only ones considered to be fit for active service. They sailed with Sir W. Keir's force to the Persian Gulf on November 3rd, arriving at Ras el Khyma on December 2nd. On the following morning the troops landed about two miles E.S.E. of the town. Our flankers, and those of the Marine Battalion, were formed into a Battalion under Captain Deschamps, 1st/3rd. On the 4th, at about 9 a.m., all the Light Companies, under Captain Backhouse, of the 47th Regiment, were ordered to advance and take up a position under cover of a sand-bank about 900 yards from the Fort. This was effected without loss. Some works were required to be thrown up about 400 yards from the Fort. The European Light Companies advanced to form the covering party. The advance brought them to within pistol-shot of the walls, where they maintained a skirmishing fight with the enemy, in which from their exposed position they suffered considerably. The Light Company, 1st/3rd, was a good deal exposed when dragging 6-pounder guns from the first position to within 400 yards of the Fort. The trenches were opened on the night of the 4th. A battery, mounting two 18-pounders, was completed on the morning of the 6th, and commenced to batter down a breach. Two other batteries, with 6 more guns, were formed, and the breach was pronounced practicable on the 9th. Our flank Company formed a part of the storming party which advanced to the attack. The fort was taken without opposition, the enemy having evacuated it during the night.

Shortly after the capture of Ras el Khyma, a detachment under Colonel Warren was sent to take another piratical fort, named Zayah, eleven miles distant on the coast. Finding the force he took with him inadequate to the speedy reduction of Zayah, Colonel Warren applied to Head-quarters for reinforcements. Our flank Companies, with those of the 47th, were accordingly sent. The siege was now closely pressed. In two days a breach was effected and the enemy capitulated. Our Companies returned to Ras el Khyma the following day, and remained there until the end of January (1820), when with the exception of a small force left to garrison Ras el Khyma, the troops all embarked to effect landings at Sharga Murgaween, Bodabee, and other places on the pirate coast. The enemy offered no resistance, and these forts were dismantled without molestation. After this, the fleet sailed across to the Island of Ken to water, preparatory to taking its departure to Bombay, the principal object of the expedition having been accomplished.

The native troops landed on the island and remained there till nearly the end of February, when with the European force they sailed for Bombay. A less agreeable fate awaited the flank Companies of the 1st/3rd and Marine Battalion, for Captain Thompson, on whom the command at Ras el Khyma had devolved, deeming the garrison insufficient, wrote to Sir W. G. Keir for an addition to it, in consequence of which, when the European troops set sail for Bombay, our flank Companies were sent back to Ras el Khyma, reaching it on February 28th. Here they remained until the demolition and abandonment of the Fort on July 21st. On July 22nd the force was moved to Derristan, from whence it sailed in the *Ernaad* for Bombay, touching at Muscat for four days, where the men were allowed to land for refreshment.

The following copy of the General Order, published on the demolition of Ras el Khyma, will be of interest here, showing the satisfaction of the Military authorities on the carrying out of this campaign:

"The Honourable the Governor in Council having received the official reports of the demolition of the town and Fort of Ras el Khyma and the removal of the troops to the Island of Ken, desires to express his acknowledgments to Captain Thompson of His

Majesty's 17th Dragoons, the Officer Commanding, for the judicious manner in which these arrangements have been effected. Captain Price of the Corps of Engineers and the whole of the Officers and privates of the detachment of Artillery 1/2nd Bo. N.I., Det. 1/3rd Bo. N.I., Det. 1/11th Bo. N.I., Det. Pioneers, Detachment in the Persian Gulf, together with Captain Malliand, Lieut. Macdonald and the Marine Branch of the service have equally merited the commendation of Government by their unremitted exertions and zealous co-operation in the execution of these arrangements. The laborious duties to which the troops were continually exposed, under privations of no ordinary nature, have been performed with the utmost cheerfulness and alacrity; and the Honourable the Governor in Council has great pleasure in recording his high sense of the exemplary conduct of the detachment stationed at Ras el Khyma from the capture of the place up to the period of its final evacuation.

"By order of the Honourable the Governor in Council.

"(*Signed*) J. B. SIMSON,

"Secretary to Government."

The flank Companies arrived at Bombay on August 27th, and on September 9th embarked in boats to proceed to join the Head-quarters of the Battalion at Boondi, arriving there the following day.

A small expedition under Captain Thompson had been sent in aid of the Imâm of Muscat against the pirates of Lashkari or Beni-boo-Ali during the Persian Campaign. This was unfortunately unsuccessful. It therefore became necessary to take measures for wiping out the disgrace of failure attaching to the British name in that quarter. Consequently a force under Major-General Smith, consisting of H.M.'s 65 Regiment, the 1st/2nd B.N.I. and the flank Companies of the 1/3rd, 1/4th, and 2/9th, was despatched early in January 1821, and reached Sohar on the 27th, going into action before Beni-boo-Ali on March 2nd. The flank Battalion —of which our flank Companies formed a part—was in the reserve, about four hundred yards directly behind the 1/7th B.N.I., who were hotly engaged with the enemy. The pirates having been defeated and dispersed, our success was followed up by an immediate occupation of the fort and town of Beni-boo-Ali. The object of the expedition being fully accomplished by the annihilation of the tribe, the flower of whom had fallen in the action, the force only remained for four days to destroy the defences of the fort, and then marched back to Sohar, whence it embarked for Bombay on March 19th, 1822, and arrived on the 28th. This period of active service lasted not quite three months. The flank Companies rejoined the Head-quarters of the Battalion now in Bombay.

On October 26 the Battalion, under command of Lieut.-Colonel J. J. Smith, embarked in boats for Mandavi in Kutch (Cutch), at which port it disembarked on November 20th. From thence, the Battalion marched to Bhuj, where it relieved the 1/6th N.I.

New Colours were presented to the Battalion on May 19th, 1823, by Lieut.-Colonel Mackonochie, Commanding the Station. On September 27th Lieut.-Colonel J. J. Smith died, and the command devolved on Lieutenant W. J. Hewitt as senior officer.

In 1824 the Battalion was renumbered as 5th Regiment Bombay Native Infantry.

On June 14th the honorary badges, "Seringapatam" and "Seedaseer" were awarded to the Battalion by General Orders of May 24th, 1824, and were affixed to the colours on this day, having been received from the Adjutant-General on June 12th.

Lieut.-Colonel W. Sandwith joined the Regiment this year. Under his command the Right Wing and Head-quarters marched to Mandavi, arriving there on

December 31st. From this port they embarked for Surat on January 3rd, 1825, to relieve the 21st Regiment.

The Left Wing under Captain McKeever marched from Bhuj on February 14th, reached Mandavi on the 19th and Surat on February 24th.

On September 27th–28th the Regiment embarked at Surat for Gogha, whence it marched to Wad in Kathiawad, arriving on October 15th. There it remained encamped till November 18th, when it marched to Wankanir, which place it reached on the 20th and continued there until January 20th, 1826, when it marched to Rajkot and arrived in cantonments on the 21st.

On September 8th the Battalion formed part of a Brigade which marched against the Fort of Bohna, a small but strong hill-fort belonging to Chily Kachee, one of the Kathiawad Chiefs. Kathiawad, a place a few miles distant from the Fort, was reached on the 12th. The Fort surrendered and was forthwith occupied by a detachment of our troops. A detachment of 400 rank and file of the 5th was left with the 19th N.I., to overawe the Kathiawad Chiefs. The remainder of the Battalion returned to Cantonments at Rajkot.

The Regiment marched from Rajkot in February 1827 and arrived at Baroda on the 22nd of that month.

The Right Wing and Head-quarters of the 5th were brigaded for Field Service with one squadron 1st Light Cavalry, the 3rd Regiment N.I., and a Detachment of Artillery with two 6-pounders. This force marched from Baroda under command of Major Gibbon on April 2nd, 1828, reached Dubhai on April 6th, when, after taking possession of the Gaekwar's sequestered districts of Dubhai, Bahadurpur and Sirnoor, the Brigade returned to Baroda on the 15th. It was there joined by the Left Wing of the 5th, and marched to Petlad, which it reached on the 19th. It then marched to Lehgaon and Kurri, reaching the latter place on

May 1st. The whole of the sequestered districts were occupied by detachments from the Regiment (amounting to 700 men). The Brigade returned to Baroda on May 14th and was broken up on the 15th.

The Regiment under the command of Major James Gibbon marched on April 11th, 1829, from Baroda, and proceeded to Tankaria Bunder, where they embarked in transport boats for Sevendroog. In consequence of the non-arrival of three of these transport boats, a detachment consisting of two European officers, 2 Subadars, 2 Jemadars, 9 Havildars, and 161 rank and file, were delayed at Tankaria Bunder. The Regiment, marching via Amboli Ghaut, Sattara, and Bundipur, reached Sholapur on May 16th.

On July 9th the Right Wing, Head-quarters, and flank Companies (total strength 500 bayonets) under command of Lieut.-Colonel Gibbon, started at 10 p.m. on Field Service, having had but two or three hours' previous notice. The object of attack was the Fort of Akalkot. The Fort was reached after long and arduous march, which the men accomplished with great vigour and cheerfulness. The same spirit was shown during the fortnight's siege of the Fort, though this duty led to much hard work and exposure in the worst of weather. The scourge of cholera too was added to other hardships, and the Regiment lost 1 Subadar, 1 Havildar, 2 Naiks, 1 Drummer and 12 Privates. After 14 days the Fort capitulated, and the Regiment returned to Sholapur. The entire force engaged in the siege was: two 6-pounders, No. 4 Troop R.H.A.; 500 men 5th Bo. N.I.; 300 men 9th Bo. N.I., under command of Lieut.-Colonel Robertson, Resident at Sattara.

Before the separation of the Brigade, Colonel Robertson tendered his warmest thanks to all ranks.

"Short as the service has been," he said, "it had not been wanting in circumstances calculated to evince the advantages arising from discipline and zeal. In the first instance, the troops moved from cantonments on very short warning, and after performing a long night march, encountered the following morning a degree of fatigue with a cheerfulness which nothing but devotion to duty could produce. During the stay of the Brigade at Akalkot, the calls of duty which the nature of the service required, and which led to much exposure in the worst of weather, were obeyed with a promptness and alacrity that could not be surpassed."

Under command of Lieut.-Colonel Gibbon, the Regiment left Sholapur on December 8th, 1830, and marched to Dharwar, which they reached on the 27th, relieving the 18th Madras Native Infantry.

Three years later, the Right Wing of the Regiment, under command of Captain Keys, marched from Dharwar on November 10th, to Poona, arriving there on the 10th of the following month. The Left Wing and Headquarters, being relieved by a Wing of the 1st Grenadiers, marched from Dharwar under command of Lieutenant Heath, on December 11th, reaching Poona on January 9th, 1835.

On January 1st, 1837, the Regiment was still at Poona, but it left at the end of the year, under command of Major Spiller, for Malligaon.

The Regiment lost two young officers from cholera in 1838. Captain B. Justice died on May 1st, whilst in command of a Detachment at Dhoolia, and Lieutenant Cruickshank died on July 7th after an illness of only six hours.

By General Orders of July 12th, 1838, Regiments of the Bengal and Bombay Armies were increased from 75 to 85 men per Company, and by a subsidiary Order of September 3rd they were further increased by Havildar, 1 Naik, and 10 Privates per Company, making each Regiment consist of 800 men.

CHAPTER XIV

FIRST AFGHAN WAR

We now come to the first great Afghan War of 1839. In this campaign our Regiment took part and gained for itself undying renown for its glorious defence of the Fort of Kahun against attacks of overwhelming numbers of Afghans. But before describing the operations, it will be as well to enter into the causes which led to this war.

For many years Russia had held a menacing attitude. She had encouraged the Shah of Persia to attack Herat; she had supported Dost Mahomed, Ameer of Afghanistan, who had driven the rightful Ameer, Surajah Dowlah, out of the country, and had seized Peshawar from Runjeet Singh, the "Lion of the Punjab."

The continual intrigues between these northern neighbours and the Chiefs of Scinde had caused the Government of India great anxiety as to the safety of the country on the north-west.

England had made every endeavour, by treaties with these various Chiefs, to arrive at a friendly agreement with one and all. How her efforts failed is a matter of history. But the immediate cause of the war was that the old Ameer of Afghanistan, Surajah Dowlah, who, after being driven out by Dost Mahomed, had taken refuge and lived for many years in India, appealed to the Government to regain for him the lost throne of his ancestors. In return he promised to give back Peshawar to Runjeet Singh, the latter thus giving proof of his desire to become our staunch ally in the event of any attack from Persia or Russia. These promises were accepted as a wise solution of the north-west danger, and the advance of an Expeditionary Force was decided upon.

The advance was to be on a grand scale. The main force was to come from the Bengal Presidency, and as it was impossible for the Bombay Division to join it by land, it was ordered to Karachi in Scinde. There it was to disembark and proceed up the Indus to join the Bengal Division and advance up the Bolan Pass to Kandahar, where the great ceremony of re-instating Sarajah Dowlah was to take place. It was naturally expected that this Division would be afforded every facility in its advance, as, under the treaties with Runjeet Singh and the Ameers of Scinde, we were on friendly terms with them and had a Resident in the latter's capital of Hyderabad. Unfortunately there were differences between the three principal Ameers of Scinde. One favoured the British, and two were opposed to us. Great friction arose, and before the military plans for the general advance could be carried out, it became necessary to adopt punitive measures against these Powers. The Bombay Division was placed under the command of Lieut.-General Sir John Keen, K.C.B., and on September 8th, 1838, our Battalion marched from Malligaon to Bombay, and on November 18th it embarked on transports for Scinde, landing at Bomankot, a small village on one of the channels of the Indus Delta near Karachi. The Regiment was brigaded with the 2nd Queen's Royals and the 1st Grenadiers, under Major-General Wallace, C.B. Great delay was caused by the non-arrival of camels from Cutch, and an advance could not be made until February 3rd (1839), when the Bombay Division of the Army of the Indus broke ground, and marched via Kotri to

Sehwan. The Brigade then advanced to Tatta and from thence to Larkana, via Hyderabad.

On March 10th the Regiment was transferred from the 1st to the 2nd Brigade, and proceeded to Sukkur on the banks of the Indus, for the purpose of escorting convoys for the Advance Army, which proceeded up the Bolan Pass to Kandahar during April. The main portion of the Bombay Division joined up on May 4th.

The 2nd Brigade, to which the Regiment had been transferred, did not proceed with the main army under Sir John Keen. It was left to conduct operations against the rebel Baluchis, these being necessary in order to protect the main force. On May 1st a detachment of the Regiment, 150 strong, with a detachment of Golandaz with a 6-pounder, marched for Khojan, a village in the desert, and attacked the fort of Khangurh, which was held by 400 Baluchis. They took it by storm. Unhappily this brilliant little feat of arms was not effected without loss to the Regiment, and amongst the killed was an old and much-honoured Native Officer, Sirdar Bahadur Subadar Mahomed Khan. He met a most honourable death in the 40th year of his meritorious service, while leading his men to victory. Ensign Stanley was wounded during the assault. The Baluchis lost one Chief and 45 men killed, and a Chief and 46 men wounded and captured. The detachment returned to Sukkur on June 15th.

On October 20th the Light Company, under Captain Brown and Ensign Stanley, proceeded with the Headquarters of the 1st Grenadiers under Major Billamore, against two Baluchi tribes, the Murrees and Boogtees, who lived in the hills which bound the Kutchee plain to the eastward. Kahun, the chief town of the Murrees, was taken without resistance, and Deyra, the principal city of the Bogtees, was taken after some opposition. Bibruk, the Chief of the Bogtees, was made prisoner, and a large quantity of grain captured. The Light Company then rejoined the Head-quarters.

On January 14th, 1840, the force marched to Sheeber in the plains, for the purpose of keeping the country quiet. Fifty men under Captain Heath were detached to Dadar, and 210 men under Captain Brown were sent to Kahun, the chief town of the Murrees. On April 3rd, 1840, the Kahun Detachment left Lehree where they were delayed in consequence of the commissariat supplies not being ready, until May 2nd, when they commenced their march to Kahun, accompanied by a 12-pounder howitzer, under Lieut. Erskine, and 40 Scinde Horse, under Lieut. Walpole Clarke of the 2nd Grenadiers. An additional party of the 5th, consisting of 2 Native Officers and 50 rank and file, accompanied Captain Brown for the purpose of bringing back the baggage camels from Kahun to Lehree. During the halt at Poolaji, Subadar Pandu Laar, an old and deserving Native Officer, died from the intense heat, and Ensign Taylor had to be sent back from the first halting ground in consequence of a severe attack of fever.

Kahun was reached after nine days of trying marching over an almost impassable hill-track, under the intense heat of a Scinde sun in May. During the march, the howitzer had frequently to be drawn by our men, the bullocks being, from the nature of the country, nearly useless. The Detachment arrived safely at Kahun, having experienced no molestation from the Murrees, with exception of a few shots fired at them from the surrounding heights, while the men were toiling to get the gun and commissariat stores up the hill of Nafusk. After three days' halt at Kahun, the return party of the 5th, in company with Lieutenant Clarke and his 40 Horse, commenced their return march to the plains, in charge of the camels. Captain Brown, having heard that the Murrees had assembled in force in his vicinity, sent an additional party under Subadar Baji Jadow, consisting of 3 Havildars and 78 men, with orders to accompany the party under Lieutenant Clarke, until he had safely passed the hill and defile of Nafusk.

The two parties proceeded together for about twelve miles, when Lieutenant Clarke, having seen no sign of the enemy, directed Subadar Baji Jadow to return to Kahun, and the return party, under Lieutenant Clarke, proceeded towards the plains.

When the party arrived at the first watering-place about twenty-three miles from Kahun, the Murrees were seen collecting on the surrounding hills, and by the time the *bhistis* (water carriers) had obtained water for the men, some two or three thousand of the enemy had assembled. Lieutenant Clarke ordered the camels to be made to sit down, and placed the Horse to protect them. He then fell in with the men of the 5th, wearied with a twenty-three mile march over a hill-track, in a burning sun, and called on them to follow him to the attack on the heights, where the enemy seemed to be most densely massed. The call was readily and cheerfully responded to, and a small hill about five hundred yards off was at once carried by a gallant rush. Fearing to follow his success further, lest his active enemy should seize the opportunity to attack the cavalry guarding the convoy, Lieutenant Clarke halted his men, and commenced to fire on the ever-increasing enemy. The Murrees now took the offensive, but were beaten off by the fire of the 5th until their ammunition ran out. The position of the Detachment was now desperate, surrounded on all sides by a fierce enemy who were rushing to the attack with sword and shield. With their ammunition expended, nothing remained but to attempt to cut through the enemy's attack. Only one Havildar and 11 men broke through. Lieutenant Clarke and the whole of the rest of the Detachment died for the honour of the Regiment, fighting against overwhelming odds.

Subadar Baji Jadow's party of 78 men was surrounded in a pass on its way back to Kahun. All that good discipline could effect was, that it enabled the men to sell their lives dearly and die where they stood in the ranks. Again the superior numbers of a tribe reckoned as the bravest men and the best swordsmen in Southern Afghanistan won the day, and Subadar Baji's party, undaunted to the end, were killed to a man.

Thus in one day the Regiment lost 3 brave Native Officers, 6 Havildars, and 141 rank and file, and these mostly the best men in the Regiment.

Captain Brown's force, being much reduced by these heavy losses, commenced strengthening the Fort by every available means, and from the probability of another convoy not being able to reach him in time, he put his garrison on half rations, they having only two months' supply of grain with them. There was no possibility of procuring anything in the adjacent country, as no party could be sent out of gunshot of the Fort without being attacked by large bodies of the Murrees (chiefly Horsemen), who kept a constant look-out from a position in the dry bed of a river about one and a quarter miles from the Fort.

Frequent reports arrived that the Murrees were collecting to make a night attack on the Fort. Thus every man was on duty at night and employed working on the fortifications by day. This severe duty, combined with the effects of bad water, half rations (and those of a bad quality), together with the total want of vegetables and *mussalas*,[1] soon put the greater part of the men in hospital with scurvy, Scinde ulcers and fever, from which many died.

[1] Condiments, specially used by Indians in cooking.

On August 31st a convoy with a party of the 1st Grenadiers, under Major Gibbon, attempted to relieve Kahun, but the convoy was attacked by the Murrees at the Pass of Nafusk and driven back with heavy loss. Ensign Stanley of the 5th was with this party.

A communication from Major Forbes, commanding in Upper Scinde, was received by Captain Brown at this time, to the effect that he considered Kahun untenable, and that he regretted that owing to the total want of camels, and the scarcity of troops, he was unable to afford further aid. Captain Brown was instructed to take what steps he might think most advisable for the safety of his men, either by making terms with the enemy or by a rapid night march.

The garrison's rations were now further reduced, and Captain Brown opened a negotiation with Doodar Khan, Chief of the Murrees, which was completed on September 27th on the following terms:

"That the garrison should evacuate the Fort of Kahun, taking with them the whole of their guns, arms, ammunition and baggage, and that Doodar Khan would guarantee that they should not be molested on their road to the plains."

Thus from April to September, through fearful heat and hard work by day and night, did a mere handful of men, weakened by miserably short rations, sickness and death, hold Kahun, the capital of the Murrees.

CHAPTER XV

DEFENCE OF KAHUN

On December 28th, 1840, the Detachment commenced its march for the plains, having destroyed everything they could to lighten their baggage, except a portion of the ball cartridge, and having broken up the ammunition-wagon and body of the forage-cart, as the gun-bullocks were so weak from want of fodder that they were unable to draw them. The 12-pounder howitzer and limber of the forage-cart only were taken. Most of the men, being unable to march owing to sickness and debility, had to be mounted on camels. After eighteen hours' hard work the gun was eventually dragged over the Pass of Nafusk, but the men were so knocked up that they had to abandon the forage-cart limber, being still eleven miles from the first watering-ground.

The Detachment reached Poolaji, in the plains, on October 3rd, having then only forty men in the ranks, the rest being obliged to come in on camels or dhoolies that were sent out for them. After a day's halt at Poolaji, the Detachment marched on to Lehree and joined the Head-quarters.

We must here refer to a despatch addressed to Captain Brown from the Commander-in-Chief, which will be found in full in the Appendix. In it, His Excellency most highly commends the skill, judgment, and perseverance which Captain Brown had displayed in holding the Fort of Kahun for so long, under circumstances, as he says, of unusual trial and difficulty. The Commander-in-Chief expressed the very highest praise of Captain Brown and all those serving under him, and as a mark of his sense of the high order of services rendered, he nominated Captain Brown a Brigade-Major in the force assembled in Scinde.

Added to this commendation from high quarters, came also a letter from Major-General Brooks, Commanding in Scinde, expressing the very great satisfaction he had in publishing to the troops composing the Field Army a letter he had received from the Secretary to the Government of India, conveying the high approbation of the Governor-General in Council of the discretion and courage which had characterised the proceedings of Captain Brown, 5th Bo. N.I., in the critical position in which he had been placed at Kahun, and also of the admirable support afforded him by Lieutenant Erskine and Dr. Glasse and all the men composing the garrison. General Brooks was requested to convey this recognition of his indefatigable work and bravery to Captain Brown and his Detachment. (See Appendix.)

During the time that Captain Brown's Detachment was at Kahun, the Head-quarters remained at Lehree, where many men died from the intense heat. The strain moreover was great on one and all from being kept unceasingly on the alert by rumours that the neighbouring hill tribes were in motion. They were also harassed by raids from plundering parties of horsemen who came down from the hills to try to carry off camels and cattle. After Major Clibborn's brush with the enemy at Nafusk, there remained only eighty men fit for duty, the remainder being in hospital. The lines were entrenched in consequence of a report that the Murrees, Bhoogtees and Kojucks had joined the Brahuis under Naseer Khan, the son of Miral Khan of Khelat, with the intention of attacking the outposts of Dadar, Lehree, Poolajee, and Shanpur, in detail.

Orders were received on October 5th, from Major Forbes, commanding in Upper Scinde, for a Detachment to march forthwith upon Dadar to reinforce that post, then occupied by a Detachment of the Regiment under Captain Heath and Lieutenant Symonds, together with 240 men of the 23rd Bo. N.I., under Captain Watkins (in command of the post), three 6-pounder guns, and about 200 of the 1st Bengal Local Horse.

The Kahun Detachment, with the sick men and recruits, remained at Lehree under Captain Brown, being reinforced by the 1st Grenadiers. The rest of the Regiment marched to Dadar, taking with them 120 men of the 1st Grenadiers, two guns under Lieutenant Erskine, and 50 of the Scinde Horse. This Detachment consisted of the following officers and men of the Kali Panchwin:

Captain Heath.
Lieutenant Symons.
3 Subadars.
3 Jemadars.
16 Havildars.
146 Rank and File.

Relieving Force:

1 Major.
2 Lieutenants.
2 Ensigns.
1 Assistant Surgeon.
6 Native Officers.
260 Havildars, Rank and File.

It was reported that Naseer Khan had assembled a force said to be 7,000 strong at Bibi Nani, in the Bolan Pass, about thirty-three miles from Dadar. The Regiment started the night of October 6th, on the march to Dadar, via Bhag, but were detained at the latter place by the requisition of the Political Agent there, for the protection of that town, which was threatened to be plundered by a body of Brahuis under Kammel Khan, about 1,800 strong. These men had collected in the Gundara Pass and had ravaged the country up to within 30 miles of Bhag.

On October 29th Naseer Khan attacked the entrenched camp at Dadar which had been chiefly constructed by Captain Heath previous to the arrival of Captain Watkins and the Detachment from the 23rd Regiment. The Brahuis were beaten off with loss, our casualties being only 2 Naiks wounded. On the night of the 31st the Brahuis plundered the town of Dadar, the gates having been opened to them by the irregulars employed to defend the town. At the same time another attack was made on the camp and was repulsed.

On November 1st a wing of the 40th, and the 38th Bengal Regiment, under Major Boscawen, arrived at Dadar, having about 300 Scinde Horse with them. The force at once proceeded to attack the Brahuis' Camp, about four miles from our lines. Captain Heath and Lieutenant Symons, each taking charge of a 6-pounder gun—there being no Artillery Officer present—accompanied them with some of the Kali Panchwin men, leaving the main portion of the Detachment under Captain Watkins to protect the camp. On the arrival of our troops the Brahuis fled to the hills, leaving the murdered body of Lieutenant Lindsay, whom they had taken prisoner at Khelat, and the greater part of their baggage on the ground.

The Regiment having been relieved at Bhag on November 3rd by the 23rd Regiment under Major Newport, proceeded to Dadar in charge of upwards of 2,500 camels. Arriving on the 15th, the Regiment left Dadar on November 20th, and marched again for Sukkur. On reaching Jagan, December 2nd (a day's march from Shikarpoor), it received orders to reinforce the convoy under Colonel Wymer, 38th Bengal Regiment, which was proceeding to Dadar, 300 Brahuis having been reported as assembled at Karda across the desert.

The Regiment arrived back at Dadar on December 12th, but again commenced its return march to Sukkur, finally arriving there December 28th, accompanied by 6 European Officers, 11 Native Officers, 1 Sergeant, and 439 Havildars, Rank and File. The Kahun Detachment, sick men and recruits, had been previously sent down the river to Karachi. The Head-quarters were ordered to remain at Sukkur until further orders.

On February 17th, 1841, the Regiment embarked in river boats and proceeded to Umer Bundar, one of the mouths of the Indus. It arrived there March 5th and re-embarked for Bombay. After three days' halt on landing, the Regiment marched to Poona, where Captain Brown's Detachment was awaiting it, having preceded it from Karachi.

It was notified in General Orders of April 5th, 1841, that the badge "KAHUN" was to be worn on the colours and accoutrements of the 5th Bo. N.I. Six months' batta was given to the survivors and heirs of the killed of the Kahun Detachment, and Captain Brown was gazetted as Brevet-Major for his defence of the Fort. The Regiment was completed up to its established number, by drafts from the Recruit Depot, consisting chiefly of Hindus.

By General Orders of May 10th, 1841, the Regiment was made "*Light Infantry*," an honour conferred for its services in Afghanistan. Under instructions from the Adjutant-General of the Army, 150 General Service recruits were transferred to other regiments, in order to enable the 5th to enlist men better adapted for Light Infantry soldiers.

By General Orders of March 11th, 1842, an additional or 10th Company, consisting of 2 Native Officers, 12 Non-Commissioned Officers, 2 Buglers, and 100 Privates was to be added to each Native Infantry Regiment of the Bombay Presidency, and Commanding Officers were directed to adopt immediate measures for bringing up their respective Corps to the new strength.

By the end of the year the Kali Panchwin had completed bringing its Corps up to the new strength, having enlisted about 350 recruits, almost all being drawn from the Deccan, Konkan and Ghauts.

By General Orders of February 2nd and March 10th, 1843, the establishment of each regular Regiment of the three Presidencies was reduced by 1 Havildar, 1 Naik, and 10 Privates per Company.

On July 15th of this year four Companies of the Regiment were detached to Bombay for garrison duty, and on October 24th the Head-quarters and remaining six Companies marched to Bombay, arriving November 1st.

The following year, the Left Wing of the Regiment, under Major Smee, left for Field Service and embarked for Surat on September 9th, returning, however, on October 8th following.

By General Orders of March 26th and June 14th, 1845, the strength of each Company was again raised to 2 Native Officers, 6 Havildars, 6 Naiks, 2 Buglers, and 100 Privates.

The Right Wing and Head-quarters of the Regiment, under command of Captain Bayly, embarked on November 4th of this year, for Deesa, where they were joined by the Left Wing, under Major Smee, on January 8th of the following year.

By General Orders dated February 2nd, 1846, 1 Native Officer, 1 Havildar, 7 Naiks, and 50 Privates were transferred to the 27th B.N.I. The Regiment was to be still further denuded in strength, for the following year by General Orders, dated February 15th, 1847, the establishment of each Native Infantry Corps belonging to the Bombay Presidency was reduced by 10 Havildars, 10 Naiks, and 200 Privates, leaving the strength of each Company only 1 Subadar, 1 Jemadar, 5 Havildars, 5 Naiks, 2 Buglers and 80 Privates.

The Right Wing and Head-quarters of the Regiment, under command of Major Bayly, left Deesa on November 3rd, the following year, and marched to Ahmedabad, where they arrived on the 12th. The Left Wing, under Captain Rudd, joined them there on December 4th.

The Regiment left Ahmedabad for Karachi on November 10th, 1850, and under command of Major Bayly marched via Mandevi, arriving at Karachi on December 14th.

Ordinary Regimental routine and the usual Regimental annual Inspections, appear to be the only items recorded in the Records about this time. We pass on to 1852, when the Regiment made another move, and under command of Lieut.-Colonel Bayly embarked at Karachi for Vingorla, thence proceeding to Dharwar, where it arrived on April 23rd. The Regiment remained at this station until November 1st, 1885, when it marched to Bombay, Major J. C. Heath commanding.

CHAPTER XVI

THE INDIAN MUTINY

We now come to the despatch of the Bombay Forces to Persia, the cause for which is described in General Sir F. J. Goldsmid's Biography of Sir James Outram, as follows:

"At the end of the year 1855, the relations of the Government of India with the Court of Teheran, the Capital of Persia, were very unsatisfactory. Not only was our Envoy treated with want of civility, but the tone of the Persian correspondence was actively discourteous. So great was the tension that our Envoy withdrew to Bagdad in December of that year. The Shah immediately sent a large Military Expedition under his Royal Uncle, Murad Minza, to take possession of Herat, which was not only in direct defiance of our treaties with Persia and Afghanistan, but a blow to England's Eastern policy. News arriving that Herat had been occupied on October 26th, 1856, whilst negotiations were going on diplomatically at Constantinople for the withdrawal of the Persian Force, it was decided to take action."

A strong Expeditionary Force was in consequence quickly assembled at Bombay, consisting of 5,765 fighting men, of whom 2,270 were Europeans, and 3,750 followers,[1] together with 1,150 horses, 420 bullocks, 3 war steamers, 7 small steamers, and 30 sailing vessels.

[1] This number of "followers" may astonish some of our readers, but it must be remembered that the Indian Army was not provisioned by Government as a European one would be. The Sepoys received the

This force, under the command of Major-General Foster Straker, K.C.B., comprised the 1st Division of the convoy. It landed at Bushire on February 3rd, 1857, captured an encamped position at Barasjan, and on February 8th fought the battle of Khush-áb, where it was attacked on its retirement to Bushire. It was in this action that the Bombay Cavalry made its renowned charge on the Persian square, breaking it up and defeating it entirely. After the defeat of the Persians at Khush-áb, Lieutenant-General Sir James Outram, who had left Bombay on January 15th to take over command from General Straker, arrived at Bushire on January 27th, and immediately proceeded to attack the Persian Forces.

We now turn to the Second Division, which was ordered to mobilise at Bombay on January 13th, under the command of Major-General Havelock, C.B. The Light Battalion—of which the 5th gave its Light Company—formed part of the Second Division. It encamped on May 14th, and was present at the bombardment and capture of Muhamra on March 26th by the forces under command of Major-General Sir James Outram. We are told that the Persians had greatly strengthened the defences of Muhamra, with 13,000 troops and 30 guns, but evacuated it during the night, leaving behind all their camp equipment and 17 guns.

equivalent in money and found their own food. Consequently a considerable number of "Wandering Provision Merchants" with butchers, bakers, and other workers, as well as goats and beasts of burden, accompanied the Army into the field. To give instances of the number of non-combatants on an Indian campaign, General Harris took with him 35,000 combatants and 120,000 non-combatants in his expedition against Mysore, and Lord Hastings opened the campaign of 1817 with 610,000 men, of whom 500,000 were "followers." This very large percentage of non-fighting men in its train, with the necessary accompaniment of camels and oxen, must have greatly hampered the movements of the Army when on active service.

Many officers of the Regiment were employed during these operations: Captains Boodle and Taylor, with the Land Transport Corps, Lieutenants Des Voeux and Fellowes with the Light Company, Captain Mackechnie as Brigade-Major of Colonel Hale's Brigade, and Lieutenant Hogg as Adjutant of the First Scinde Irregular Horse. All these officers were present at the capture of Muhamra. Peace was proclaimed on April 4th, and an advance on Ahwaz abandoned. The Europeans were sent back to Bombay, whilst the natives were kept at Bushire.

Sir James Outram went to Bagdad, left on June 9th, and on the 17th left Bushire, and arrived in Bombay on the 26th. We are not told when the Light Company and their officers returned to Bombay. Barely were the troops brought back into India, when the great Mutiny in the Bengal Army broke out and spread rapidly throughout the Punjab, Oude, and Bengal, and later to the Central Provinces and still farther south. It was in connection with the operations of Sir Hugh Rose that the 5th took part in helping to quell this terrible outbreak.

The cause of the Mutiny is well known, but we quote the words of Sir John Lawrence, which describe it briefly from his own personal knowledge and well-balanced judgment:

"The Mutiny had its origin in the Army itself. It was not attributable to any external or antecedent conspiracy whatever, although it was afterwards taken advantage of by disaffected parties, to compass their own ends. The approximate cause was the cartridge affair, and nothing else."

Another reason, however, was that we had treated the Nana Sahib of Bithoor in Oude—descendant of the Peshwa—badly, in not giving him the Pension granted to his father, when he was transferred from the Deccan after the battle of Kirkee in 1817. This enraged the Nana so greatly that for years he set about spreading dissatisfaction against the Government in every direction, with the aid of the King of Oude. The latter's administration was so bad that the Governor-General, Lord Dalhousie, had been forced to annex his kingdom and place it under British rule. Then came the report, which spread like wildfire, that the cartridges had been greased with the fat of cows and pigs, with the object of destroying the caste of both Mahomedans and Hindoos.

The preposterous tale was believed by ninety-nine out of a hundred, and a feeling of immediate alarm for their religion and caste spread through every regiment from Calcutta to Peshawar. The whole Army, in fact, was enveloped in a blaze of mutiny. The great storm of rebellion occurred when the 11th and 20th Native Infantry at Meerut attacked the Europeans, shot their officers, and after firing the town and slaying every English lady and child they could find, went off to Delhi. There they were joined by all the Sepoys in that great city, and commenced their fearful work of destruction. The flame of rebellion had now spread throughout the whole of Hindustan, and in twenty different places at once, the Sepoys mutinied and murdered all the English they could lay their hands on.

We now come to the part taken by the 5th Battalion Bo. N.I. in the operations connected with the suppression of the Mutiny throughout the Bombay Presidency. The Regiment's Head-quarters and six Companies left Bombay on Field Service on July 15th, 1857, under command of Lieut.-Colonel Heath, and arrived at Poona on July 19th. On December 20th Captain Mackechnie—who was on duty at Asirgarh—was sent with a small Detachment, accompanied by

THE RESIDENCY, LUCKNOW, 1857.

Lieutenant Des Voeux, and Subadars Umrao Singh and Ittoo Larr, against a rebel named Yeshwant Rao Kadam, who was in arms against the Government, in the Fort of Khundaree, fifty-six miles from Asirgarh. The Detachment seized the Fort, captured Yeshwant Rao and twenty of his followers, together with all the arms that had been collected. They also disarmed about two hundred fanatical Mussulmans, inhabitants of Viramgaum. For this service they received the thanks of Lieut.-Colonel Le Mesurier, the Officer Commanding at Asirgarh.

The following letter from H. L. Anderson, Esq., Secretary to Government, dated July 29th, 1858, also testifies to the Detachment's good work:

"Sir,—With reference to your letter dated 19th instant No. 428 and its enclosures detailing the operations of the Detachment under Captain Mackechnie, I am directed to state for the information of His Excellency the Commander-in-Chief, that the operations appear to have been conducted with judgment and activity, and that in the opinion of the Right Honourable Governor in Council, the Detachment has performed good service.

"(*Signed*) H. L. Anderson,
"*Secretary to Government.*"

The Head-quarters of the Regiment, under the command of Lieut.-Colonel J. C. Heath, marched from Poona on September 12th and arrived at Ahmednagar on September 17th. From thence a Detachment of 200 men under Captain Olliver, Lieutenants Ramsay, Fellowes and Browne, formed part of a Field Force under Captain Pottinger, Bombay Artillery, in pursuit of a party of Bheels, under Ragoji Naik, leaving Ahmednagar on September 27th.

New colours were presented to the Regiment on

December 5th by Brigadier-General Blood, Commanding at Ahmednagar.

During practically the whole of the following year (1859) the Regiment was employed in furnishing escort parties for conveying treasure and ammunition, etc., for the Field Forces in Central India. In November a Detachment accompanied Colonel Tapp's Field Force from Ahmednagar, Captain Mackechnie being Brigade-Major, and Lieutenant Des Voeux Commissariat Officer. Three Companies, under command of Lieutenants Browne and Mackenzie, proceeded with a force under Major Marsh, 3rd Dragoon Guards, into Khandeish and the Nizam's dominions. Lieutenant Hogg was appointed Staff Officer to the Force.

The Regiment was paid a high compliment in regard to general efficiency, drill, etc., by the Brigadier Officer who reviewed it this year. (See Appendix.)

The Head-quarters of the Regiment, under command of Major Stanley, marched from Ahmednagar on Field Service on February 20th, 1859, halted at Mominabad in the Nizam's territory for a few days, and then marched on to Kaladji, arriving there on March 31st. Detachments of the Regiment were employed on outpost duty on the frontier of the Southern Mahratta Country at the following places: Bijapoor, Badami, Bagalkot, Mudgal.

In June the Regiment was reduced to 700 rank and file.

Intimation that the Regiment was to be sent again on foreign service arrived in a letter to Major Stanley from Bombay Head-quarters, informing him that the Commander-in-Chief had nominated the 5th Bo. N.L.I. as one of two Native Infantry Regiments required for service in China. In order to make the Battalion complete, the two extra Companies that were raised in July 1857, and which had been transferred to the 1st

Extra Battalion Bo. N.I., were to be retransferred back to the 5th Bo. N.L.I. and incorporated in the Regiment's Companies as the Commanding Officer thought fit.

Following this, Major Stanley received a letter from the Adjutant-General, conveying the Commander-in-Chief's gratification at receiving a most favourable Report in all respects of the 5th Bo. N.L.I. In communicating this to Major Stanley, the Commander-in-Chief, Sir Henry Somerset, desired the Adjutant-General to add that he feels assured that the good conduct and discipline of the Regiment will be uniformly upheld by all ranks and be conspicuous during its service in China, for which country they are about to embark.

A " Farewell Order " followed, which we must give in full, though it will be found in the Appendix.

" FAREWELL ORDER

" SOUTHERN DIVISION OF THE ARMY,
" BELGAUM, *January 23rd*, 1860.

" Her Majesty's 5th Regiment Bo. N.L.I., being on the point of quitting this Division and embarking on Foreign Service in China, Major-General Farrell considers it not less a pleasure than a duty, to state that the old and well-known reputation of this Regiment, extending over half a century, has been fully maintained during the period that they have served in his Command. Major-General Farrell in thanking Major Stanley, his officers, and men, can assure them that he feels certain that all their comrades whom they are now leaving, unite in wishing them all honour and success in the forthcoming campaign.

" (*Signed*) J. C. COLES, *Major*, D.D.A.G., S.D.A."

CHAPTER XVII

WAR WITH CHINA

Before proceeding to detail the operations in China in which the Regiment took so prominent a part, it is as well to touch on the causes which led to this war with the Chinese in 1860, 61, 62.

For long past there had been continued friction between the reigning Emperor and the Home and Indian Governments, on the opium traffic, and other commercial and political questions. Treaties had been carefully drawn up and agreed upon by the Chinese and British Administrations, and continually broken by the former. Attacks, naval and military, had been made on our settlements by the Chinese forces, and by organised pirate fleets. These "pirate forces"—the curse of the Chinese—though not actually encouraged by them, were never openly restrained by the Chinese authorities. At last, the Home Governments determined to send an Ambassador to interview and remonstrate personally with the Emperor of China. On arrival at Pekin he was informed that he must "kow-tow" when he was admitted to the presence—that is, he must kneel down and make *obéissance*, as always insisted on at such interviews. This the Ambassador refused to do, as derogatory to the Royal Representatives of Her Majesty the Queen of England, so he was ordered to leave immediately. This final action forced the English Government to declare war.

The 5th Bo. N.L.I., having received its Orders for

active service, marched from Kaladji on January 6th, 1860, via Belgaum, to Vingorla, which was reached on January 24th. According to "General Orders" of December 28th, 1859, the Regiment had been increased to 1,000 Privates.

Companies, Numbers 8 and 10, under command of Lieutenants Haig and Ramsay, and Ensign Stratton, embarked on board the *Prince Arthur* on February 20th for China. Four Companies under Captain Taylor, on the transport *Ally*, on March 16th, and the Head-quarters of the Regiment, under command of Major Stanley, on the transport *Malabar* on March 19th. The latter proceeded to Canton, arriving there May 2nd. Captain Wallace, Lieutenants Des Voeux and Ramsay, proceeded to North China, with the Force under Sir Hope Grant, G.C.B., and were present during the operations ending in the surrender of Pekin. Ensign R. G. Stratton died at Macao Fort on the Canton River, on July 24th. (The Regiment lost two other officers this year. Captain R. W. Mackechnie died in England, and Captain C. E. Boodle died at Jacobabad on December 16th.)

General Sir Hope Grant, after reviewing the Head-quarters of the Regiment at Canton the following year, expressed himself as being much pleased with its efficiency generally, both on parade and in barracks, and also in regard to hospital arrangements, etc. The same praise was given to the Regiment a month later by Major-General Sir J. Michel, K.C.B., who, after reviewing it, desired the C.O., Major Stanley, to make known to his men after parade, before marching to quarters, the very sincere gratification he experienced from what he had just witnessed, and how efficient he considered the Regiment in all respects.

On the evacuation of Canton by the British troops in the autumn of 1861, the Head-quarters left on October 4th for Hong-Kong. The Brigadier-General issued a "Farewell Order" expressing his unqualified approbation of the high state of discipline and efficiency of the Regiments and Corps comprising the Garrison at Canton, the 5th Bo. N.L.I. being specified amongst them. The Brigadier-General went on to say, that he was aware that the two Native Regiments from Bombay came to China in full expectation of participating in active service in the field, and were disappointed at being retained for garrison duty. They had, however, performed everything required of them, most cheerfully and satisfactorily, and to both these Regiments he tendered his best thanks for their good conduct in quarters and their constant attention to their duties.

These two Regiments having been reviewed in the presence of Brigadier-General Sir Hope Grant, and General Sir J. Michel, both concurred in expressing the highest praise of the steadiness and precision of drill of the 5th Bo. N.L.I., and its perfect state of discipline and general efficiency, which was pronounced not to be surpassed by any regiment in Her Majesty's Service. All praise was accorded to Major Stanley, not only for the high standard of proficiency in which they found the Regiment, but also for his own close attention to the comforts and welfare of his men. The Brigadier-General stated that he should have much pleasure in bringing to the notice of the Commander of the Forces the valuable services rendered by the Kali Panchwin, and the very favourable opinion entertained of it by all the distinguished Generals who had reviewed the Regiment. A personal letter to Major Stanley from General Sir J. Michel endorsed all this high praise.

On the arrival of the Regiment at Hong-Kong on October 10th, the Governor-General of the Colony made an urgent application, in consequence of the amount of crime and the inefficiency of the Police, for the services of a certain number of men from the Regiment, to be placed at the disposal of the Civil Authorities, for duty in the Constabulary Force at Hong-Kong. The Commander-in-Chief in China acceded to this request. The men evidently gave complete satisfaction in this duty under Civil control, as the following letter from the Governor shows:

"SIR, HONG-KONG, *May 8th*, 1862.

I have the honour to acknowledge the receipt of your letter No. 25 of the 22nd ultimo, and in reply, beg to state that the men of the 5th Regiment N.L.I. were handed over this morning.

I have much pleasure in adding that these men, while attached to the Police Force of the Colony, by their steadiness in performing their duties, have given great satisfaction.

(*Signed*) HERCULES W. ROBINSON,
Governor and Commander-in-Chief.
True Copy
(*Signed*) JAS. H. RAMSAY, *Lieutenant,*
Adjutant 5th Regiment N.L.I."

The Head-quarters of the Regiment—strength as follows:

Major Taylor,	5 Subadars,
Lieutenant Ramsay,	5 Jamadars,
Lieutenant L. G. Browne,	33 Havildars,
Lieutenant W. T. Brown,	447 Rank and File,
Lieutenant R. A. C. Hunt,	12 Buglers,
Lieutenant M. R. Chambers,	7 Bhisties—
Assistant Surgeon Langley,	
Lieutenant Leacock, } Attached,	
Ensign Walcott, }	

commanded by Lieutenant-Colonel Stanley, embarked at Hong-Kong on board Her Majesty's Transport *Vulcan* on March 17th, 1862, for Shanghai to form part of the allied forces against the *Taepings* (Chinese forces) under Brigadier-General Stavely, C.B., commanding the Army in China during this expedition.

The Regiment was first in action at an attack and capture of the entrenched camp at Wang Kaza on April 4th. On April 17th it embarked on a gunboat soon after daylight and proceeded some twenty-five miles by water. Disembarked at about 9 a.m., and marched on Tseerpoo, an entrenched town about 8 miles from the boats. At about 3.30 p.m. this town fell to the allied forces after feeble resistance. The Regiment marched back to the boats late in the evening, and on the following morning returned to Shanghai.

On April 26th the 5th marched to the city of Nazean, twelve miles from Shanghai, *en route* to Kahding, and bivouacked for the night among the ruins of that city, having found the Taepings strongly stockaded in a position about one-quarter of a mile north of Nazean. On the 27th a close reconnaissance of the enemy's position was made, during which Lieutenant W. T. Brown was dangerously wounded.

On April 29th the stockade was attacked in force, and after sustaining a sharp artillery fire from 15 guns for twenty minutes and seeing the Infantry moving round to cut off their retreat, the enemy abandoned the position which they had so stoutly defended, and fled to Kahding.

On May 1st the walled town of Kahding was bombarded and captured by the allied forces. Lieutenant-Colonel Stanley, Lieutenant Ramsay, Lieutenant Hunt, Ensign Walcott, Subadar Ittoo Larr, Subadar Khandar Singh, Jemadars Munoo Connbee, Ragonat Singh, Ranoojirao Chowan, Randbir Singh, with 100 men, were present at the capture. The remainder of the Regiment, who were left at Nazean, rendered most important service by working the flotilla containing heavy guns, and all military and naval stores required at Kahding, through a most difficult shallow canal which intersected Nazean. Their exertions in this work were most cordially acknowledged by the naval officers who witnessed them.

Major Taylor was nominated to command the garrison of Kahding, and a Detachment of the 5th Regiment (strength 2 Officers, 2 Subadars, 2 Jemadars, 9 Havildars, 200 Privates) formed part of the garrison.

On May 3rd the Head-quarters of the Regiment returned to Shanghai, and on the 7th embarked in a gunboat for Soong-Kong (about forty miles by water) *en route* to Tsingpoo.

On May 12th, after about two hours' bombardment by the combined Artillery of the French and English, the walled town of Tsingpoo was stormed and captured by the allied troops. The Regiment returned to Shanghai on May 15th, and its C.O., Lieut.-Colonel Stanley, was appointed to command the garrison there.

On the 19th information was received at Shanghai that a large Taeping army from the north was marching on Kahding for the purpose of retaking it. Lieutenant Chambers was instantly detached in command of a party of the Regiment—i.e. 2 Lieutenants, 2 Native Officers, 5 Havildars, 2 Buglers, 93 Privates—and ordered to reinforce Major Taylor's garrison. This move was satisfactorily effected. On May 22nd a Taeping Force under Chung Wang, a notorious rebel leader, designated "Prince," with the reputation of never having lost a battle, encircled Kahding, cutting off all communications with Shanghai.

On May 20th Subadar Khunday Singh, in command of a party of 15 Sepoys, was ordered to proceed to Kahding, with 2 Officers and 17 Seamen of the Royal Navy, in charge of stores. They were attacked on the 21st at Nazean and forced to retire by an overwhelming number of the rebels. The men of the 5th, covering the retreat, lost 1 Naik and 5 Privates killed (nearly half of their small party). The naval officers spoke highly of the gallant conduct of the Sepoys on this occasion.

Kahding was beleaguered by the Rebel Forces for three days and three nights. Major Taylor and his garrison were kept constantly on the alert during that time, and notwithstanding that the rebels appeared in front of Kahding in countless thousands, they were overawed by the arrangements Major Taylor had made to meet the attack. They therefore sought to obtain their object by stratagem, and sent some twenty-five men disguised as coolies into the town. This attempt did not succeed, for they were discovered to be rebels and were beheaded. No further effort was made to divert the allegiance of the Imperialist soldiers, who formed part of the garrison, and Chung Wang finding that the gates of Kahding were not to be opened to him, moved off in the direction of Nazean with his whole force, early on May 25th. The strength of Major Taylor's garrison was:

99th Regiment—2 Officers, 1 Assistant Surgeon, 30 Privates.
French—3 Officers, 125 men.
5th Bo. L.I.—4 Officers, 300 men.
Ward's Chinamen—3 Officers, 125 men.
Imperialists—1,000 strong.

On May 29th a column under Lieut.-Colonel Stanley was despatched to Kahding and the garrison was withdrawn. Lieut.-Colonel Stanley was obliged to proceed on sick certificate to Europe in November.

The Head-quarters of the Regiment, under Captain A. Des Voeux, left Hong-Kong on November 29th, 1862, to return to India, and reached Bombay January

5th, 1863. From Bombay, via Poona, they marched on to Belgaum, which was their destination. The Right Wing, under command of Major Taylor, which did not leave Shanghai till June 1863, rejoined the Regiment that autumn.

There appears to be nothing special to record of the years 1864, 1865, and 1866. Taking advantage of a quiet time, the Regiment turned its attention to building new Lines. The Sanitary Commissioner commented on them in his Report, in terms of the highest praise, stating that the whole had an appearance of stability, neatness, and good order, such as in his opinion had never been surpassed, if equalled, by any other Native Regiment in the Bombay Presidency.

CHAPTER XVIII

ABYSSINIAN WAR

THE lull and the peaceful occupations did not last for long. Four years after the Regiment returned from China it was again warned for active service—this time for another continent. Trouble had been brewing in an unlooked-for corner of north-east Africa, over the aggressive behaviour of the Ruler of Abyssinia towards British subjects. That country's King Theodore had possessed himself of the throne of Abyssinia in 1855 after deposing his father-in-law Raj Ali. Theodore was thought to be rather an enlightened Prince, but he proved himself to be a man of most violent temper and suspicious of everyone around him. On becoming King, he dismissed all the Roman Catholic missionaries in his kingdom, replacing them by Protestants. Two unfortunate missionaries, Stern and Rosenthal, incurred his wrath and were beaten and imprisoned. The next victim was the English Consul, Colonel Cameron, who was suddenly arrested and imprisoned. This treatment of a British officer was the more astounding as only the year before (1863) King Theodore had despatched a letter to Queen Victoria, begging for an alliance with England.

On the news of Colonel Cameron's imprisonment being received in London, Mr. Hommyd Rassan, a Christian Arab, Assistant to Colonel Mereweather, the Political Resident at Aden, was sent on a mission to King Theodore, to demand the release of the prisoners.

The request was refused, and Theodore had his prisoners conveyed to the strong fortress of Magdala, between four and five hundred miles from the coast.

Rassan was recalled, and a more important mission, consisting of two English representatives, Lieutenant Prideau, Assistant Political Agent at Aden, and Doctor Blanc, the Resident Medical Officer, together with Mr. Rassan, were despatched to endeavour to bring Theodore to reason. He received them in a friendly manner, and then suddenly imprisoned them, keeping them as hostages he affirmed, whilst he sent his representative, Mr. Illard, to England with the design of obtaining workmen to carry out some improvements in his country. This emissary was received in audience by Queen Victoria, who sent him back with an autograph letter, impressing upon the Abyssinian King the necessity of instantly releasing the prisoners and promising a more peaceful policy.

This letter had no effect, and Illard himself was imprisoned on his return.

In April 1867 the British Government sent an ultimatum to Theodore, demanding the release of the prisoners within three months. He continued to maintain a defiant attitude, and war was declared against him. A strong Expeditionary Force composed mostly of Bombay troops was despatched to Abyssinia, under the command of General Sir Robert Napier, towards the end of 1867.

The 5th N.L.I. was not included in this first Expeditionary Force, but followed later when reinforcements were sent for. It may, however, be noted that Lieutenant Arthur Poole (who commanded the Regiment in 1885–6) and Lieutenant Reginald Hennell, who later on joined the Regiment and also subsequently became its C.O. (in 1886–9), both served throughout the

Abyssinian campaign, the latter acting as Quartermaster of the 25th Bombay Light Infantry.

Massowah had at first been selected as the port of disembarkation for our Army, but Napier finally decided on Annesley Bay, though there was not a drop of fresh water there, and the only entrance to the uplands of Abyssinia lay over twenty miles of desert and through a defile seventy miles in length. At places this was so narrow, that it could be blocked from the hills alone by merely rolling down the overhanging boulders.

Our Army landed at Annesley Bay in the last week of 1867, and as the various units arrived, the troops were sent forward on the long march through the formidable Sooroo Defile in the Senafe Pass, to Adigerat, where the first garrison was formed. Fortunately the Tigré Prince, through whose country we had to march, was entirely on our side, and he sent a deputation to meet Sir Robert Napier at Adigerat, to assure him of his complete friendliness.

The long march to Magdala of nearly 500 miles was not only arduous in the extreme, a large portion of it being over the wildest of rugged uplands, but the Force had also much to contend with from the climate. Towards the end of March, 1868, as the head of the column approached Magdala, it was reported that Theodore had determined to abandon this fort and march with his army and the prisoners to Deha-Tabor, a still stronger fortress farther away, which he believed it would be impossible for our forces to reach before the breaking of the monsoon. Sir Robert Napier telegraphed for reinforcements and further supplies, and arranged for the withdrawal of the troops to Antalo, about forty miles from the head of the Senafe Pass. There he formed an entrenched camp, with a strong garrison and long-range artillery, to command and

[*Illustrated London News.*

THE ABYSSINIAN EXPEDITION: THE DESTRUCTION OF MAGDALA, 1868.

occupy the surrounding country until the rains were over, when a fresh advance could be made on either Deha-Tahor or Magdala, wherever the prisoners should be confined.

These precautionary preparations having been made, Sir Robert Napier pushed on with a selected force of mountain guns, Cavalry, and Pioneers, picked European and Native Infantry, and arrived before Magdala on April 15th. Theodore sent out two of the captives, Prideau and Blake, to negotiate for peace, offering to release his prisoners if the Force was withdrawn. Napier sent them back with his reply, "Unconditional surrender," and commenced to storm the fortress. A preliminary skirmish took place, when the Abyssinians were routed. The resistance was feeble and the attacking force soon obtained an entry into the fort. King Theodore was found dead, either killed by a stray bullet, or, as was generally believed, by his own hand. The prisoners now being released, the return march commenced at once.

The Prince of Tigré was received by Sir Robert Napier, on the way down, at Adigerat, with great ceremony and invested with temporary Kingship. A parade of the troops was held in his honour and he was given a thousand stand of arms, a battery of seven mountain guns, ammunition, and a quantity of stores, as a reward for his neutrality, and to support him against his numerous rivals after we left. He begged for some of the naval rockets which had created such an impression when used at Magdala. When it was explained to him that they were extremely dangerous, as they were apt to come back and injure those who fired them—as in fact they did when we used them at Arogee in the battle before storming Magdala—the Tigré Prince explained that he did not wish to fire them. If it were known that he possessed *one* only, he would be able to march from one end of Abyssinia to the other and be proclaimed Emperor, as no one would dare oppose him.

All reinforcements had been countermanded, and amongst them our 5th, which had arrived on the 21st April in Annesley Bay. The Regiment had left Belgaum on March 30th, for Vingurla, under the command of Colonel W. Taylor, and embarked from Bombay on the transports *Bengal* and *Agamemnon* for Abyssinia. It was a bitter disappointment on reaching Annesley Bay to find they had arrived too late to take part in the operations. Orders met them that they were to set sail at once to return to Bombay. The strength of the Regiment that had come on this active service was as follows:

Lieut.-Colonel W. Taylor, Commandant.
Captain Des Voeux.
Lieutenant Hunt.
Lieutenant Hartigan.
Lieutenant Chambers, Adjutant.
Lieutenant Maddan, Quartermaster.
Lieutenant Oxley.
Surgeon Day.
Assistant Surgeon Raby.
8 Subadars.
7 Jemadars.
37 Havildars.
14 Buglers.
637 Rank and File.
8 Bhistis.
5 Boys.

Our Army in Abyssinia was hurried back as quickly as possible, only just in time as it proved, for the rear-guard of the 25th was cut off on two occasions in the Sooroo Defile, the road being washed away by the heavy rain. By the middle of June, the last of the Force had embarked and sailed for India.

Military historians look upon this, known as the "Bloodless Campaign," as one of the most wonderful crusades on which our nation has ever embarked. Sir Robert Napier only accepted the command on condition that he was given a free hand in arranging the constitution of the Force and its conveyance across the seas, its march up to Abyssinia, and release of the captives. Given this, he accepted the full responsibility. What this was, can only be realised when we are aware that the force consisted of 10,000 combatants of all ranks, Artillery, Cavalry, Infantry, and 20,000 noncombatants, i.e. Transport, Commissariat, etc., which had to be gathered from all parts of India, and transported from Calcutta, Madras, Bombay, and even from England. From three to six thousand miles by sea had to be traversed, and marches made of nearly five hundred miles, through mountain passes and over a country utterly desolate and devoid of any food supplies, before reaching the fortress of Magdala, where the captives were confined. The way Napier overcame all these difficulties was truly marvellous.

CHAPTER XIX

INCREASED PAY AND NEW UNIFORM

EARLY the following year the Regiment was inspected and reviewed by Lord Napier of Magdala, and the following extract from a memorandum in the Quartermaster-General's Office at Poona, dated May 13th, 1869, reporting on the same, is an interesting reference to the resourcefulness of the men of the Kali Panchwin, from a practical, constructive side :

" The 5th Bombay Native Light Infantry have built Lines that could not be surpassed in neatness and efficiency. The men cut the timber in the forests and quarried stone for the gables, to face the drifting monsoon of Belgaum. The Native Officers' houses are extremely comfortable, and much more suitable to the improved position of those officers than the old style of hut. Every hut has a border of plants or a few flowers in front of it, and the whole Lines are a model of neatness and propriety, most creditable to Colonel Taylor and the officers and men of the 5th Bo. Native Light Infantry."

His Excellency goes on to say :

" I have never seen a native Regiment more advanced in drill, discipline, and efficiency."

From the same Office, in the Adjutant-General's Letter dated May 18th, 1869, this further report was issued of the Regiment, commenting on a previous inspection of it by Brigadier-General Domville, Commanding the

Belgaum Brigade, which also testifies to the handicraft of the Kali Panchwin:

"This is a highly satisfactory report, creditable to the Commanding Officer and all.

Lord Napier of Magdala has never seen a better Regiment.

The Regiment has built an excellent set of Lines which are a model of good order and neatness.

The 5th N.L.I. is the only Regiment that has cultivated small gardens, and if they received any assistance in tools and seeds, they would emulate an European Regiment in gardening.

The school is very good.

By Order.

(*Signed*) J. H. CHAMPION,
Colonel, D.A. General of the Army."

In the Adjutant-General's Official Letter, No. 6131, it is noted that permission is accorded to the 5th N.L.I. to wear their overcoats rolled up in the form of a valise, slung over the left shoulder by sleeves, and fastened by two removable straps.

In November 1870 the Regiment was ordered to Aden, and was quartered there for three years.

During that time it was twice inspected and reviewed, first by Brigadier-General Beale, and then by Brigadier-General Schneider, and in His Excellency the Commander-in-Chief's remarks thereon he states that he considered the report on the Regiment very satisfactory, and was glad to notice that it kept up the high character it had borne for years.

The 5th left Aden on December 24th, 1872, and returned to Belgaum, arriving there on January 13th, 1873.

Commenting on the reports of its inspection and review by Brigadier-General Kirby, the following year, the Commander-in-Chief again expressed his pleasure at receiving such a satisfactory report of—as he worded it—his "old friends the 5th Bombay Native Light Infantry"; a very gratifying expression of his kindly feelings towards the Regiment, and highly appreciated by all ranks.

The Regiment was armed with the new breech-loading Snider rifle on April 7th, 1875.

On December 3rd of that year the Regiment left Belgaum for Poona. It was inspected and reviewed by Lord Mark Kerr, C.B., Commanding Poona Division, on the 25th February, 1876, when again it is recorded that His Excellency the Commander-in-Chief remarks that "the report on this Regiment is satisfactory."

An increase of pay was accorded to various ranks in the year 1877. This was as follows:

"A grant of 30 Rupees on enlistment, to every recruit, to aid in the provision of the established kit.

An annual allowance of 4 Rupees to all below commissioned ranks of not less than eighteen months' service, in aid of half mounting.

Good conduct pay at the rate of 1, 2 and 3 Rupees monthly after 3, 9 and 15 years, instead of 1 and 2 Rupees after 6 and 10 years as formerly.

Increased pay to Native Commissioned Officers at the following rates:

Subadars	½ at 100 Rupees per month.
"	½ " 80 " "
Jemadars	½ " 50 " "
"	½ " 40 " "

The allowance to all Subadar-Majors is henceforth increased from 25 Rupees to 50 *per mensem*."

It having been decided by the Military Authorities that a change in the old uniform of the Bombay Army should be made, new patterns of serge frock-coats in place of tunics, and knickerbockers and gaiters in place of trousers, were designed, and the 5th Bo. N.L.I. was selected to report upon it. The uniform was received in April 1877, and a Regimental Committee of English and Native Officers and N.C.O.s was appointed to give their views as to its suitability for general adoption. The report of the Committee being favourable, it was decided at Head-quarters to issue this new uniform, and it was accordingly given out to the whole of the Indian Army.

Following this, and the increased pay Orders, came the announcement from the Right Honourable the Governor-General in Council, that upon the recommendation of the Government of India, Her Majesty's Government had been pleased to sanction the following measures with a view to putting the pension rules of the armies of India upon an improved footing:

"1. By the grant of the superior rate of pension heretofore given after 40 years' service on the completion of a period of 32 years' service.

2. By the grant of higher rates of pension, both ordinary and superior, to Native Commissioned Officers.

Subadar	ordinary,	30 Rs. *per mensem*,	superior,	50 Rs.
Jemadar	"	15 Rs. *per* "	"	25 Rs."

CHAPTER XX

SECOND AFGHAN WAR

We now come to the second Afghan War, in which our Regiment again participated. The causes which brought about this war with Afghanistan in 1879, whilst more menacing, were almost similar to those which led to that of 1839. Ever since 1842–3 Russia had been steadily advancing south, absorbing the Khanates of Turkestan, Bokhara, Samarkand, and Khiva, one after another, until in 1876–77 she threatened to occupy Herat. This city is said to be the "Key to India," and it had been given back to Afghanistan in 1842. War was averted by the Anglo-Russian Convention, which met and estimated the situation, Russia and England agreeing to establish an Exchange in Kabul to watch over the interests of their respective countries.

Sir Louis Cavagnari was appointed British Envoy and Resident, by the Government of India. He had not been many months at his post when he was brutally murdered by the Afghans, together with his small escort or guard.

The Amir, Shere Ali, fled to Turkestan, and his son Ayub Khan, who had been given the Province of Kandahar as a separate kingdom, defied the British to advance to avenge the treacherous murder. A severe punishment was of course decided on, and it was arranged that the British Army should move forward in two strong columns, one by the Khyber Pass on

Kabul, and the other by the Bolan Pass on Kandahar. It was with this latter, called the Southern Army, that our Regiment served throughout the war.

Being warned for active service, the 5th was moved from Poona by rail and steamer to Karachi, arriving there on December 2nd, 1878. It was kept at Karachi in reserve, until January 13th, 1880, when it received its marching orders, and was provided with the new valise equipment. The following officers were with the Battalion:

Colonel Roome, Commandant.
Colonel Des Voeux, 2nd in Command.
Colonel Hunt, Wing Commander.
Major Arthur Poole, 1st Wing Officer.
Captain Reginald Hennell, 2nd Wing Officer.
Lieutenant Nicholetts, Adjutant.
Lieutenant Francis, Quartermaster.
Lieutenant Ogilvie.

Captain Hennell (who only rejoined the Regiment on December 4th, 1879, having had to travel on a long journey from Canada, where he was away on sick leave) was sent forward on the 24th with 200 rank and file, as an advance party to Jacobabad, and went into camp with the Cavalry Regiment "Jacob's Horse," already encamped there.

The Head-quarters of the 5th followed three weeks later and trained to Sibi, at the mouth of the Bolan Pass, arriving there on January 14th, 1880. The Ruk Railway had been pushed forward across what was known as "the Put"—hard white desert—at the rate of a mile a day and was opened for traffic on the 15th, but was not in thorough working order till the 27th. The Regiment had to halt at Sibi so as to take over transport animals, but on February 1st, joined by its advance party, the whole Battalion started on its march through the Nari gorge to Spintangi (called "White Rock"), a very narrow rift leading into the Harnai Valley. Here the Regiment halted, and the Headquarters and four Companies branched off and marched to New Post at Thull Chotiali, already occupied by a squadron of the 2nd Scinde Horse. The Right Wing under command of Colonel Des Voeux, with Captain Hennell acting as Adjutant, marched to Harnai to form a new post there to protect the railway to Pishin and Quetta, then under construction. Detachments of the 1st Baluchies and 2nd Scinde Horse were already encamped there. Our Companies at once started the work of preparing and entrenching the port for the protection of the Commissariat stores and railway coolies.

On March 23rd Captain Showers, acting as Political Commandant, with Baluchi Guides, passed through Harnai on his way to explore a new short route through the hills to Quetta, the old route being blocked by rebels. Though warned of the danger of attempting it, he persisted in going on, and the next day he was killed. Sir Robert Sandeman, Agent-General for the Frontier, arrived at Harnai on the 25th, and ordered out a Column to avenge the murder, and drive off the hostile Panizai Kukars tribes of the Zhob Valley—who had taken up a strong position on the Chuppar Ridge, commanding the old road to the Pishin Valley, and had sent in defiant messages to our force. A punitive column was formed consisting of four Companies of Sappers and Miners, two Companies of Bombay Native Infantry, under command of Colonel Durand, with Captain Hennell of the 5th as Staff Officer, but retaining command of his own Detachment. Sir Robert Sandeman accompanied the Column, which marched first to Sharigh, and then on to Darhai, close to the mouth of the Chuppar Rift held by the Rebels, arriving there on April 1st. Three attacking parties were organised, one to clear the left flank, one to the right flank, and one to move up and attack the Rift. No. 1, commanded by Captain Hennell, was the only one that engaged the enemy, driving them off in a running fight over the low hills. Sir Robert Sandeman, who accompanied him, had a very narrow escape of being shot. He was conspicuous by a large white solar topee he was wearing and shots went through his helmet. The following morning, when an advance was made on the main position, it was found evacuated, the enemy having fled during the night. The road was now reopened for general traffic.

The Detachment of the Regiment under command of Captain Hennell remained at the new post at Dargai till May 28th, when they returned to Harnai. The road between them and the Head-quarters at Thull Chatiali was found to be unsafe, and the whole country being in a state of unrest—especially in the Zhob Valley—the detachment was kept in a continual state of readiness against attack. Lieutenant Ogilvie of the 5th, while out with a Detachment to repair the road, was fired upon in the Sembah Pass. There were no casualties, but one prisoner was made by our men. A relief party under Major Poole was also fired on at the same place. Following this, Captain Francis was sent out with 160 men to help in repairing the road through the Sembah Pass, rendered impracticable by heavy rain; and to assist in the completion of this work, Captain Hennell proceeded from Harnai with orders to re-establish the post on it and punish the marauders. He was employed on this duty till June 10th, when he returned to Harnai.

On July 28th came the news of the unfortunate defeat of General Burroughs's Brigade at Maiwand near Kandahar. This spread throughout the neighbouring tribes, and there was a general rising. A contemplated attack on Harnai by the Zhob tribes was only frustrated by the chiefs of friendly tribes giving us timely warning of the plan.

The disaster, however, hastened the forward move, and orders were given for a concentration of all the troops from Thull Chatiali and Harnai, to join General Phayre's Division at Killa Abdulla. Skirmishes with hostile tribes took place *en route*; a party of Sowars were attacked near Lieutenant Francis's post, and two men and a horse were killed, and two men wounded. At Kooriak, the force, consisting of the 5th Head-quarters, and five Companies of the 2nd Bombay Cavalry, with two guns of No. 2 Mountain Battery, was attacked at night, firing being kept up till 2 a.m. A small body of the enemy was seen in the early morning when the force left the camp, but it was dispersed with one shell.

On August 6th the Head-quarters of the Regiment marched, via Sharigh, to Dargai, and Harnai, picking up the Detachments encamped there, and by August 9th and 10th the concentration of the Column was effected under the command of Colonel Roome, with Captain Hennell as Staff Officer. The entire Column—22 officers, 900 men, and heavy baggage—passed through the famous Chuppar Rift without a single mishap, and camped on the northern side. On the 12th, the Column marched to Kach, leaving all the sick behind there in the fort. On the 13th the force reached Gwall, 14th, New Bazaar, 15th, Kykalzai, 16th, Azud-Khan, where the Column halted to cover General Phayre's advance. News being received that after the Column had left Kach on the 13th, the Murrees had attacked the fort, and Captain Wylie, the Political Officer-in-Charge, asking for a relieving force, Colonel Hunt and Captain Hennell, with a couple of Companies, and two guns and a troop of Cavalry, doubled back by forced marches. On arrival they found that the garrison had managed to drive off the enemy; they only remained therefore one night, and then rejoined the Column at Killa Abdulla.

On August 28th an advance was made over the Khojak Pass, our Regiment leaving all tents and baggage at Killa Abdulla, so as to be in at the projected dash arranged by General Phayre for the relief of Kandahar. After camping for the night on the north side of the Pass, the march was resumed to Gatai, and Mahomed-Ameen was reached on August 31st. There, news met the force that Sir Frederick Roberts, with three Brigades from Kabul, had arrived near Kandahar and would await General Phayre's Division before attacking. The Cavalry were promptly ordered forward to go on ahead with supplies. General Phayre placed Captain Hennell of the 5th in charge of 200 carts conveying the stores. He pushed on with these, accompanied by a Detachment of the Regiment as escort, and arrived at Mait-Karez on September 2nd, where an unexpected halt had to be made on hearing that General Roberts had attacked the Afghans and relieved Kandahar. All were naturally greatly disappointed at not participating in the victory.

Captain Hennell's Detachment was ordered to move away to Morgi Chaman so as to clear the road for Roberts's Force to march back to India. The latter's supplies having run out, Major Hennell handed over some of the stores he was taking to Kandahar. The conquering Division having passed down to the Frontier, General Phayre's Division advanced again towards Kandahar, and on September 10th went into camp outside the city. The 5th, who were the only Regiment without tents, had a fresh supply sent out to them, as well as warm clothing.

On September 20th the whole of General Phayre's Division, including 2 Brigades of Infantry, and a Cavalry and Artillery Brigade, marched into Kandahar, and took up quarters in a large rectangular square on the north-west of the city, rooms and domed quarters being given to the officers. Captain Hennell was appointed Commissariat Officer, and was engaged with a Special Commissariat Staff in collecting supplies from the surrounding country throughout October. Large quantities were brought in by neighbouring chiefs. Regimental Parades, Divisional Parades, and Manœuvres occupied the Regiment during the month. Two Companies of the 5th were sent to Mundi Hassar in Pishin, at the close of September.

On September 5th orders were given for the Regiment to march to Shorawak for the purpose of collecting grass from the desert, and obtaining intelligence of the country towards Nushki and the lower portion of the Lora River. The Regiment marched out of Kandahar cheered by all the troops of the garrison, and accompanied by many bands, on September 10th. The Battalion camped at Mundi Hissar, and on the 11th crossed the Arghastan and Dori rivers. The Corps was obliged to halt the next two days, the animals being done up. The march continued on the 14th via Dubai and Amun, to Gatai. The Kojack Pass was recrossed on the 18th, and Gulistan-Kharez, the largest and strongest fort on the line of march, at the mouth of the Rughani Pass leading to Shorawak, was reached on the 20th. Major Poole and Lieutenant Seddon with A and K Companies remained there as garrison.

On September 21st and 22nd the Battalion marched through the Pass, down the defiles and over ridges, and reached the camp at Shorawak on the 27th, where a Field Column was formed of a Squadron of the 2nd Madras Cavalry, 80 Sappers, two 7-pound Jacobabad

[24] ENTRANCE TO KANDAHAR, SHOWING THE GUNS TAKEN FROM AYUB KHANH, 1880.

Mountain Batteries in Head-quarters and seven Companies of the 5th Bombay N.L.I.

Major Hennell received a letter from G.O.C. asking him to superintend the cutting, etc., of the grass supplies for the line of communication, and at once commenced the work. The whole Regiment was employed in helping to carry this out; Native Officers, N.C.O.s and men, under the personal superintendence of Captain Hennell, being engaged in sorting, binding and pressing bales, loading these up on camels and carts, and despatching them to Gulistan, under escort, for the lines of communication between Kandahar and Quetta. The estimate was 33,600 bales, weighing 46,000 maunds, to be turned out in fifty-six days. The Shorawak *Mallicks*,[1] who contracted to collect and bring in the grass, also supplied fruit and vegetables and other supplies, and the Sirdars Almed Khan from Nutki, and Rah Khan from Nushki, came into camp to report on the desert grass supplies and assisted in its collection.

On March 15th, 1881, Major Loch, Political Officer, visited the camp and presented *longees* (turbans) to the Mallicks of Shorawak in recognition of their loyalty and help.

The final despatching of the grass to Gulistan having been completed, Captain Hennell was ordered to proceed with an escort from Gulistan to Quetta, to hand over all the accounts of the three months' operations to the Deputy Commissariat General, which he did on April 15th. The Shorawak Mallicks accompanied him, and took quite a touching farewell.

The Regiment started on its homeward march at the beginning of April, arriving at Quetta on the 23rd. Thence it moved via Siri-Ab, Durnaze, Dozan, Bibi-Nani, South Kitra to Kundi-Lani the Junction of the Sibi Railway, where it entrained to Karachi via Jacoba-

[1] Headmen, or Overseers of villages.

bad. At Karachi, the Battalion embarked on May 6th, on the British India steamer *Tenasserim*, and arrived at Bombay on the 9th. Their destination was Deesa, and the Regiment proceeded there at once by train to Pallampur, marching into the Cantonment on the 12th.

Thus came to an end the second War in Afghanistan, lasting a little over seventeen months. Strenuous as were the heavy marches over the long monotonous stretches of rock and sand, there were yet opportunities, during halts or when encamped at outposts, in which to indulge in occasional games and shooting, when the stern realities of the expedition could be for a time forgotten. In spite of having to be ever on the alert to watch for the appearance of hostile tribesmen, there were some quiet hours of tranquillity and leisure, as the officers' diaries show, when those who were in isolated posts and might otherwise have felt somewhat lonely could wander around and fill their notebooks with sketches or maps. And those who were flower lovers or botanists could take pleasure in collecting specimens of the beautiful flora, that, desolate and arid as most of the country is, yet spring up to cheer the landscape with their glorious colours. Amongst these are the pretty blue flower of the lily tribe, that the natives call *ghobar*, which grows in vast quantities amongst the wheat; the crimson lily, *stur-ghatol*, and the yellow specimen of the same. The *shimsbak*, a beautiful deep blue-bell, and many others, grow also in profusion in those districts and delight the eye with their brilliant hues of many shades.

Though the health of the troops was on the whole fairly good during this campaign, there were occasional outbreaks of sickness. These were especially trying when coming, as they sometimes did, to the small isolated detachments where no doctor was available and the sick had to be dependent upon such help and treatment as the officers and men themselves could give. Once or twice cholera broke out, as well as dysentery, and the hospitals established in forts that were annexed on the line of march were at times quite full, more especially on the homeward march. But when the campaign was over and the regiments were safely at home in their Indian quarters, many looked back with feelings of actual pleasure on this long period of active service and forgot all its hardships. For it is at times like these, in sharing toil, danger, privations, and sickness, as well as the hours of relaxation and amusement, that officers and men are brought closely together, and learn to know and value one another as they could never have an opportunity of doing in the ordinary station life. Many an act of unselfishness and devotion by officer or man is treasured up and remembered by the recipient with a warmth of gratitude and sense of comradeship that will linger in his memory through the rest of his life. In no Indian Regiment could this feeling of good fellowship and appreciation between officers and men be stronger than it was with the 5th B.N.L.I.—the Kali Panchwin—on their return from this Afghan Campaign.

The casualties amongst the British officers during the war were: Captain P. C. Heath and Brigade-General Burroughs, killed at the battle of Maiwand July 27th, 1880.

After its arrival in Bombay on May 9th, the Regiment proceeded to Deesa, where it was quartered for two years. General Sir Robert Phayre, K.C.B., in whose Division the Regiment had served during the late war in Afghanistan, reported very favourably on it. The annual Inspections in 1882–3 were also very satisfactory, His Excellency General Harding, C.B., Commander-in-Chief, expressing himself very much pleased with the Regiment both as regards discipline and drill, especially complimenting it on the manner in which it performed the proposed New Double Company Formation.

The Regiment lost its Adjutant, Lieutenant C. H. Seddon, this year. He died at Deesa, June 19th.

At the end of 1884, the Regiment was moved from Deesa to Mhow, marching via Lunawara, Dohad and Dhar, arriving at Mhow January 18th, 1884. This march was specially ordered through the Bhul country as it was in a somewhat disturbed condition. The Rajah of Dhar gave the Kali Panchwin a warm welcome *en route*.

Lieutenant C. H. Brackenbury, Wing Officer, died at Karachi on July 13th, 1885, of enteric fever, which had been contracted on transport duty whilst on the N.W. Frontier, Rundiland Sibi.

CHAPTER XXI

WAR IN UPPER BURMAH

In April 1886 the Regiment was warned for field service in Upper Burmah.

To understand the situation in Burmah which made it necessary to send an Expeditionary Force into that country, we must take a brief backward glance at the causes of the two earlier wars there in 1824–6 and 1852 (in neither of which were Bombay troops employed).

Alompra, the first Sovereign of the present dynasty of Burmah, was described as a talented adventurer. Having led his armies against the Chinese and other neighbouring countries, with brilliant success, he became so inflated by his victorious career as to conceive the idea of laying hands on the English settlements in Burmah. Although these were outside his frontiers, he claimed them as his own and demanded that they should be given back to him. He wrote peremptory letters to the Governor-General, and in 1823 attacked the island of Mahgrin on the coast of Arakan, and slaughtered the British garrison there. Again and again the Viceroy had remonstrated with the Court of Ava, but to no purpose, and this last action led to the first Burmese War of 1824–6. The ultimate result of this was a treaty, by which the neighbouring States of Assam, Tenasserim, and part of Arakan, were ceded to the British Government. The Burmese King was made to defray the cost of the long-drawn-out campaign, and also to consent to receive a British Resident at his Court at Ava.

Notwithstanding these concessions, from this time onwards the Burmans continued a course of constant hostility towards British traders. They were insulted and imprisoned on every possible pretext. At last, as no action was taken beyond stormy protests, the Burmans went to the length of besieging the Residency at Ava and openly insulted the Resident himself. He at once withdrew from the capital and reported the state of affairs to the Government at Calcutta. Ample apologies, and compensation for the outrages and loss to English merchants, were demanded. These requests were insultingly refused, in fact the Government in India was openly defied. There was therefore no option but to go to war, and this was declared in 1852.

Rangoon was taken on April 15th. The Princes and people of Lower Burmah received our Army with every demonstration of friendliness, welcoming the English as deliverers against their tyrannical conquerors in Upper Burmah.

An advance was made up the Irawadi, but the Burmese leader Myahtan put up a stout resistance, for many months inflicting heavy losses on the Bengal and Madras troops. The Burmans were, however, ultimately defeated, and Myahtan fled. England then annexed Pegu, and the people of Lower Burmah were freed from their oppressors. Thus the second Burmese War was brought to an end.

The causes that led to what may be called the third Burmese War, in which our Regiment took part, were briefly as follows.

The result of the last war in 1852 had only embittered the Rulers more strongly than ever against us, and though at times a peaceful attitude was taken, it never lasted for long. In 1878, Theebaw, a King of the old type, full of hatred against England, succeeded to the throne, and it was evident that the relations between the two Governments would soon become overstrained. His first act was brutally to murder all his near relatives so as to render the throne more secure to himself. Theebaw then proceeded to persecute all British merchants who sought to trade with his people, to such an extent that it became no longer possible for an Envoy to remain at the Court at Mandalay, to which place it had been transferred from Ava, Mandalay having been proclaimed the capital of the country shortly after the conclusion of the second Burmese War.

In 1885 the inevitable crisis arose. Theebaw inflicted a huge fine on a British commercial company, and threatened, if not paid, to confiscate the whole of their property. Remonstrance being unavailing, an ultimatum was sent, with which the Burmese King refused to comply. An Expeditionary Force was in consequence sent from India. Mandalay was taken within a fortnight and Theebaw made a prisoner and deported to Schycher.

It was hoped that the country would quiet down on the removal of its tyrannical Ruler. His army was disbanded, but unfortunately this was only a temporary measure. After a brief interval it was allowed to reform, with the consequence that in a very short time a number of the leading Bohs who had served under Theebaw began a series of raids against one another. They looted their rural districts and produced chaos throughout the country. Isolated British posts, scattered far apart from one another, were continually being threatened, and being only weakly held, were in danger of annihilation. Reinforcements were urgently called for, and, amongst other Regiments, the 5th was summoned to start at once for Burmah.

Our Regiment left Mhow by rail for Bombay, and embarked on the B.I.S.N. Company's steamer *Newassa* on April 30th, disembarking at Rangoon on May 10th.

The following composed the strength of the Regiment during the campaign:

Colonel Poole, Commandant.
Major R. Hennell.
Captain Nicholetts.
Lieutenant A. Beale.
Lieutenant P. Holland.
Lieutenant A. Milne.
Lieutenant Fisher.
Lieutenant C. H. Macdonald.
Lieutenant W. S. Delamain.
Lieutenant W. Ayerst.
Lieutenant R. Williams (attached).
Surgeon Quicke.
Surgeon Ward.
13 Native Officers.
28 Havildars.
497 Rank and File.
24 Public Followers.

Later on, Lieut.-Colonel F. S. Leacock, replacing Colonel Poole when invalided, as Commandant, and Major Tandy and Lieutenant E. R. Haughton, joined the 5th.

The Regiment was conveyed without delay from Rangoon by steamer up the Irawadi to Mandalay. C Company remained there as Head-quarters in five *poongyi kyoungs*, at the north-east corner, outside the city, covering the lines of the 2nd Madras Lancers, and E and F Companies, under Captain Nicholetts, formed a post at Shemaga, about 20 miles above Mandalay on the right bank of the river. D, G, and H Companies were conveyed farther up the Irawadi and landed at Kyoukmyoung, about 50 miles above Mandalay, D Company to form a post under Lieutenant Macdonald and G and H Companies forming part of a garrison at Shwebo.

A and B Companies, under Lieutenant P. Holland, had been left at Myinmoo, about fifty miles below Mandalay. This Detachment was badly stricken with cholera, and was taken over by Major R. Hennell when he arrived in Burmah on July 1st from British Columbia, where he was away on leave when the Regiment was called on active service. He found that twenty men had succumbed to the disease, and that about thirty sick, out of one hundred and thirty all ranks, were still in hospital. No doctor and no medicine.[1]

The next day Major Hennell moved the camp to a new position, two miles inland from the river, on rising ground, with the happy result of immediate improvement. General Low and Colonel Durand, who inspected the camp on July 22nd, expressed their entire approval, though Major Hennell, feeling that prompt measures must be taken, had acted on his own initiative in shifting the camp.

It is somewhat difficult to enter into any detailed account of this war. It differed from all others in which the Regiment had served, owing to the nature of the country we had to deal with. Open fighting was rendered impossible on account of the dense forests in

[1] *Editor's Note.*—One of the men, remembering Major Hennell's successful treatment of some cases of cholera at an outpost in Afghanistan, exclaimed when he came into the hospital tent, "Ah, Sahib, now that you have come we shall soon all get well." Knowing that faith in being cured is more than half the battle, Major Hennell followed up this remark by showing them a small disinfectant vaporiser that a member of his family had put in his portmanteau on his hurried rush through England, for burning in his tent to keep off the mosquitoes. "Here is the last new cure for you from England that I have brought with me," he said, placing the vaporiser on a table in the centre of the tent and lighting the little lamp. The sick men's faces lit up at once with hope, and their confidence in the cure, added to the fumes of the disinfectant, undoubtedly had an excellent effect on the invalids.

Upper Burmah. In practically all engagements with the enemy we had to fight an invisible foe. The dacoits waylaid our troops as they came up the river in boats or by road marches, and lying concealed in the thick jungle along the river banks, poured forth a heavy fire upon the advancing forces as they got within range. Not only was it difficult to locate the enemy in their hidden lairs, but our men laboured under the vast disadvantage of having to force their way through the close undergrowth of an unknown forest, whilst the enemy knew all the ins and outs of their tangled labyrinths and were able to keep concealed. As a rule they contented themselves with firing several volleys on our troops and then bolting, knowing that they were safe from pursuit. Our only means of punishment was to burn their villages. These as often as not we found deserted, news of our approach generally preceding us. Occasionally they mustered in force to defend a large village, and put up a sharp resistance, keeping up a steady fire upon their assailants. But when they found themselves getting the worst of it, they invariably managed to effect their escape from some corner of the village into the cover of the surrounding thicket, though often with heavy losses.

Added to being so greatly handicapped in carrying on a warfare under these conditions, was the serious danger of an even more formidable enemy, namely malaria, that lurked in the unhealthy jungles. We also had outbreaks of cholera—as already mentioned—and our troops, weakened by illness, were often little fitted to carry on their pursuit of the elusive dacoit, but many deeds of valour are recorded. The courage and endurance of all ranks under trial of sickness were beyond praise. The heat at times was excessive and caused cases of sunstroke. On the other hand, after heavy rains, the marches were rendered very heavy, through mud so thick that some of the men had to be lifted out, and it is mentioned in the records of the Regiment, that two men strained their legs so badly in these quagmires that they became unfit for further service. But all hardships were borne with that unvarying cheerfulness which characterised the Regiment throughout the operations in Upper Burmah, as it had done in all its former campaigns.

It would weary our readers to read all the daily entries from the Regimental Records and officers' diaries during these two years. They form a long list of expeditions against the dacoits, of the latter's constant worrying attacks on our camps and small outposts, and of our incessant efforts to catch the ringleaders. We must confine ourselves merely to quoting a few instances. In this campaign there were no brilliant battles to stand out as distinguishing features. But though it lacked the outward glory of striking military feats of arms, the vigilance, tactics, and skilfully devised manœuvres that resulted in bringing about a successful issue were none the less of the highest order. Many officers and men were especially mentioned in despatches and received the medals and military decorations they so richly deserved, and our 5th added yet another fine record to the Regiment's war services.

CHAPTER XXII

THE ELUSIVE DACOIT

The following extracts from the Regimental Records will enable our readers to judge for themselves, from these personal instances, of the kind of warfare that had to be carried on with the dacoits, and something of the general nature of the whole campaign. Our own Regiment's experiences were much the same as those of others composing the British Punitive Force.

Owing to the difficulty of obtaining information as to the whereabouts of the leaders, important captures were only made by slow degrees. Our flying columns were, however, on constant duty and the Bohs were kept in perpetual fear. Quarrels were rifé amongst themselves, and one troublesome chief (Hilaoo), at least, was murdered by his followers. The flying column of the 5th was directed in person by Colonel Leacock with untiring efforts during his command out there.

In reading the following little descriptions of the 5th's share in the effort to restore peace and a proper respect for the people's rights and property which it was the aim of our nation to enforce, a general idea of the difficulties encountered during this campaign may be gained.

"On the 4th of June, 1886, Lieutenant W. S. Delamain marched with 50 rifles to Thadan (16 miles), and on the next day to Payaban (10 miles), where he met with about two hundred dacoits. They fled at his approach after discharging about 100 firearms without taking any effect. Half the dacoits tried to escape across a large tank, and about twenty of them were hit and drowned. The Regiment lined the bank of the tank and fired volleys at them from 400 to 700 yards, the range being found by observing the bullets striking the water. One gingal, a few muskets and sixteen prisoners were taken, and a lot of stolen cattle recovered and restored to their owners. The marching was very trying, through mud and water, often knee-deep.

"On June 29th, Lieutenant W. Ayerst and 20 rifles, returning from a survey up the river in two native boats to Shemaga, were suddenly fired on by a body of a hundred dacoits, at Phogon, on the right bank of the river. Four of the party were wounded, namely Lieutenant Ayerst, Subadar Shaik Kasim, Lance Naik Ramdyal Chaube, slightly, Private Sidu Kakre, dangerously (he died at Mandalay). The party effected a landing with some difficulty and drove the dacoits out of a village and pagoda they had occupied. On the party re-embarking, the dacoits came back and opened fire, but without doing further damage. Several dacoits were seen to fall, but their exact casualties were not ascertainable, the party being too small to pursue them into the hills.

"On the 13th July, Lieutenant W. S. Delamain, with 50 rifles, formed part of a Column to attack the rebels who were occupying the fortified village of Yeutha in force. The 5th were told off to attack the N.W. angle of the high earthern wall covered with dense thorn hedge surrounding the village, while the remainder of the Column attacked the S.W. The 50 rifles extended about 400 yards, when the enemy immediately opened fire from bullet-proof firing places on the top of the wall. The 5th advanced by sections firing steady volleys. The final rush was made at the same time as the Mounted Infantry charged on the other side. As the 5th climbed the wall, the enemy fired a misdirected volley and swarmed out of the opposite side of the village. They lost 33 killed, including a Boh, and 92 prisoners. Privates Chandru Sakpal and Raoji Powar were mentioned as having displayed much dash in the attack.

"On the 15th July, 50 rifles under Lieutenant Beale, forming part of a punitive expedition under Lieut.-Colonel Baker, Hants Regiment, with two guns, 50 rifles Hants Regiment, and 100 rifles 43rd Gurkhas, left Mandalay with orders to burn four villages situated amidst forest in the Shan hills N.E. of Lamaing. The Column was reinforced by 50 rifles of the 12th Madras Infantry from that post. After a few skirmishes with the enemy *en route*, the first village was reached and burnt by the Gurkhas and Hants men, the 5th forming a cordon in the jungle round the direction in which the rebels had retreated. From this point the 5th formed the advance guard, the Hants following with the guns and the Gurkhas bringing up the rear. The second village was reached without resistance, surrounded, searched, and burnt by the 5th, after which the advance continued in the same order. As the Europeans came to a clearing by a stream, a jingal from the opposite side opened fire. The Sergeant marching at their head, fell seriously wounded. The Column had to halt and a brisk fusillade broke out on both sides. The enemy were invisible, though quite close on the farther side of the stream. As soon as their fire had been silenced, the column advanced. The next check was the final engagement at the village of Zeebyobin. The Shans had made a very strong stockade at the foot of the rise on which the village and phoongyi kyoung were situated. It was known that the enemy would make a decided stand at this point, both their flanks being protected by a winding stream that had to be crossed before reaching the village, and their stockade commanded the only approach to the river. The orders were, on the head of the Column coming under fire, to extend and reply. Owing to the denseness of the jungle on either side, extension was a difficult matter. The

GROUP OF DACOITS AWAITING TRIAL, BURMAH, 1886.

Shans, having their guns and jingals pointed on the spot where the Column would have to debouch, reserved their shots, and as soon as the 5th was within 150 yards of them, the Regiment was subjected to a murderous fire until one of our guns came into action and silenced the enemy's jingals. The 5th then charged into the river, which was only waist-deep and about 40 yards wide, but as the ford did not lead straight across, some time elapsed before the path, which was blocked with fresh abattis on the other side, was found. A party being left to watch the path, the 5th forced an opening through a by-path lower down the stream. When they had formed on the bank near the village where the jungle was less thick, no Shans were to be seen, but it was deemed probable that another stand would be made in the village and at the phoongyi kyoung on the crest of the rising ground. A rapid advance was accordingly made by alternate sections, firing volleys at the supposed position. On arriving at the top the place was found deserted, and the 5th extended along the outer edge, lying down, glad to rest, while the main body halted at the kyoung, the Gurkhas skirmishing through the jungle on both sides. The following is a list of the Regiment's casualties :

KILLED

Private Ittu Powar.

WOUNDED

Havildar Bahadur Khan, severely.
Private Genu Thorat, ,,
Private Babu Kadow, ,,
Private Babu Ghatkar, ,,
Lance-Naik Mith Singh, slightly.
Private Shaik Mohideen ,,
Private Shola Singh, ,,
Private Balu Powar, ,,
Private Laxman Mhadik ,,

"Owing to the narrow front, the Hants and Gurkhas

could not come into action. The enemy managed to keep unseen throughout, owing to the denseness of the undergrowth and their knowledge of the ground. At sunset the Column returned to Lamaing after setting fire to the village and the Kyoung.

"On the 10th August, 1886, 30 rifles under Lieutenant A. H. R. Milne, crossed the Irawadi from Shemaga in native boats and attacked a band of about 60 dacoits under Boh Nga Thaung at Shainwa, killed ten of their number, captured fifty-three gold coins, 504 Rupees, six muskets, three spears, two ponies and a boat, besides a quantity of dishes and cooking-pots.

"There was only one casualty on our side, though the attack was made under hot fire from the dacoits who ensconced themselves behind numerous pagodas. Havildar Binda Singh was conspicuous for coolness and dash.

"On the same day, 40 rifles under Lieutenant R. Williams, left Shwebo with 20 Mounted European Infantry and 15 Lancers, and on reaching Tebin, 18 miles from the Moo River, found about 100 dacoits of Boh Hlaoo's gang, four times that number having crossed the river on hearing of the approach of the British troops. The 100 men made a feeble resistance, firing a few shots and then throwing themselves into the river as the 5th advanced into the village. Owing to the thick jungle and elephant grass, and the swollen state of the river, pursuit was impossible, but seven dacoits were taken prisoners by the Cavalry. Bugler Dasratji Bedar and Private Powar distinguished themselves by their untiring pluck during and after the long march in intense heat from Shwebo."

Another distinct success was achieved by Subadar Ambar Sing.

"Starting at 8.30 p.m. on the 18th December with 30 rifles and skirting all villages to conceal his movements, he marched fourteen miles to a cave in the hills about two miles west of Mingoon on the Irawadi. Arriving at 2.30 a.m. he waited till 4.30 a.m., when he closed in on three entrances of the cave. There happened to be a fourth outlet of which he had no information. They found the dacoit sentry asleep under a tree, his post being at the top of it, where he had left his gun. On this sentry waking and giving the alarm, some shots were fired from the cave, the 5th returned the fire and killed 6 dacoits, 4 more were wounded, but escaped out of the fourth outlet into the jungle behind. 26 guns, 22 lbs. of powder, a quantity of bullets and a pony were captured."

With this last extract we will close our abbreviated account from the Regimental Diary of the 5th's participation in the Burmah campaign, merely mentioning that on the last day of 1887, four strong Companies, under Lieutenant A. Beale, took part in the Proclamation Parade at Mandalay, earning praise by their smart appearance and steadiness. Also that for six weeks in the opening of the next year, the Regiment was divided into patrols of 20 to 30 rifles, under their Native Officers, to patrol the whole of the Sagaing district between the military posts held by the Regiment. This patrolling was carried out with great energy and intelligence, and the Native Officers' services were acknowledged in a letter from the Deputy Commissioner of the District.

In March 1888 the relief of the outposts began and by April 4th the Regiment was concentrated at Sagaing, the last Detachment recalled being the Ongdaw Detachment, one of 30 Infantry and 30 Mounted Infantry, under Lieutenant Fisher. The services of the latter earned the thanks of the Officer Commanding Mounted Infantry in Upper Burmah.

The Regiment was relieved from active service by the 15th Madras Infantry on April 13th.

The following highly satisfactory Report dated Mandalay, April 23rd, 1888, signed by Brigadier-General

Low, was given of the Regiment on its departure from Burmah :

"Conduct and discipline in the Field exceedingly good.

"The Regiment had a lot of hard work on Flying Columns, etc., and has always done well. Dress and turn-out, exceedingly good. Sanitary conditions and efficiency very satisfactory, taking into consideration the continuous Field Service on which the Regiment has been employed."

Colonel A. Poole, Major R. Hennell, Captain C. O. Nicholetts, and Lieutenant P. Holland, were specially mentioned in Despatches by the Commander-in-Chief, General Sir George White, and Major Hennell received the Distinguished Service Order.

Unhappily the strain from overwork, fatigue, and illness, resulted in the death of Surgeon G. J. Ward, two Native Officers, and 48 men during the campaign, and Colonel A. Poole, Major R. Hennell, a Native Officer, and 69 men were invalided from Burmah before the Regiment was relieved.

CHAPTER XXIII

CENTENARY CELEBRATIONS

THE Regiment embarked at Rangoon on April 17th, 1888, for Bombay. There had been a scare of cholera on the way down the Irawadi, a few cases having broken out amongst the men, but these were left behind in the hospital at Rangoon and happily no further cases of the disease developed. Bombay was reached on May 1st, and six Companies proceeded by rail to Baroda. E and H Companies were detained for three weeks in Bombay owing to cholera prevailing at Surat, for which place they had been detailed. They moved up to Balsar on May 23rd, and on to Surat a month later.

The Regiment suffered a sad loss that same day in the death of its C.O., Lieut.-Colonel Leacock, who was accidentally drowned whilst bathing alone in the swimming-bath at Baroda. Colonel Watling took over temporary command until Lieut.-Colonel Hennell returned to duty from sick leave the following November, and was appointed Commandant.

On September 17th, 1888, the Regiment celebrated its Centenary.[1]

To commemorate the event, a three days' Rifle Meeting was thrown open to all Native Corps within practical reach, and the teams who took advantage of the invitation were hospitably entertained. The Regi-

[1] This centenary date was reckoned from the establishment of the Kali Panchwin as an individual Battalion. Previously it had formed only part of a large Battalion of ten Companies (see pp. 31, 33, 35).

mental Officers, European and Native, gave two nautches, as well as prizes for the Rifle Meeting and Athletic Sports. H.H. the Gaikwar also kindly presented prizes, and he likewise gave a banquet, followed by fireworks in honour of the occasion. Sir Olive St. John, K.C.S.I., R.E., Agent to the Governor-General at Baroda, presented a Centenary Challenge Cup, which was won by F Company, commanded by Subadar Sikandar Khan.

At noon on this eventful day, a summary of the Records of the Regiment, curtailed and translated into the native language by Jemadar Rancharn Singh, was read out by him to the Regiment in the presence of all the European Officers. Captain Francis presented a handsomely bound book for holding the Regimental Records as a Centenary gift, and lastly—though not sent till some years afterwards—a water-colour drawing presented by Colonel R. Hennell, to commemorate the Regiment's Centenary, should here be mentioned. It depicts the men's dress as worn a hundred years ago, and the dress of to-day. The names of the battles in which the Regiment had distinguished itself, and the various medals and decorations won by officers and men, are shown on the design. Before it was sent out from England, Her Majesty Queen Victoria graciously consented to see it, and it was taken to Windsor Castle for Her Majesty's inspection. The Queen expressed herself greatly pleased with the design and sent a letter to the Regiment complimenting it on its fine record of service. The letter was framed and sent with the picture, and now hangs below it in the Officers' Mess Room, a cherished and greatly honoured possession.

The following year, in accordance with a General Order by the Government of India (No. 378, dated April 1889), the word "Mysore" was authorised to be inscribed on the colours and appointments of the Regiment, in commemoration of services rendered in the past century during wars in the Carnatic and Mysore.

In this year, the "Order of British India" was presented to Subadar-Major Ramchandrao Chauhan, 5th Bombay Light Infantry, in recognition of excellent service rendered during a period of 31 years.

In November 1889 the Regiment again had to have a change of Commandant. Colonel Hennell was obliged to retire from the Service owing to ill-health. He was succeeded by Colonel H. Scott, 3rd B.L.I., who was appointed to the command of the 5th and arrived at Baroda in January 1890, Captain C. O. Nicholetts having been appointed to officiate temporarily during the intervening months after Colonel Hennell left India.

The Regiment moved from Baroda the following year to Bombay, where it was quartered in the Borce Bundar lines.

Medals for long service and good conduct were given to Naik Gonnak Bhagnak and Private Deoji Bedar, by Brigadier-General Bugden, D.S.O., on a Brigade Parade on September 11th, 1891. During this year, the Garrison Reserve was disbanded in accordance with the Military Department Order No. 1994 of 10.7.91. (The men of the Reserve were discharged in August 1891.) The same order directed that the late active Reserve should be styled "Reserve."

Martini-Henry rifles (Mark IV) were issued to the 5th in November of this year, and the old Snider rifles withdrawn.

CHAPTER XXIV

NEW COLOURS

THE Regiment was presented with new Colours by Lady Harris on the general Parade Ground Esplanade, Bombay, on March 6th, 1893.[1]

A carpeted enclosure had been marked off on the west side of the Maidan, where the British Standard was hoisted, and a large gathering of Bombay Military and Civilian Society assembled there. Outside the railings there was a big assemblage of the general public. The 5th mustered strongly on parade in full dress, there being eight Companies and the Band present, under the command of Lieut.-Colonel Scott. The following is the account of the ceremony from the *Times of India*, which paper kindly gives permission for its insertion here:

"The Regiment in preparation for the Ceremony, which is of a description seldom witnessed in this city, was drawn up in line at open order. The old Colours, with four Sergeants of the colour party and double sentries, being in front of the left of the line, and the band and drums formed in front of the right of the line at right angles with it and turned inwards opposite the Colours.

"When Lady Harris arrived on the ground accompanied by His Excellency the Governor, Lord Harris, and attended by Captain R. M. Poore and Captain

[1] The Colours were to have been given on the celebration of the Regiment's Centenary, but the Clothing Department was unable to meet the demand at the time.

Fowle, A.D.C.s and Staff from Government House she was met by Brigadier-General Bugden and his staff, and having been conducted to the enclosure, Colonel Scott, the Commandant, gave the order for the Regiment to present arms, after which the colours were trooped.

"The band and drums then played a slow march proceeding from the right to the left of the line, and on arrival near the Colours changed front, halted and ceased playing. They then played a quick march from left to right and changed front, halted and ceased playing again when in front of the line. The Company on the right of the line which formed the escort for the colours preceded by the band playing 'The British Grenadiers' then moved out at quick time the distance of a company and a half from the line formed to the left and marched straight to the Colours.

"The escort was halted at about company distance from the Colours and the ranks opened, the band wheeling to the left, halting and turning about. The two Jemadars of the escort then came forward and received the Colours from the Serjeant-Major and turned about. The escort presented arms and the band played 'God save the Queen' and turned to its front again. The escort then formed to the left to slow time, preceded by the band playing the 'Grenadiers March.' The music stopped as the escort approached the left of the line of officers.

"The escort on reaching this point turned to the left and when its leading file arrived at the left file of the front rank of the line the order was given to wheel to the left. The Commandant then ordered the Regiment to present arms and the band recommenced playing.

"The officers of the escort then moved along the front of the line of officers, the Jemadars carrying the Colours following them abreast of the escort, the front rank of the drummers in rear of the rear rank. Proceeding thus the escort on arrival at the right of the line was ordered by its Captain to halt, front and present arms, the band having ceased to play just before the escort halted and then formed on the right of the line.

"The Commandant then ordered the Regiment to shoulder arms, and afterwards closed the ranks. And here commenced the most interesting part of the ceremony, as the Regiment then bid a loving, yet sad and pathetic, farewell to the old Colours which had borne their part so gallantly for the last thirty-five years and the tattered remnants of which bore testimony to many a hard-contested engagement. The old Colours on reaching the right of the line, after they had been 'trooped,' took post in front of the escort, which then advanced about ten paces, formed to the left, and in that order proceeded to the left of the line, the band following, playing 'Auld Lang Syne.' The escort then returned to its place by the rear, the old Colours, cased, remaining in rear of the left of the line, under charge of the Colour-Sergeants. It was an impressive spectacle even to an on-looker, while it must have been with full hearts and dimmed eyes that the faithful soldiers of the brave old Regiment took their last adieu of the sacred emblem that they had defended in days of yore with such courage and true soldierly devotion. The Regiment having been then formed three sides of an oblong, the drums were piled in the centre, and the new Colours placed against the pile of drums, one on each side, the Queen's Colour being on the right. Major Nicholetts, the senior Major, and the senior Jemadar having taken charge of the Queen's Colour, and the junior Major and the next senior Jemadar of the Regimental Colour, these officers unfurled the Colours and replaced them against the drums. The senior Major then handed the Queen's Colour to Lady Harris, from whom the senior Jemadar received it, going down on the right knee. The Regimental Colour was in like manner handed to the junior Major and received by the next senior Jemadar, both Jemadars then rising.

Lady Harris, as the handsome flags were unfurled to the breeze, addressed the regiment as follows:

"'Colonel Scott, Officers, Non-commissioned Officers, and Men of the 5th Bombay Light Infantry—it is a great pleasure to me to have the opportunity of presenting to you for your earnest and watchful guard a new set of Colours in place of those which you have hitherto borne so gallantly. It is an additional pleasure to me to perform this ceremony in the case of a Regiment which was under the command of my husband's ancestor at the Siege of Seringapatam. To follow the history of the Regiment, Colonel Scott, which I am sure you feel it an honour to command, would take me too long. It is enough to notice that on the scroll of its war services are to be found expeditions to Ceylon, China, the Persian Gulf, Burmah and Abyssinia as well as the operations of the latter part of last century against Tippoo Sultan, the Pindharees, and the Mahrattas, and in 1880 in Afghanistan, and in the Burmah Campaign from 1887 to 1889. The Laurels that your Regiment lays claim to, Colonel Scott, have been won in several countries and in many a battle-field, and it may well be that in the course of so many years of such arduous services it has been necessary to renew the regimental Colours more than once. But whilst Colour may fade and silk may wear, the spirit of the men who guard them neither fades nor wears out. That has stood the strain of time and of conflict untarnished. That spirit, which has carried your old Colours so gallantly forward in the past, still lives, I feel sure, and I, therefore, consign these new Colours to your care, confident that it will enable this Regiment to carry them to the front when it gets the order to advance, guard them valiantly and jealously in the stress of battle, and bring them safely back with new lustre added to the brightest of their fame.'

"Colonel Scott, the Commandant, replied as follows: 'In the name of the Officers and Men of the 5th Bombay Light Infantry, I beg to tender to your Excellency our heartfelt thanks for having honoured us by presenting the Regiment this day with new Colours. We also thank your Excellency for speaking in such appreciative terms of the services of the Regiment since it was raised in 1768. We all naturally feel an honourable pride in belonging to a Regiment that can show such a favourable record, and if we cannot hope to excel we will try to emulate, such services, and always follow the high example set us by our honoured predecessors. In receiving these Colours from your Excellency this day, we promise to guard them as a sacred trust for our Queen and country; and should necessity arise, we will, in the hour of danger, make these precious emblems our rallying point and defend them with our lives as becomes true and faithful soldiers.'

"The line was then re-formed, and the Colour party, with the new Colours unfurled, turned towards the centre; the ranks were opened, and the Colours received with a general salute. The Colour party then marched in slow time to its place in the centre of the line, the band playing 'God save the Queen,' the ceremony being concluded by the Regiment marching past in column, after which it returned to its lines, while we understand the old Colours will be eventually placed for safe keeping in Satara Church, that station being the regimental centre of Colonel Scott's Regiment.

"The following officers of the Regiment were present:

"Colonel W. Scott, Commandant.
Major C. O. Nicholetts, Second-in-Command.
Captain J. C. Francis, Wing Commander.
Captain A. Beale.
Lieutenant F. A. Fisher.
Lieutenant A. H. R. Milne.
Lieutenant C. J. Windham.
Lieutenant E. R. I. Chitty, Adjutant.
Lieutenant S. H. Westropp.
Lieutenant C. H. C. Grace, Quartermaster.
Lieutenant H. Brand.
Lieutenant A. A. West."

CHAPTER XXV

PERIM EPISODE

In August 1893 the Regiment was ordered out to suppress riots, for which it received the thanks of the Brigadier-General and the Bombay Government.

It was in this year that orders were received from Head-quarters, under the Adjutant-General, No. 1712, C/17–3, dated August 4th, 1893, to form "Caste Companies," as under:

A Company . .	Rajputs.
B Company . .	Dekhani Mahrattas.
C Company . .	Konkani.
D Company . .	Bedars.
E Company . .	Pardhesis.
F Company . .	Konkani Mahrattas.
G Company . .	" "
H Company . .	Dekhani Mahomedans.

Recruits were obtained from Satara, Ahmednagar, and Rajputana. The introduction of these class Regiments produced a great change in the Indian Army and had very far-reaching effects.

It is interesting to note how very much the composition of the Regiment was altered some fifteen years later. In 1908 the 105th Mahratta Light Infantry consisted of four Companies of Dekhani Mahrattas, two of Konkani Mahrattas, and two of Dekhani Mahomedans. Bedars and Pardhesis are now only enlisted for the Band, and Sikhs, who had at one time two

Companies in the Regiment, are no longer enlisted in it.

In March 1894 the Regiment received orders to proceed to Baluchistan. Prior to its departure, it was inspected by Brigadier-General W. Gatacre, D.S.O., who reported that the Regiment was in very good order in all respects and reflected great credit on Colonel Scott and its British and Native Officers.

The Regiment left Bombay for Karachi by steamer and reached Sibi on March 23rd. A detachment of 200 rifles from A, B, and C Companies, under Captain C. Dretton, railed to Quetta *en route* to Kelat. The remainder of the Unit railed to Yaru Karez, from whence it marched to Shelabag, relieving the 24th Baluchistan Regiment on March 30th. On November 24th the Regiment moved on up to Quetta. The duration of its stay there, however, was very much curtailed, for hardly had the men settled into the barracks, than orders were received for the Regiment to march on to Pishin. After being stationed there for a very short period, the 5th was again on the move, this time to return to India. The Regiment reached Bombay at the end of March 1896, and proceeded by rail to Ahmedabad, a Detachment being sent to Rajkote. Major W. O. Nicholetts—now Colonel Nicholetts—assumed command of the Regiment, vice Colonel W. Scott, retired.[1]

A General Order regarding officers' dress came into force this year, which abolished the Glengarry Cap, and a peace manœuvres cap was authorised in its place. The pattern for the Regiment was dark green;

[1] *Editor's Note.*—The Regiment was greatly gratified at this time to receive the news that its previous Commandant, Colonel Reginald Hennell, had been appointed Clerk of the Cheque and Adjutant of the Royal Body Guard of the Yeomen of the Guard, especially as he was the first and only officer of the Indian Army who had been honoured by holding an appointment in the Sovereign's Ancient Guard.

Austrian patterns with red piping, and a silver bugle with the numeral V in the centre. The following year, a new pattern sword was introduced for British Officers, with the Royal Cipher V.R.I. below the crown on the hilt.

Under Army instructions, shoulder belts and swords for Drummers, Buglers, and Musicians were ordered to be discontinued, about this time, and short sword bayonet frog substituted. Native Officers received Webley pattern revolvers in place of the old Enfield ones.

Shortly after the arrival of the Regiment at Ahmedabad, it was inspected by Brigadier-General Hogg, who reported that it had suffered from the disadvantage of having too many Detachments. The following year when the Regiment moved from Ahmedabad to Rajkote—with a Detachment at Deesa—at an inspection of the regimental lines, workshops and institutes, the G.O.C. Deesa District remarked that these were all "perfect." A later report, after an inspection by General Hogg, also gave the warmest praise to the Regiment, remarking, "The 5th Bombay Light Infantry is in a satisfactory condition. It drills well and is very good in musketry training. Fit for active service." The Commander-in-Chief endorsed this by saying, "The Regiment appears to be efficient in every respect, for which Lieut.-Colonel Nicholetts is to be commended."

In February 1900 the Regiment received orders to go to Aden, and embarked at Port Bandar on the 25th, reaching Aden on March 4th. On account of quarantine regulations, however, it was not allowed to land. Detachments were sent to Bulhar and Berbera, in Somaliland on the opposite coast of Africa, and to Perim. The latter is a small island in the Straits of Bab-el-Mandeb, the eastern entrance to the Red Sea from the

Indian Ocean. Being right in the middle of the narrow channel, it holds a commanding position and has rightly been called the "key to the Red Sea." It is a long, narrow strip of rock and sand hillocks, only $1\frac{3}{4}$ miles across, and 10 miles in length. Ever since Aden became one of England's seaports, this important little island had been looked upon as part of that possession, though no troops were kept on Perim. An amusing episode is told of how, owing to this lack of forethought, we very nearly lost the key to the ocean highway between Europe and Asia. It happened this way. A French man-of-war put into Aden one day and an invitation was sent by the Garrison to the officers on board, to come on shore and dine at the English Mess. They accepted, and an excellent dinner was given to the French guests. Under the genial influence of their hosts' hospitality one of the French officers let out that they were on their way to Perim. The English Commandant made no comment, but a little later as they sat over their wine and cigars he asked to be excused for a minute and left the room. He then gave orders for an Indian troop-ship to take a few soldiers across to Perim at once and hoist the Union Jack on the highest point. When the French got there the next morning, they were very much taken aback to find the island flying the British flag, for they hoped to have placed their own there! Since then, we have always kept an English officer and fifty men at Perim. Rather a lonely billet for the unfortunate officer, as the author knows from experience, though sailing and fishing offer helpful distractions.

In July 1901 a small force of three arms was sent out from Aden to the boundary of the British Protectorate, as a punitive expedition against Turco-Arabic incursions into the territory of the friendly Sultan of Lakej. There were eight Companies of Infantry (four from the

5th, and four from the West Kent Regiment) and Artillery, one section, two guns. The force, commanded by Major Rowe, West Kent Regiment, started in the hottest weather on July 14th, in a blinding sand-storm, and on the 26th fought a successful action ending in a downpour of rain, at Ad-Dareja, in the hilly country about 70 miles above Aden. The enemy force was strongly posted on a steep hill from which they were dislodged by a smart attack and driven back into Turkish territory. Mahomed, commanding the Turco-Arabic forces, fled, and the Toll Tower built by him at Ad-Dara-ja, was blown up. Our casualties were Subadar Hanwati Gaekwar, and one Private killed. On October 11th the Regiment left Aden for Bhuj, landing at Mandvi on October 26th.

In July 1902 Colonel Anthony Beale took over the command of the Regiment from Colonel Nicholetts.

During the years 1903–4 the Regiment remained at Bhuj with Detachments at Charber and Jask. In March of the latter year Lieutenant Delmé Radcliffe, 114th Mahrattas, was transferred to the 105th, and appointed Adjutant. In 1905 the Regiment moved to Karachi and was quartered there till 1908, when it had orders to proceed to Hong-Kong. The following officers were with the Battalion:

Colonel A. Beale.
Major E. R. I. Chitty.
Major C. H. C. Grace.
Major M. E. Nuttall.
Capt. A. Delmé Radcliffe, left behind to command depot at Sattara, his adjutancy having expired.
Major E. J. H. Haughton, Quartermaster.
Lieutenant G. N. Ford, newly appointed Adjutant.
Lieutenant M. E. C. V. S. Monteith.
Lieutenant W. B. Benton (at depot).

Lieutenant G. G. Richardson.
Captain A. Proctor, I.M.S. (attached).
Captain J. M. Balderson, 120th Rajputana Light Infantry (attached).
Lieutenant E. G. J. Bryne (104th Rifles, Wellesley).
Lieutenant Weaver (114th Mahrattas).
Lieutenant D. H. Powell (103rd Mahratta Infantry, later appointed to the 105th Mahratta Light Infantry).

In March the Regiment embarked for Hong-Kong in the R.I.M.S. *Dufferin*, and arrived there in April 1908, under command of Major E. R. I. Chitty.

The Regiment was accommodated in barracks built of boards with rush roofing of a temporary nature, reputed to be strong; but in July a typhoon of tremendous force razed the whole of these barracks to the ground. In the evacuation, made in a blinding storm of rain and sand, only one man was hurt. The new barracks built in consequence of this, are now typhoon-proof, and the accommodation much improved.

In February Colonel H. C. B. Dann, 110th Light Infantry, arrived from England, and took over command from Major E. R. I. Chitty, and in March of this year Major-General R. H. Carew-Hunt, a former Commandant, was appointed to be Colonel-in-Chief of the Regiment.

In February the following year the Regiment left China and sailed for Bombay *en route* for Poona. The following officers joined the Regiment: 2nd Lieutenant H. R. B. Irwin from Oxford and Bucks Light Infantry, and 2nd Lieutenant Chapman from Suffolk Regiment. Captain E. J. H. Haughton proceeded to Bombay on embarkation staff duties.

On its return from China, the Regiment was inspected by the Commander-in-Chief in India, Sir

THE COMMEMORATION OF SEEDASEER DAY, SHOWING THE ANCIENT UNIFORM.

O'Moore Creagh, and Sir Edmund Barrow commanding the Southern Army. After this, the whole Regiment was granted $3\frac{1}{2}$ months' furlough.

On March 6th—Seedaseer day—Regimental Sports were held in commemoration of the battle. Drill of the period in the dress of that date was performed and much appreciated by a large crowd of onlookers.

In April Captain G. N. Ford vacated the adjutancy of the Regiment to proceed to Russia, in order to study the language. The adjutancy was taken over by Captain E. J. H. Haughton.

Colonel Sir R. Hennell being on a brief visit to India visited the Regiment on December 29th, 1913. The day following, Colonel Dann gave a rehearsal of the Seedaseer Memorial Parade for him, showing the drill and uniform of the period of the battle of Seedaseer. Sir Reginald Hennell also saw the practice march past next morning which the Regiment performed splendidly, winning the congratulations of Sir A. Barratt commanding the 6th Poona Division. Colonel Sir R. Hennell left for England on New Year's Day, all the British and Indian officers assembling to give him a great send-off at the railway station.

In February Colonel H. C. B. Dann vacated command, and the Regiment was taken over by Lieut.-Colonel E. R. I. Chitty, who had served with it for twenty-four years.

CHAPTER XXVI

THE GREAT WAR

On the declaration of war on August 4th, 1914, the three linked Battalions of the Mahratta Light Infantry Group—the 103rd, 105th, and 110th—were all stationed in and around Poona in the VIth Poona Division: the 103rd at Ahmednagar, 110th at Belgaum, and 105th at Poona. These three Battalions being in the same Division, resulted unfortunately for the 105th when the Poona Division was despatched on active service. It was deemed impossible, under the then existing means of obtaining reinforcements, for any group to have all its Battalions away on service together, so one had to be taken out. This chanced to fall to the lot of the 105th, a misfortune which caused much heart-burning to its officers and men. The 104th Wellesley Rifles were chosen in its place, and the Poona Division went off to Mesopotamia in November.

The 105th were detailed to take over various detachments on the railway, to cover and protect important bridges. No. 3 Double Company strength about 140 rank and file, under Major A. H. P. Waller, proceeded on railway defence duty to Bulsar on the B.B. & C.I. Railway with Detachments at Surat, Dahanu Roa, and Bhusaval.

All the recruiting parties were considerably strengthened, several others being sent out to collect all the men they could. Already there was a call from the various fronts for officers and men to fill up gaps, and the Regiment supplied some of these. During August and September, Captain W. B. Benton and Lieutenant H. R. B. Irwin were sent to the 117th Mahrattas to complete their numbers; 3 N.C.O.s and 72 men went as a draft to the 110th Mahratta Light Infantry: and 14 Sepoys to the same Regiment for Field Service.

In October Reservists were called out for service. Two N.C.O.s and 130 men went to Bhusaval, under Captain Delmé Radcliffe; 1 Indian Officer, 7 N.C.O.s, and 49 men to Igatpuri, under Captain F. E. Thornton, who had joined in September from the 21st Royal Scots; 1 Indian Officer, 3 N.C.O.s, and 27 men to Kalyan; and 3 N.C.O.s and 23 men to Lanada—all on railway defence duty. Colonel Chitty, commanding the Regiment, went to Bombay as Officer Commanding Railway Defences. Captain D. H. Dowell went on Field Service as A.D.C. to General Aitken in East Africa; and in November Captain Delmé Radcliffe went on Field Service to France, as G.S.O. III, 2nd Cavalry Division. Major Grace retired from the Service:

Lieutenant Irwin was wounded at the battle of Zahil, 30 miles south of Basra, in November.

In accordance with a Special Indian Army Order dated September 24th, 1914, the strength of the Regiment had by this time been increased to 1,049 men.

Orders were received in December for the following Detachments on railway defence, to close as below:

Pulgarh, Surat } on Bulsar.
Bhusaval, Manmad } on Igatpuri.

During this month the following officers joined the

Unit from the Indian Army Reserve, and were put under the Adjutant for training:

2nd Lieutenants, J. H. Carol; R. R. B. Maclean; R. H. Burne; W. S. Halliley; and J. H. Cardew.

On January 10th, 1925, Major A. P. Waller, with 3 Indian Officers, 103 N.C.O.s and men, and 6 followers, closed from railway defence at Bulsar; and Captain F. E. Thornton, with 3 Indian Officers and 112 N.C.O.s and men closed from Railway Defence at Igatpuri, on Poona, on the 26th. The latter left next day for Belgaum, with No. 2 Double Company, but orders for their return were issued on February 21st, when the Regiment was informed that it was to move to Dacca in Eastern Bengal, to relieve the 11th Rajputs. The move occasioned much surprise and conjecture as well as disappointment among all ranks, as their chance of seeing active service appeared to have grown less.

The Regiment arrived at Dacca on March 2nd. Detachments were sent to Sattara (recruiting centre) and to Chittagong, Mushiganj, and Barisal, in and around Dacca. The strength of the Regiment had been so considerably increased that the work entailed on the few officers now available to carry it on was very much augmented. These Officers were:

Colonel E. R. I. Chitty.
Major A. H. P. Waller.
Major Ross.
Captain F. E. Thornton.
Captain E. J. H. Haughton.
Captain A. N. Thomas, I.M.S.
Lieutenant Mildmay. }
Lieutenant Halliley. } I.A.R.O.
Lieutenant R. B. Maclean. }

The paying out of the family allotments alone every month to the dependents of the Unit on service caused a great deal of extra work on the clerical establishments, especially on the Quartermaster and Adjutant's clerks, but they buckled to the task uncomplainingly and great credit is due to them for their efforts. An Order was published by the Government of India to meet the increased strength of men, permitting one Havildar and one Naik for every 20 men or portion in excess of 912. These promotions were to be temporary. One extra promotion to commissioned rank was allowed for every 114 men over 912.

In February Lieutenant R. H. Burne proceeded to France to join the 59th Rifles. Ten Sepoys were again sent as a draft to the 110th Mahratta Light Infantry during this month.

In March, Captain Thomas, I.M.S., proceeded to Mesopotamia with the 131st Cavalry Field Ambulance, and 2nd Lieutenant W. S. Halliley went to join the 7th Rajputs, on the same front. 2nd Lieutenant Rogers joined the Regiment.

The 105th received new Colours this month.

In April the bad news was received that Captain Delmé Radcliffe had been dangerously wounded near Neuve Chapelle on the 9th of this month, but happily he recovered.

In August the Regiment moved from Dacca to Lahore via Goalundo, by steamer, and thence by rail. At Goalundo two more young officers joined the Unit, i.e. 2nd Lieutenant Leigh Bennett and 2nd Lieutenant Robertson.

On arrival at Lahore, the Regiment was ordered to furnish guards at Ravi Bridge, Kaiser-i-Hind Bridge, and Budha nala; all connected with Railway Defence and the internal security of the Lahore area.

At this time, Orders were received to form two Emergency Companies for Field Service with the 103rd and 110th Regiments, these two linked Battalions having had severe casualties in Mesopotamia. The composition of the two Companies was to be 2 Indian Officers and 100 rank and file each. One Company named J Company, to be composed of Dekhani and Konkani Mahrattas, and the other Company named K Company, to consist of Konkani Mahrattas and Dekhani Mahomedans. These two Companies left for Active Service in October, under command of Captain Gunn of the 110th Mahratta Light Infantry, and 2nd Lieutenant Leigh-Bennett, of the 105th Mahratta Light Infantry. The majority of these men, alas, died in the siege of Kut-el-Amara.

The official strength of the Regiment at this time was fixed at 1,275, plus the Emergency Companies, but no restriction was laid on the number of recruits from the Poona area. The total number enlisted between the months of August 1915 and March 1916 amounted to 904, an average of 120 a month. This represented nearly one-third of the total enlistment of Mahrattas in the Konkan and the Deccan.

During the next five months, drafts were being sent from time to time to Units and Field Hospitals in Mesopotamia, the majority going to the 103rd and 110th Mahratta Light Infantry, the total number of men despatched from August 1914 till December 1916 being 889 Indian ranks.

Captain Benton was wounded on November 22nd, 1915, at the battle of Ctesiphon, close to Bagdad. He rejoined the 105th in December, and was subsequently awarded the Military Cross for gallantry when in command of the Machine Guns of the 16th Brigade at the battle of Shaiba, near Basra, in Mesopotamia.

Subadar Khema Jagdale was killed in action on November 23rd, 1915.

Captain D. H. Powell was twice mentioned in Despatches for good staff work in East Africa.

The following officers of the Indian Army Reserve were posted to the 105th and drafted to other regiments during 1915:

2nd Lieutenant R. B. Maclean, sent to 103rd Mahratta Light Infantry.
2nd Lieutenant Cantlie, sent to 103rd Mahratta Light Infantry.
2nd Lieutenant Kirwan, sent to 103rd Mahratta Light Infantry.
2nd Lieutenant Mildmay, sent to 110th Mahratta Light Infantry.
2nd Lieutenant Leigh-Bennett, sent to 110th Mahratta Light Infantry.
2nd Lieutenant McCombe, sent to 110th Mahratta Light Infantry.
2nd Lieutenant Hillier, sent to 110th Mahratta Light Infantry.
2nd Lieutenant Huss, sent to 105th Mahratta Light Infantry.
2nd Lieutenant Young, sent to 105th Mahratta Light Infantry.
2nd Lieutenant Tomlinson, sent to 105th Mahratta Light Infantry.
2nd Lieutenant Glyn, sent to 105th Mahratta Light Infantry.
2nd Lieutenant Normand, attached to Staff.
2nd Lieutenant Cardew, sent to 117th Mahrattas.
2nd Lieutenant Rogers, sent to 18th Depot.
2nd Lieutenant Robertson, sent to 5th Infantry.
2nd Lieutenant Harrison, sent to 13th Rajputs Depot.
2nd Lieutenant Hobbs, sent to 9th Infantry Depot.
2nd Lieutenant Jenkins, sent to Grantee Camel Corps.
2nd Lieutenant Gildea, sent to Aden.

2nd Lieutenant Tierney, remained with the Unit.
2nd Lieutenant Falcon, remained with the Unit.
Captain John, attached to General Barrett's Staff in Lahore.

Major A. A. P. Waller was appointed 2nd in command of the 103rd Mahratta Light Infantry and proceeded to join them on December 9th, 1915.

Captain Ford, who since November 1914 had been Brigadier-Major at Poona, proceeded on Field Service as Staff Captain, 30th Brigade, Force D, Mesopotamia, in December of this year.

The following drafts proceeded to Mesopotamia in January 1916:

2 Non-commissioned Officers, 36 men, and 1 follower, to 117th Mahrattas.
1 Indian Officer, 2 N.C.O.s and 45 men to 1 Bhisti, to 11th Mahratta Light Infantry.

These latter drafts never reached the Units for which they were intended, as the 103rd and 110th Mahratta Light Infantry and the 117th Mahrattas were surrounded at Kut, and reinforcements could not reach them.

The Military Authorities now formed two Composite regiments in Mesopotamia, the one to which the 105 Mahratta drafts were being called the "Composite Mahratta Regiment." This Regiment fought magnificently at the battle of Sheik-Saad, in January 1916, and suffered very heavy casualties, after which it was taken out of the front line.

The experiment of putting Mahrattas with officers who knew nothing of them was not a success, and it was decided to form a second Battalion of the 103rd Mahratta Light Infantry, of which Major H. Ross was appointed Commandant. This officer originally belonged to the 103rd, but had been posted to the 105th Mahratta Light Infantry. The Regiment greatly regretted his departure as 2nd in command. Major Ross commanded the 2/103rd Mahratta Light Infantry with conspicuous success, and was given command of the Rangoon Brigade after the war.

In January 1916 Subadar Chimaji Garud was presented by the Viceroy with a Sword of Honour and a *khillat*, at a big Durbar before 2,000 pensioned officers. Following an old Mahratta custom, he chose as his *khillat* a gold bangle with an inscription. These rewards were bestowed for good recruiting work. The Regiment had enlisted 850 recruits since leaving Poona.

Captain E. J. H. Haughton left on February 23rd for Basra, where he was sent as D.A.Q.M.G. embarkation. This officer had completed four years as Adjutant with the Regiment, and was given a magnificent send-off on leaving for the front.

Orders were received for a double Company of the Kashmiri Mahomedans, domiciled in the Punjab, to be formed by the Unit. This double Company filled up very quickly, and orders for another to be formed of the same class were received.

In April the strength of the Regiment had reached 1,700, not including 680 still on service. Up to this date, the Unit had lost 100 killed or died of disease, and 200 wounded, some of the latter having rejoined.

In response to a request from Army Head-quarters, for a Band to be sent to our troops in Mesopotamia, that of the 105th volunteered *en masse*, headed by the Bandmaster, Mr. Bailey, an old soldier himself. The Commander-in-Chief was very pleased and sent a message to the Regiment to that effect.

In July came the eagerly awaited call for the Regiment to go to Mesopotamia. It left Lahore 627 strong, and took over 200 men from the 2/103rd, now being re-formed and on their way back from Mesopotamia. The effect of the order to mobilise at once made apparent how welcome was the call in the Regiment to active service. The hospital cleared automatically.

Captain Ford, who had returned from Mesopotamia and was still unfit for active service, was sent to Belgaum in command of the Depot, the strength of which was 1,264, many of whom were likewise unfit, and invalided from active service. This number also included Kashmiris who were under orders for transfer to another Unit.

CHAPTER XXVII

THE MAHRATTA AS SOLDIER

JUST before the 105th left for Mesopotamia, the following interesting appreciation of the Mahratta as a soldier, written by " Eye Witness," was published in the *Civil and Military Gazette of India*, April 28th, 1916. By the kind permission of the paper we insert it in this story of the 105th Mahratta Light Infantry, feeling sure that it will interest our readers and give those who are not personally acquainted with India and its peoples a little insight into the character of the present-day inhabitants of the Mahratta country, called by the people themselves Maharashtra.

IN MESOPOTAMIA

THE MAHRATTA

(By " Eye-Witness ")

ORAH CAMP, *March* 30, 1916.

I saw it stated in a newspaper the other day that one of the surprises of the war had been the Mahratta. " Surprise " is hardly a tactful word; and it points back to a time when two or three classes of Sepoys were praised indiscriminately to the disparagement of others. The war has brought about a readjustment of values. Not that the more tried and proven types have disappointed expectation; the surprise is that less conspicuous types have made good.

In France one heard a great deal about the " Garhwali." The Cinderella of the Indian Army here is undoubtedly the Mahratta.

That his emergence is a surprise is illogical. The Mahratta horseman was once a name to conjure with, and the sword of Sivaji has left a dent in history legible enough. He was once the "Malbrouck" of Hindustan. If the modern Mahratta has fallen under eclipse, the cause has been largely geographical. Our frontier campaigns have never offered the Indian Army active service enough to go round; certainly the Bombay Army has not come in for its share, and Zahil on November 17th, 1914, was the first pitched battle in which a Mahratta regiment, constituted as such, had been engaged. What honour he earned before that went to swell the collective prestige of class company regiments, for it was not until the Indian Army was reorganised in 1897, that the Mahratta battalion came into being. The British officer, of course, in these regiments knew his Sepoy. He believed that the Dekhan and the Konkan produced as stout a breed as any other soil, and he would tell you so in most definite terms. But then no one ever listened seriously to a regimental officer when he talked about his own men.

The Sapper in a Field Company with diverse races under his command is listened to with less suspicion. It was a Sapper who first opened my eyes to the virtue of the Mahratta, and that was before the war.

"Who do you think the pick of your lot?" I asked. "The Mahratta," he replied unhesitatingly. "Because he can dig?" "None better. But it is his grit I was thinking of. I'd as soon have a Mahratta in a scrap with me as anyone."

One heard little or nothing of the Mahratta in France. Yet it was a Mahratta who earned the Médaille Militaire (I believe the first bestowed on an Indian) for an unobtrusive bit of work at Givenchy on December 11th, 1914. We took a German saphead that day and drove the Huns down their communication trench and then we had to sap back to our own lines while another sap was being driven forward to meet us. For 23 hours the small party was cut off from the rest of the line and they worked steadily with their backs to the enemy, bombed at and fired on the whole time. Supplies and ammunition ran short and we threw them a rope with a stone on it and they dragged ammunition and food and bombs into the trench, bumping over the German dead, and the Mahratta took his turn at the traverse covering the party, as cool as a Scot.

There were but a sprinkling of them in Flanders, a few Sappers and Miners and two Companies of the 107th Pioneers. It was left to Force "D" to discover that the Mahratta has as big a heart for his size as any Sepoy in the Indian Army. To follow the exploits of the Mahratta Battalions from the battle of Saihan on the 14th November, 1914, to Ctesiphon is to follow the glorious history of the 6th Division. Up to and including Ctesiphon no Mahratta Battalion was given a position to attack which they did not take, and in the retirement on Kut-el-Amara their steadiness was well proved. It is a record which is shared with other regiments, but this article is concerned with the Mahratta alone. They were in nearly every fight, and for a long time they made up a fourth part of the whole force.

It was the 117th who with the Dorsets took the wood and cleared the Turks out of their trenches at Saihan. It was the 110th with the Norfolks who led the attack on Mezairam village on December 4th, clearing the left bank of the river; and a double company of the Regiment captured the north face of the Qurnah position four days afterwards. Two Battalions of the Mahrattas were in the front line again at Shaiba, when the Turks were routed in one of the hardest fought and most critical battles of the campaign. They were at Nasiriya and Amara, and they were a tower of strength at Sinn, which gave us Kut-el-Amara. Here all three Battalions were engaged. They went without water and fought three consecutive engagements in forty-eight hours. The 117th with the Dorsets and the 22nd Company of Sappers and Miners were the first troops to enter the enemy's trenches. They broke through the wire and rushed the big redoubt, led by a Subadar-Major when all their British officers had fallen. At Ctesiphon again they covered themselves with glory. The British Regiment brigaded with them speak well of these hard-bitten men and many a villager of Dorset, Norfolk or Oxford will remember the Mahratta and think of him as a person one can trust.

"What was the Indian Regiment on your right?" I heard a Norfolk man ask another, discussing some obscure action on the Tigris of a year ago.

"The—Mahrattas." The Bungay man nodded. "Ah, they wouldn't leave us up a tree. Not likely."

And being familiar with the speech of Norfolk men, who are sparing of tribute of admiration or surprise, I knew that the Mahratta had received a better *chit* than even the Sapper had given him.

It was in the trenches and I had been getting the Norfolks to tell me about the thrust up the river in the winter of 1914.

There was a lull in the firing, the Turks, 200 yards ahead, were screened from us by the parapet; and as I stood with my back to this looking eastward there was nothing visible but earth and sky and the Norfolk men, and a patch of untrodden field like a neglected lawn, running up to the next earth-work, and yellow with a kind of wild mustard. The flowers and grasses and a small dwarf yellow trefoil—Nordeum, dwarf mallow and shepherd's purse—were Norfolk flowers. They and the broad familiar accents of the man made the place a little plot of Norfolk. Nothing Mesopotamian impinged on the homeliness of the scene.

And beyond the traverse were the Mahrattas, sons of another soil. They were a new draft, most of them mere boys who had come straight from the plough into this hard school. They looked dreamy and pensive with a not very intelligent wistfulness, but they were ready for anything that was going on. Two of them were sniping from a loophole. One of them was shot in the shoulder through a sandbag while I was there. Soon after dark I saw a batch of six with an officer step over the parapet into that particularly horrid zone called "No-Man's land." They were to look for surface mines and to be careful not to tread on one. The bullets cracked against the parapet, but they were as casual as if they were going to pick mushrooms.

The "mines" are charged shell-cases lying flat on the ground. The difficulty with these young recruits was to prevent them feeling for them with their feet or prodding them with a bayonet. They were quite untrained, but there was the same stuff in them as in the men who fought at Shaiba and Ctesiphon, and boasted that they had never been beaten by the Turk. A boy of seventeen who had gone out a few nights before was shot in the leg and lost his patrol. In the morning he found he was crawling up to the Turkish trenches. He was out all that day, but got back to his regiment at night, and all the while he hung on to his rifle.

The subaltern had been a little depressed with this new batch of recruits. There was so little time to knock them into shape and he was particularly pleased that Ghopade had brought back his rifle. "They've got the right spirit," he said. "It's only a question of a month or two. But look at these children."

They certainly did not look very smart or alert or particularly robust.

"This one doesn't look as if he could stick a Turk," I said, and pointed to a thin, hatchet-faced lad who could not have weighed much more than eight stone.

"Oh, I expect he'd do that all right. They are much wirier than you would think. It's their turnout I mean."

"They've been in the trenches a week," I said by way of extenuation. But the subaltern and I had passed by the —th and the —th[1] in the same brigade,

[1] Cut out by War Censor.

equally trench-bound, and they were comparatively spick-and-span

The Mahratta Sepoy is certainly no swashbuckler. To look at him you would not take him for a member of a military caste. No one cares less for appearance; and his native dress, the big flat *pagri dhoti* and large loose shoes of the Dekhan and Konkan, do not lend themselves to smartness. Nor does the King's uniform bring with it an immediate transformation. The unaccustomed military turban, which the Sikh or Pathan ties deftly as if with one fold, falls about the head and down the neck of the Mahratta in the most capricious convolutions. If he is a Bayard he does not look the part, and looks, no doubt, as well as his geographical position, have stood in the way of his finding himself. Anyhow, the men who move the pawns on the board in the war game had long passed him over. The Mahratta Battalions are not strictly speaking class regiments, for they each contain a double company of Dekhani Mahomedans. These, but for their inherited religion, are not very widely separated from the Mahratta. They too have brought honour to the Dekhan. At Ctesiphon a double Company of them were attacking a position. They lost all five officers, the British subaltern killed, two Jemadars wounded, two Subadars killed. One Subadar, Mirza Rustum Beg, was wounded twice in the attack, but went on and received his death within twenty-five yards of the enemy. The rest of the Company went on, led by the Havildars, and took the trench at the point of the bayonet.

That is not a bad record for a class of Sepoy who has probably never been mentioned in the newspapers during the war. But it has been a war of "surprises," and one of the morals of Mesopotamia is that one ought not to be surprised at anything. What the Mahratta and Dekhani Mahomedans have done might be expected from them, and has indeed been unparalleled by other hardened stocks. With good leading and discipline and the morale that tradition inspires, you can make good troops out of the agriculturist in most lands, provided he is not softened by a too yielding soil.

A Mahratta has no very marked characteristic to distinguish him from other Sepoys. He is just the bed-rock type of Indian cultivator, the real backbone of the country. And he has all the virtues and limitations which you will find in the agriculturist, whether he be Sikh, Rajput, Dogra, Jat, or Mussulman, whether he tills the land in Dekhan or Peshawar. A prey to the priests and money-lenders, quarrelsome, contentious and unsophisticated, but of strong affections, long-enduring and brave. The small landowner, where the soil resists him and the elements chastise, is much the same all over the world.

CHAPTER XXVIII

FIGHTING IN MESOPOTAMIA

To return to the Regiment and its movements. It arrived at Basra and proceeded up the river at once to Shaikh Saad, arriving there on August 10th. A case or two of cholera unfortunately breaking out soon after, the Regiment had almost immediately to go into a segregation camp. Ten men died, amongst them Subadar-Major Chanderao More, the first Konkani Mahratta who had been appointed a Subadar-Major.

The Regiment left Shaikh Saad in half-battalions, on September 9th and 11th, in charge of convoys, and joined the 9th Brigade of the 3rd Lahore Division, at the Narrows on the right bank of the Tigris, opposite the Sanna-i-Yat position, about 7 miles south of Kut-el-Amara.

On September 12th the Regiment came under shell-fire for the first time, the Turks shelling the camp heavily. The Kali Panchwin Band was called upon to cheer up the troops in the front sectors, and their playing was greatly appreciated. It moved from Brigade to Brigade, spending a few days with each. On September 14th the musicians had just fallen in, preparatory to playing, when the Turks opened fire. The band "went to ground" by orders, but when the shelling stopped it commenced its programme as if nothing had happened. This cheery reply to their guns must have been a bit mortifying to the Turks.

These sudden bombardments were made pretty fre-

PRESENT-DAY UNIFORM OF KALI PANCHWIN.

quently. The Turks would run up a couple of batteries on the left bank of the river, fire a hundred rounds and then dash back to their former positions some 1,500 to 3,000 yards farther back. The bombardments did singularly little damage as the camps were well dug in, and the moral effect was nil—in fact, it tended to raise the spirits of the troops owing to the slight injury effected. Our guns on both banks invariably opened fire on the Turks' batteries directly they were located, but owing to the visibility, as well as the rapidity with which these movements were carried out by the Turks, equally little damage was done to them by our return fire. These bombardments were always carried out on the Turks' part in the evening, when the sun was behind them, making it most difficult for our gunners to see the enemy and at the same time making our movements most distinct. On the other hand, when the sun was rising we could see the Turks without their being able to observe us, so our bombardments, or "strafes," were usually morning efforts, as theirs were evening ones.

During October and November 1916 the Regiment spent part of the time on the outpost line, the other part at Brigade Head-quarters. The 3rd Division occupied a line from Twin-canals Dajaila Redoubt, and the Narrows, one Regiment occupying each of these places in turn.

Writing from camp about this time, Colonel Chitty mentioned a novel idea emanating from the Regiment in respect to bomb-throwing. This was an adoption of the Mahratta *gopan*, or sling for the purpose. An additional ingenious device, invented by an attached officer, rendered it quite safe to sling bombs in this manner. A special exhibition was given before the Divisional General, and many of the men slung 80 yards or so. Two of them slung over 100 yards.

(The normal throw is 40 to 50 yards.) Seeing that other regiments were copying the device, Colonel Chitty wrote to the Inventions Board Head-quarters to register it as the invention of the 105th.

In December 1916 operations for the relief of Kut-el-Amara started, and considerable fighting took place south of Kut. Various orders, such as to be ready to move at a moment's notice and to "dump" all extra kit, gave the Regiment warning that something special was pending. The 13th and 14th Divisions were moved up north of where the 105th were posted, south-west of Kut-el-Amara. The Regiment was not in the first assault on the Turks' position, being kept in reserve, but was close enough to realise it was a pretty severe attack. From the commencement of the bombardment, which was terrific, a succession of our aeroplanes passed overhead all day, dropping bombs and circling back for fresh supplies, with the result that no enemy aeroplane dared to go up.

The 9th Brigade, of which the Unit formed part, was relieved after this attack and withdrawn to Highland nullah. On the 17th December it marched at half a day's notice to Sinnabtar, and the Regiment was sent on next day to relieve the Manchester Regiment of the 8th Brigade, in the trenches, some 1,200 yards from the Tigris, east of Kut. The relief was ordered to take place by day. The trenches were incomplete, and the only possible method of advance was in extended order across the open. The Turks opened shell-fire, but the steadiness of the young soldiers under their "baptism of fire" in the open was remarkable. The lines advanced with intervals correctly kept, as if on a manœuvre parade. Thirteen men dropped and as each man was wounded, each that could, fixed his bayonet and stuck his rifle upside down in the ground to mark his position, in accordance with his training.

Stretcher-bearers moved out under fire to tend the wounded.

The Regimental Head-quarters were in a nullah about a hundred yards away from the men who were in the trenches. On the 22nd a reconnaissance was ordered to the river bank. It met with no resistance, and the information obtained earned the thanks of the Corps and Divisional Commanders, and indirectly resulted in a forward movement of the whole line.

After digging day and night for some days extending the trenches, the Regiment was relieved and retired for a rest at Head-quarters. On December 30th orders were received to drive a sap forward with a "T" head, 300 yards towards the enemy trenches. The 105th provided the covering party throughout the night, and the digging fatigue from 6 to 10 p.m., another Unit supplying the fatigue from 10 p.m. to 2 a.m. The working party was apparently unnoticed till 1.30, when heavy firing commenced. The party was somewhat disorganised, but rallied by Captain Benton from "C" picket, and resumed work. A party of 70 or 80 Turks crept up unseen and tried to rush the "T" head just after dark.

The garrison stood firm though almost surrounded, and a counter attack by two platoons gallantly led by Captain Wilson, of 103rd Regt., and Lieutenant Huss, drove the enemy back into their trenches.

Orders were received on January 8th for an assault on the Turkish position the following day, in the Abul Hassan Bend. The 9th Brigade, 3rd Division, was selected as one of those to carry this out. The 105th, Bombay Light Infantry, 93rd Burmahs, and 1/1st Gurkhas were the regiments detailed to attack, the 105th to be in the centre. The attack opened with a heavy bombardment, and the first lines went over at 8.45 a.m. The formation for the 105th was eight lines of platoons, at three paces' interval, lines at 50 yards' distance. B Company Konkani Mahrattas, under Lieutenant C. R. Glyn, on the right, C Company Dekhani Mahrattas, under Captain H. R. Wilson on the left, in the first four lines. A Company Dekhani Mahrattas, under Captain W. B. Benton, and D Company under Major Greenstreet, next four lines. The last two lines were to be in reserve, at the disposal of the Officer Commanding, Colonel Chitty. Bombers of Companies were on the outer flanks of their platoons, at the disposal respectively of Lieutenant Huss on the right, and Lieutenant Mumford on the left.

The morning was very misty, and the lines when started disappeared from view almost at once. The first line of enemy trenches was just in front; then came an open space with four nullahs running perpendicular to the advance, then a second position, and finally the river bank.

The attack started on a front of 200 yards, but the flanks converged, being limited on the right by a nullah and the flank of the 93rd Burmahs, and on the left by the Kut "East Mounds," along which the 1/1st Gurkhas were working. The left flank directed, and to avoid crowding, the Companies on the right were ordered to close in on reaching the nullah, following up the nullah bed. C Company had orders to halt on reaching the 2nd line of trenches at the end of the Mounds, allowing the Companies in rear to pass through, thus giving two, more or less fresh Companies, for the next objective, whilst B and C Companies could reform and become the support and reserve.

The attack was carried out with great élan, and numerous Turkish prisoners were captured almost at once. Unfortunately both Lieutenants Huss and Glyn were wounded at the start of the action. Lieutenant Glyn was able to go on and led his men most gallantly, though badly wounded in the hand. He was mortally wounded by a Turkish Officer in the 2nd position. His death was much felt by all ranks, with whom he was most popular.

Owing to the mist, formations became a little mixed, but both the leading Companies reached their objectives without check. The Turks were bombed down the nullahs with great success. Captain Wilson, leading C Company, was wounded early in the action. The leading platoon was led by Subadar Chimaji Garud. He was held up by a Turkish Machine Gun, but with two Privates he dashed forward gallantly to attack the men working the gun. His two comrades were killed before they reached it. The Subadar rushed on by himself, and with his revolver, shot both men working the gun, which was dismantled and brought in by Lance-Naiks Sawlaram Barhate and Kondiba Wagh, two men who had followed up the Subadar on seeing him dash on alone. The Subadar was granted the I.O.M. for this gallant action, and received the congratulations of the Army and Corps Commanders.

Lieutenant Mumford was killed whilst courageously leading his bombers. His party showed conspicuous gallantry and initiative, before and after his death, and were mentioned in despatches. During a check in one of the nullahs, six out of the bombing party of eight were killed. The two men left alive, collected the bombs of the dead men and bombed the enemy back. The enemy counter-attacked, but were again bombed back by the two surviving men, Privates Vithoba Jagtap and Gem Powar. When all their bombs were exhausted they called for help and stood their ground till a party from the 1st Gurkhas arrived.

Subadar Bala Bhor's platoon, followed by that of Jemadar Balkrishna Kanse, deceived by the mist, went too far to the right, and found themselves behind the bombers of a regiment of the 8th Brigade. As these bombers had used up all their bombs, our men were allowed to go through. The enemy now advanced and the Regiment through whom our bombers had passed fell back. Subadar Bala Bhor's party repelled the enemy's counter attack with rapid fire and bombs at short range, and following them up, seized and held a small bank. The bombers of the 105th had now joined Subadar Bala Bhor, and held the small ditch, repelling several counter attacks, saving this flank from a nasty situation. Subadar Bala Bhor was mentioned in despatches, also Jemadar Balkrishna Kanse and the four men with him.

A Company reached its objective, D Company under Major Greenstreet, followed B, and met with little opposition until they were close up to the front Companies, when Major Greenstreet was killed and many of the rank and file, causing a slight check. A party consisting of a platoon, organised and gallantly led by Subadar Sayed Suleyman, enabled the Company to advance. Naik Amir Khan showed great courage in climbing up the nullah bank under fire and throwing over bombs on to the enemy. Captain I. C. De, I.M.S., also worked magnificently all day under heavy fire with a scarcity of stretcher-bearers, tending the wounded.

The following were mentioned in despatches:

Lieutenant H. Huss.
Lieutenant A. G. Mumford.
2nd Lieutenant C. R. Glyn.
Naik Shankar Rane.
Naik Krishna Powar.
Lance-Naik Pandurang Desai.
Subadar Chimaji Garud.
Lance-Naik Sawlaram Barhate.
Private Kondibawagh.
Private Nama Thange.
Private Lakshman Tambe.
Private Dada Deshmukh.
Naik Narayan Shinde.
Naik Shankar Shinde.
Naik Ragnuath Godse.

Lance-Naik Bhau Bhacke.
Lance-Naik Ramchandar Shinde.
Private Vithoba Jagtap.
Private Gem Powar.
Subadar Bala Bhor.
Jemadar Balkrishna Khanse.
Havildar Lakshman Jadhao.
Private Bauder Hazare.
Private Gaupat Khedkar.
Private Yedu Kaloar.
Private Galavrao Kalbhar.

Altogether the events described in this last engagement brought great praise to the Unit, and Colonel Chitty had reason to feel very proud of his men. He wrote just after the action:

"The praises of the Regiment ring from Basra to Kut. The men fought like tigers (I quote the words of the Corps Commander). Some Gurkhas turned out to cheer them, led by their Colonel, and the Corps Commander congratulated a British Regiment on being brigaded with us!"

Writing in another part of his letter of Subadar Bala Bhor's dashing piece of work, he said:

"I asked him if he felt justified in charging the enemy *en masse* with one platoon; he answered quite simply, 'Sahib, when so many of the Regiment were being killed, who would want to come back?'"

Colonel Chitty goes on to say:

"There were many acts of heroism unrecorded, and many poor boys earned the cross which was beyond human gift. Their reward is that they have given their lives nobly to perpetuate the name of the Regiment, and to prove beyond all question the fighting qualities of the Mahrattas."

The Regiment's losses in the action were 4 British Officers killed, and 3 wounded, and 214 Indian rank and file.

Following this fight, the Unit lost men daily in the forward posts along the river, and was serving as support, or part of a flank to regiments in other Brigades who were carrying out direct attacks on trenches. The slaughter by our guns in these attacks was appalling. When the Turks evacuated their position, eight lines, each 80 yards long, of enemy dead were seen laid out for burial and their final trench was practically filled with corpses.

CHAPTER XXIX

FALL OF BAGDAD

It is needful to digress at this point from the story and say a little as to the general operations.

General Sir Stanley Maude, Commander-in-Chief in Mesopotamia, had evidently planned to consolidate the right bank of the river Tigris, right up to Shat-el-Hai, that is to a point south of Kut-el-Amara. The design was then to attack the immensely strong Turkish positions on the left bank at Sanna-i-Yat, and turn the Turkish position at Kut-el-Amara. Since April 1916, the Turks had held Sanna-i-Yat, with many positions behind it stretching almost to Kut-el-Amara itself. In 1916 thirty to forty thousand men had been killed and wounded in the attempts to take this position, which was situated about twelve miles from Kut-el-Amara, with a wide lake called the Suweikeh Marsh, on its north, and the Tigris on its south. The extent of the front of the trenches was not more than 1,000 to 1,200 yards. The enemy trenches had been intermittently bombarded for ten or twelve days before the attack, and for eight to ten months the Artillery had shelled them almost daily.

On February 17th, 1917, the 21st Brigade were detailed to attack. The offensive started well, but eventually failed dismally. The 19th Brigade of the 7th Division was then ordered to make the attack on February 21st. This was carried out with great dash by the Seaforth Highlanders and 92nd Punjabis, and the objective taken by 10 a.m. The frontal extent of the 19th Brigade was 500 yards, making a wedge between the river and the trenches occupied by the

Turks, running from that point to Suweikeh Marsh. At 3 p.m., the same day, the 28th Brigade went over and attacked the remaining position of Sanna-i-Yat, the 51st and 53rd Sikhs leading. This attack was temporarily held up, but the Leicesters arriving in support of the 51st and 53rd, carried them on and the position was taken. The next day, a bridge was thrown across the Tigris at Shomran, and crossed by our troops. The Turks, now caught on two sides, had nothing to do but to fall back, their retreat developing into a rout. It was estimated that 7,500 prisoners had been taken since January, including several of their Generals. The whole plain was strewn with Turkish corpses, and only a few disorganised bands were left to straggle into Bagdad.

The 14th and 13th Divisions, followed by the 7th and 3rd, in the order named, pursued the Turks and advanced without much opposition till just north of Ctesiphon, when the 14th and 13th Divisions advanced up the left bank. The 7th Division, with the Cavalry, crossed the river at Bustaiv on the right bank, the 3rd Division protecting the long line of communication till Bagdad was in our hands.

Just prior to the taking of Bagdad, the 13th Division had a very arduous fight in the crossing of the Diala, but eventually managed to force a passage after many gallant contests. The 7th Division, on the right bank, had two very severe encounters with the enemy at Shawkhan ruins, but on the morning of March 11th, the "Black Watch," of the 21st Brigade, were in Bagdad just as the last Turkish train left the main terminus, a station built by the Germans some years before.

One of the French nuns who nursed General Von der Goltz, the Turkish Commander-in-Chief, who had died some time previously, told the British that Bagdad would fall fourteen days after the capture of the

Sanna-i-Yat trenches. This prophecy was almost correct, and would have been quite so, had not matters been delayed by Sir Stanley Maude having to telegraph to England to obtain permission to push on to Bagdad!

The 105th arrived there on March 18th, 1917, having marched up the left bank of the river, crossed the Diala and proceeded to Bakuba, Abu-Jisrah, and finally to Nahorina Canal, where the Regiment had to dig in.

On the night of March 24th the 8th and 9th Brigades proceeded towards the Jebel Hamrin Mountains, with orders to attack at dawn a Turkish position very lightly held. In the morning, aeroplanes reported that the lower spurs of the Jebel Hamrin were held by comparatively few Turks, and the 9th Brigade, commanded by General Clarke, had therefore orders to proceed to the attack.

Owing to the information that the slopes were so lightly held, the Brigade advanced on a broad front, the 1/1st Gurkhas on the left, the 2nd Dorsets in the centre, and the 105th Mahratta Light Infantry on the right. The 93rd Burmah Infantry were in support and the 8th Brigade in reserve.

The Regiment went into action with D Company on the right, in command of Lieutenant Bland; B Company in the centre, Lieutenant Douglas commanding; A company on the left, Captain Benton in command; and C Company in support under Lieutenant Fleming.

It was found that the Turks were holding a position in the nature of an amphitheatre, and the 9th Brigade was held up by the very accurate fire of the Turks, who appeared to be in large numbers instead of the position being so sparsely held as the aeroplane information had led the General to believe. The Brigade however managed to push on, and advanced for about four miles, in spite of very heavy casualties, before the Turkish position was reached. After four hours' fighting, the

Brigade was ordered to retire, as it was seen to be impossible to take the post without large reinforcements.

The order to retire was given at 3.30 p.m., the 105th —which had been in the attack—now forming the rearguard. The retirement was extremely well carried out by all three regiments, but the casualties were very heavy, every Commanding Officer and Second in Command being killed or wounded. Colonel Chitty, commanding the 105th, was unhappily amongst the severely wounded. Lieutenants Douglas and Fleming, with two Sepoys, attempted to carry him back. Whilst doing so, Lieutenant Fleming was wounded. Lieutenant Bland then came up to assist, and it was decided that he should remain behind with Colonel Chitty whilst the others went for aid. Colonel Chitty's wounds were so serious that it was seen at once that he could not possibly recover. Lieutenant Bland remained by his side until ordered by him to go. His body was never found. Major F. E. Thornton had been killed instantly earlier in the battle. Both he and Colonel Chitty were greatly mourned by all ranks. Colonel Chitty had served twenty-four years in the Regiment, and though Major Thornton had only joined the 105th in 1914, he had been with it in every action, and he, as well as his Commanding Officer, was greatly respected and popular with all ranks.

The following list shows the casualties in this last engagement:

	Killed.	Wounded.	Missing.
British Officers	2	2	—
Indian Officers	—	3	1
Indian other ranks	25	132	121

Captain Benton	Were wounded.
2nd Lieutenant Fleming	
Subadar-Major Gaupate Kenjle	
Subadar Daulet Rao Bhole	
Jemadar Goomda Dhamne	
Jemadar Hamza Khan	Missing.

The latter had remained with Colonel Chitty, and was captured. When the prisoners were liberated he returned, and is now in the Unit as a Subadar.

After this battle of Jebel Hamrin, which resulted so disastrously in losses for the 105th, the Regiment returned to camp near Shakravan, and was for some time in and around Bagdad on garrison duty.

On April 18th Major P. M. Heath, 110th Mahratta Light Infantry, was sent to take command from Captain Benton, temporarily officiating as Officer Commanding. During May and June the Regiment was at Kazimain, providing escorts, and training. This was one of the hottest years known in Mesopotamia, and the Unit, like all others out there at the time, suffered from fever and sunstroke. Major Heath unhappily fell a victim to the latter and died on July 12th.

On July 17th Major Delmé Radcliffe rejoined the Regiment, and took over the once more vacant Command.

The following officers were with the 105th during the period January 1st to July 1917 :

Colonel E. R. I. Chitty.
Major F. E. Thornton.
Major Delmé Radcliffe.
Major P. M. Heath.
Captain W. B. Benton.
Captain M. E. C. Monteith.
Captain F. E. Welsh.
Lieutenant H. H. Bland.
Lieutenant A. E. Douglas.
Lieutenant Harding.
Lieutenant I. A. Warren.
Lieutenant J. N. Cloudbury.
Lieutenant R. W. B. Wright.
Lieutenant B. B. Graveston.
Lieutenant Fleming.
Lieutenant E. E. Priestley.

CHAPTER XXX

INDIANS' REPLY TO GERMAN PAMPHLET

HERE it seems again necessary to turn from our narrative and describe, roughly, the general events taking place in Mesopotamia just at this time.

After the capture of Bagdad, the 7th Division was sent up the right bank of the Tigris to capture Samarra, which fell on April 23rd, 1917, after many sanguinary battles along the eighty miles separating it from Bagdad. The 14th and 13th Divisions occupied posts north-east of Bagdad, at a considerable distance from that place, and the 3rd Division eventually went to Beled and Istabulat. To establish the positions for the hot weather of 1917, all three Divisions had considerable fighting, but after April, affairs quieted down, the Turks showing no signs for a time of wishing to resume hostilities. Large numbers of officers, N.C.O.s, and men were granted a month's leave to India. This much-needed privilege was, needless to say, greatly appreciated.

The positions occupied outside Bagdad—such as Samarra, and the immediate posts—were very strongly entrenched and fortified, in view of the rumours that the Germans and Turks were going to attack us in Mesopotamia in the autumn, with greatly increased forces. In consequence of these moves, the 9th Brigade was ordered to Beled in September, and the Regiment took part in the immense entrenching operations necessary to place this area in a defensive state. It was here, on a big parade, that Lieutenant Bland was presented with the Military Cross for gallantry on several occasions, and Subadar Maroti Bodke, and 410 Ranks, were awarded the Indian Distinguished Service Medal.

In October the Turks made a small attack on Samarra. This was really a feint to find out in what strength we occupied the place. General Sir Stanley Maude decided to attack the enemy, and in consequence, the 7th Division, with the 8th Brigade of the 3rd Division, marched off from Samarra on October 28th. The operations lasted ten days, the Turks being defeated at Daur, twenty miles north of Samarra, and on November 6th heavily defeated at Tekrit. Though the 105th took no active part in this engagement, it had to march from Samarra to Aujanala, four miles south of Tekrit, to be in readiness should it be required. This march was an exceptionally fine performance.

The Regiment started at 10 p.m., marching in the Brigade commanded by General Luard. The march continued all night. At daybreak, a halt of one and a half hours was allowed to water animals, etc. At 11 a.m. the force had reached a point on the right bank of the Tigris, south-west of Daur, after a march of twenty-three miles. The battle of Tekrit could be seen going on straight ahead. At this point, the Brigade had orders to take up a position in reserve, and await developments. Further orders were received to move into line. The Brigade then marched on another 7 miles into Aujanala. Night was falling when it arrived, and as it happened the battle was then over and won, and the Turks were in full retreat. The men did not, however, know this, and were ready to join in the fight at once, tired out as they were. The Battalion had marched thirty miles in twenty hours, believing itself to be marching direct into action—without a single man falling out. During the hours of darkness it furnished a rear-guard of one Company under Captain Welsh, behind the Brigade transport. This Company never got a halt all through the night, yet not a man fell out excepting one with dysentery, and one with fever. Both rejoined before the end of the march.

The following British Officers, Indian Officers, and N.C.O.s were mentioned in the November Despatches:

Colonel E. R. I. Chitty.
Major P. M. Heath.
Major F. E. Thornton.
Major E. J. H. Haughton.
Captain W. B. Benton.
Subadar Sayed Suleiman.
Subedar Marote Bodke.
No. 2572. Naik Shankar Rane.
No. 2719. Naik Krishna Powar.
No. 3504. Lance-Naik Sawlaram Barhake.
No. 3211. Lance-Naik Pandurang Shinde.
No. 2511. Lance-Naik Ramchandar Shinde.
No. 3241. Sepoy Vithoba Jagtap.
No. 2271. Nama Thange.

There was a lull after this last action, and life for the Regiment for the time being was much as it would be at a camp of exercise during peace times in India. One of the officers wrote: "Our days are taken up with training and keeping ourselves up to the mark. The feeding and clothing of the army in Mesopotamia are now quite excellent. We are all—officers and men—thoroughly well off and contented. The spirits of the men are splendid, and they are very fit, playing football, hockey, and their own national games, with great zest."

An enemy aeroplane flying over the camps dropped a lot of pamphlets for the Indian troops, telling them that they were foolish to fight for the British, that British Officers had falsely informed them that the war would be over in three months from its beginning, and that they would capture Berlin in that time. The pamphlet went on to say that England was now starving, and would not be able to feed and clothe them any more, etc., etc. This was written in Hindi, and many men of the Regiment picked up copies. They were intensely amused by them and brought the papers to their British Officers, regarding it as a great joke. The Indian Officers wrote a reply and requested that one of our aeroplanes should drop it on the enemy's camps! Their reply to the Germans was to the following effect:

"Our British Officers at the beginning of the war, far from telling us that the war would be over in three months, told us that the accursed Germans had been preparing for this war for the past forty years. No doubt this is true, and that is why the war has lasted so long, and why it is likely to last a considerable time longer yet. As to the likelihood of our being starved and insufficiently clothed, we have never been better clothed or fed than we are at present, not even in India. The prisoners we take from you, however, are in rags. We will never cease to fight for the King-Emperor George V, until the evil Kaiser of the Germans is utterly trodden into the mud, as was the ten-headed demon Rawan by Shri Ramchandarji."

Thus did the 105th receive their first dose of enemy propaganda!

The Regiment remained encamped at and around Samarra till the following March, when it was ordered to move to an unknown destination. This proved to be Palestine.

The Regiment left Samarra on March 13th, 1918, reached Basra April 6th, and left Mesopotamia on the H.T. *Jeddah* on April 16th, arriving at Suez April 30th, 1918, completed disembarkation by May 2nd, and marched up to the front line via Moascar, El Ferdan,

Kantara, Ludd, and Haditeh. At the latter place, A Company was transferred to a newly raised Battalion, the 3/153rd Infantry. Lieutenant Gravestone went with this Company. A large number of these men returned to the Kali Panchwin when the 3/153rd Regiment was broken up and disbanded in 1922.

On June 23rd the Regiment reached El Mezeipah and took over the support line held by the 1/10th London Regiment of the 162nd Brigade of the 54th Division. On July 4th the Regiment relieved the 93rd Burmah Infantry, in the right sub-sector of the 3rd Lahore Division. The relief was carried out by night. This portion of the line consisted of a series of strong posts with a continuous line of wire in front, some portions of which were double. The posts were situated on the side of rocky foothills, running out into the coastal plain.

D Company occupied the right of the Battalion line, and had two strong posts. C Company was in the centre with three strong posts. A Company was in support, just behind the left of the Battalion sector. During the day most of the troops were withdrawn from the strong posts to Company Head-quarters, situated about 300 yards behind the centre of each Company's strong posts, a proportion of sentries and N.C.O.s being left in the front with Lewis guns.

The nearest point to the Turkish position was on the right, where it was about 700 yards off, and the farthest point was the left, where the distance was about 2,000 yards. "No Man's Land" was a succession of steep rocky hills and very deep ravines, which made patrolling extremely difficult, especially to carry out noiselessly at night. During the period this sector was occupied, there were several small skirmishes with the Turks, resulting in some casualties.

On July 18th the Regiment was transferred to the

[Imperial War Museum Photo. Crown Copyright.

GENERAL VIEW OF BAGDAD, 1917.

orange groves at Mulebbis, to act as part of sector reserve to the 3rd Lahore Division, the 47th Sikhs (8th Brigade) taking over the sector the Unit had left. Whilst at Mulebbis, the Regiment carried out extensive training, with special stress on the use of gas masks.

The following officers joined the 105th this month: Lieutenant P. C. Watson, 2nd Lieutenant E. Patterson, and 2nd Lieutenant M. P. Lancaster.

The Regiment had relieved the 51st Sikhs at Mulebbis, the latter forming the right section of the 28th Brigade of the 7th Division. Thus the 9th Brigade formed the left section of the 3rd Division. August 1st was the first day in the front line of the left section of the 3rd Division. This part of the line was situated in or about the centre of the coastal plains, which consist of a succession of low sandy undulating hills, with occasional thickets of eucalyptus trees.

The line was composed of a series of strong posts, with a continuous line of wire in front. There were seven "strong posts" allotted to the 105th. Four on the right were held by C Company and the remaining three on the left by A Company, D Company being behind A Company in support. This was the flank nearest to the enemy's position 600 yards distant. B Company was at Battalion Head-quarters in reserve, just inside Boche Wood, about 1,000 yards from the Turkish position. As usual in Palestine during the day, the troops—with the exception of a number of sentries and N.C.O.s—were withdrawn to the reverse side of the crests out of view from the enemy. The trenches were well made, so it was possible to enter the front line by day without being observed. The enemy had a number of advanced posts just in front of his main line, one especially known as "Kelly's Eye," a sniper's post, which caused the Battalion considerable annoyance.

CHAPTER XXXI

BOX-BARRAGE RAID

DURING August, the Regiment carried out many minor raids and reconnaissances. A full description of one in particular must be given, as it was said to have been one of the best and most successful raids carried out in Palestine. With Colonel Delmé Radcliffe's permission, we give this account in his own words, written to the author just after the event.

"The raiding party consisted of 124 men of D Company under Lieutenant H. H. Bland, assisted by Lieutenant E. Pattinson, and the Indian Officers, Jemadar Ramchandar Gaekwad, and Jemadar Baburao Pisal.

"The Turks had an advance post in a small work which was known to us as F.26. We had a work called E.12, which formed part of our line opposite to it, and was about 600 yards south-west of it. F.26 consisted of three lines of trenches, and its frontage from A to B was about 200 yards. It was some 600 yards in advance of the main Turkish trench line, and was on the top of a low hill. A communication trench ran back from it, connecting it with the main position—marked C C in sketch. Part of the line C C was, however, screened from view from our lines. Consequently, the Turks had not dug out the communication trench for the screened portion, but simply walked across the open by a path for this distance. (Shown on sketch by a dotted line.) D D is the Turkish line of barbed wire entanglement which lay in front of the whole Turkish line throughout its length, from the Mediterranean Sea to the Dead Sea. E E is the British line of wire.

"The Turkish line of defence consisted of a continuous line of trenches in most places, while our line consisted of a series of mutually supporting works at intervals. E.12 was one of these works. About 500 yards to the east of E.12, was another work, E.11, and about 250 yards west of E.12 was E.15. Neither of these are in sketch, but it is necessary to mention them as they will be referred to again later. The

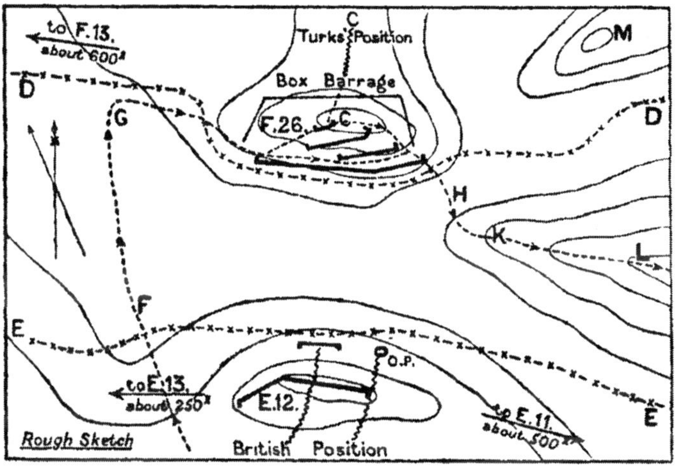

Plan of Raid (Dotted Line F G C H K L).

Turkish post F.26 used to cause us a good deal of annoyance by machine-gun fire, especially at night.

"During the period of trench warfare preceding the big battle of September 19th, raids were constantly being carried out by us on the enemy's lines, many of them with special objects, but all with the more or less general object of keeping the enemy harassed and jumpy, of giving him no rest and of being 'top dog.' The results of these raids were excellent.

"While the Battalion during August 1918 was in that part of our line, which was opposite F.26, I was ordered to carry out special reconnaissance of that work, and to report whether I considered it suitable for such a raid, and if so, to submit a plan for it. After a week's careful reconnoitring, during which some very good work was done by our scouts—especially at night—I reported that I considered a raid might very well be carried out with good results, and requested permission to undertake it, submitting my plan.

"We were then moved back as 'Battalion in support' and the 1/1st Gurkha Rifles took our place. In our support position, we prepared a piece of ground to resemble F.26, dug trenches exactly like those of F.26, put up barbed wire in front of them and rehearsed the raid, both by day and night, in anticipation of permission to carry it out. I was called up to talk over the plan, with our Brigadier, and the G.O.C.—the 3rd Lahore Division—and by the time our men had got thoroughly to know every detail of their job, the plan was approved and we were ordered to carry it out. The men were as keen as mustard by this time, and the rehearsals were really most amusing as the men insisted on acting the thing exactly like a play. Men were brought in to act as wounded, for the stretcher-bearers to practise their job, and they acted their parts most realistically, some as very badly wounded, groaning with the pain of their imaginary wounds, and were carried off on stretchers. Others had supposed broken limbs, and could only get along supported by their comrades, and so on. Special parties detailed for the job, rounded up parties of Turkish prisoners—prisoners and captors, of course, being represented by men of the Company. The rehearsals were thorough in every detail and showed how keen the men were to make a good job of it.

"The night chosen for the raid was August 18th–19th. It was to be carried out just after moonset at 2 a.m. Lieutenant Bland, who was detailed to command the raiding party, flew over the enemy's position two days before the raid was carried out, and had a good look at it from the air, which showed him exactly how certain trenches and dugouts lay, which could not be seen from the ground.

"The raiding party left our lines at 1.50 a.m. on the 19th August, about 200 yards north-west of our post at E.12, which was at this time held by the 1/1st Gurkha Rifles. The plan was that they should start just as the moon set, and move quietly across the low ground in a northerly direction, as shown by the dotted line from F to G, where they were timed to arrive at 2.15 a.m. They moved in such a formation that on arriving at G all they had to do was to turn to the right. The whole body was then in formation to attack the F.26 trenches from the western flank. On arrival at G the raiding party, after turning to the right, was to remain halted and wait for the Artillery to open fire at zero hour, which was fixed for 2.20 a.m. Punctually to the second, four batteries of Artillery opened fire simultaneously, three of field guns, and one of 4·5-inch howitzers, in addition to two heavy 6-inch howitzers. The details of the several barrages, and the changes of Artillery objectives, are somewhat complicated, but the principal barrages of interest were as follows:

"An intense barrage of shrapnel on the trenches of F.26, by one battery of 18-pounders, from 2.20 to 2.25 a.m., during which the raiding party were to advance as rapidly as possible, straight on to the trenches, where it was estimated they would—and did—arrive, at 2.25 a.m. Simultaneously with their arrival there, our battery ceased firing on those trenches, but laid down a barrage about 50 yards beyond them to prevent the enemy running away to the rear. This formed part of a 'box-barrage' which was at this time being fired by the 7th Battery (six guns), four guns of the 14th Field Battery and four guns of the 374th Field Battery. This box-barrage lasted from 2.25 a.m., for seven minutes, during which time the raiding party's task was to capture or kill every Turk found in those trenches, and to seize any machine guns and war material they could find. The box-barrage was simply to prevent the enemy from escaping. It was a line of bursting shells as shown in sketch, by a dotted line. It was a beautiful piece of work, the shells fired by batteries about 3,000 yards away, passing just over the heads of our men and bursting about 50 yards beyond them, effectually cutting off the enemy from his main position in the rear.

"After passing through the enemy's trenches, the several parties into which the raiding party had been subdivided—each having a special task—were to assemble at point H, at 2.32 a.m. and to move down the valley K L. They were then to re-enter our lines at a point chosen, farther east—or rather south-east—and beyond the limits of my sketch. The valley K L formed a deep depression in 'No Man's Land' between the enemy's lines and ours, and parallel to both. It was chosen for the return journey of the raiding party, because it was expected that by the time the raiding party had gone through F.26, the enemy's Artillery would have received news by telephone that F.26 had been raided, and would shell E.12 heavily, expecting the raiders to return that way. This they actually did, and had the raiding party returned that way, the casualties might have been heavy. Secondly the configuration of the ground made it very unlikely that the enemy would notice the party of raiders passing down the valley K L.

"What actually happened was this. On the guns opening at zero hour, the raiding party rushed forward from G, knocked down the enemy's wire without difficulty, and reached the trenches on the stroke of time. As they arrived, our shells stopped bursting there, but fell 50 yards beyond; the timing was absolutely perfect. The men swept through their objectives exactly as per programme. The garrison of F.26 had been estimated at about 30 to 50. Actually there were about 30 men there with a machine gun. Our men killed about 20 with the bayonet and took 6 prisoners—14 were lost in the dark. We captured a machine gun and brought away a number of rifles, bombs, and a few other odds and ends.

"The several parties had all assembled at H, and Lieutenant Bland had sent them all successively on their return journey towards K and L, and was just starting to follow, after checking and seeing them all through H, when he saw the Turkish S.O.S. signal go up from a place known as Brown Hill, marked M on the sketch. At this time Brown Hill was being pretty heavily shelled, and presumably the garrison got frightened and thought they were going to be attacked. At any rate the result of this was, that a pretty intense Turkish barrage of high explosive shells came down about one minute later right on the track of the returning raiding party, but luckily just ahead of them (somewhere about L and beyond, they having only got as far as K). One of the first shells killed one of our men and wounded six slightly. Bland at once passed the order down that each party was to make for our wire at the point where the fire was least, and all wheeled in perfect order and quite deliberately, making for our wire between E.12 and E.11. As no entrance had been made through our wire for them there they crawled through it—not too easy a job, and it took some time. At about 3 a.m. Bland got on to the end of a telephone and spoke to me telling me what had happened up to the time he reached K. He was unable to see what became of all his party after he reached point K, owing to the smoke and dust of bursting shells. It seemed to him that they were very close to the Turkish barrage, if not right in it. All the parties were at this time moving independently under their own Commanders, in accordance with the plan for the operation, and Bland was not at this time controlling them, nor intended to control them as it was impossible for one man to do so at this stage in the dark. All the Commanders, and in fact, each man knew exactly what they had to do, and as it turned out afterwards, everybody did his job perfectly and with absolute coolness. About 4 a.m. I received a full report that all the men were in, with six prisoners and a machine gun. That the total casualties were only one killed, ten wounded lightly, and one seriously (he died a few hours later). This was due to the cool and orderly way in which they quietly manœuvred out of the way of the enemy's barrage, which they had very nearly walked right into.

"Next day the men were just as pleased with themselves as they deserved to be, for they had done uncommonly well. In the afternoon, General Hoskins, the G.O.C. of the Division, as well as General Luard, our Brigadier (9th Infantry Brigade), came and saw the men on parade and praised them very highly. General Hoskins said that the operation had been well prepared and rehearsed, and extremely well carried out. The men had displayed coolness, determination and steadiness, and had proved that they knew how to use the bayonet. The affair had shown the new men among them, what an artillery barrage was like and how artillery could help them. He was very pleased indeed with them. Men who behaved as they had done, were of the type whom nothing can stop. That evening a telegram from the Corps Commander was received, worded as follows: 'The Corps Commander congratulates the 105th on their successful raid of last night.' To this we replied: 'The Kali Panchwin respectfully thank the Corps Commander for his kind message and hope for another chance soon.' They got that chance exactly one month later in the big battle of the 19th September, in which they did their share splendidly."

CHAPTER XXXII

ATTACK ON THE TURKS

On the night of August 23rd, 1918, the Regiment was relieved by the 27th Punjabis, and marched to camp near a Greek farm about four miles east of Jaffa, where the whole of the 9th Brigade was in Divisional Reserve. At this spot the Battalion carried out a number of practice attacks with the Brigade, over a facsimile position of the Turkish line which was shortly to be attacked.

On September 9th the 105th took over the right subsector of the left section, from the Connaught Rangers, but nothing of note happened whilst the Regiment was in the line. On September 18th it concentrated in Boche Wood in a concealed position, preparatory to the general attack of September 19th. Major-General Hoskins, the Commander of the 3rd Lahore Division, paid a surprise visit to the Battalion in its hiding place and wished it success in the attack which was to take place in the early hours of the following morning.

The main attack was carried out on a front of many miles extending from the coast north of Jaffa to the hills near Rafat about 25 miles away to the south-east. We again avail ourselves of our Regiment's Commanding Officer's own words in describing this action, and with his kind permission give the following extract from a letter that Colonel Delmé Radcliffe wrote at the time :

"On the morning of September 19th, 1918, the 8th

Brigade 3rd Division marched to its position of deployment just behind our front line trenches. The whole Brigade was fully deployed and ready to attack at zero minus 90 minutes, i.e. at 3 p.m. The Brigade attacked on a two battalion front—ourselves, and a British Battalion, the 2nd Dorsetshire Regiment, in the front line, two Indian Battalions in support. The front line posts of our trench system were held by

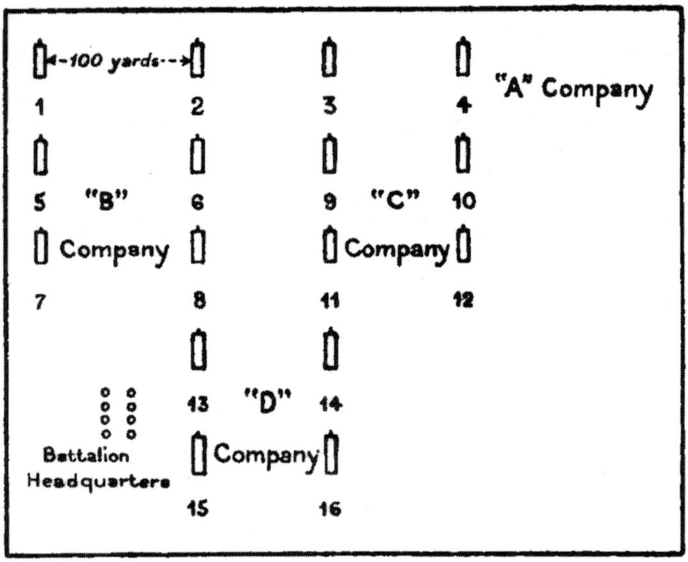

their normal garrison, furnished by other Units which followed on later.

" The enemy was indulging in an unusual amount of rifle and machine gun fire. Possibly he was suspicious that something unusual was about to happen, or perhaps it was just coincidence, which was a good thing for us as it prevented the enemy from hearing our movements as we formed up.

" The troops were all well trained in night work, and moved very silently, but large bodies of men had to move through long dry grass in places, and with the best of training a certain amount of noise was unavoidable.

"Our Brigade was to attack on a frontage of 800 yards—400 were allotted to the British Battalion on our left, and 400 to us.

"Our dispositions at the position of deployment were as follows:

"*Leading Wave.*—A Company—its four platoons in line—each platoon in fours. Interval between platoons 100 yards—the left platoon at an interval of 100 yards from the right leading platoon of the British Battalion on our left, which was the directing platoon of the brigade.

"*Second Wave.*—Two platoons of B on left and two platoons of C Company on right as shown in diagram on opposite page.

"*Third Wave.*—Two platoons of B Company on left, and two platoons of C on right exactly same as Second Wave.

"*Fourth Wave.*—D Company—central, as reserve Company.

"All intervals between platoons equal—viz. 100 yards.

"All distances between platoons also equal—viz. 40 yards from the head of one platoon to the head of the platoon next behind it.

"The formation of the British Battalion on our left was exactly the same as our own, except that the headquarters of that battalion moved on the right of its reserve company instead of the left, that being the inner and directing flank, and both battalion headquarters were thus close to their telephone wires, which were run out between the two Battalions as they advanced. They were, however, soon cut by the enemy's artillery fire.

"It is now a standing order that only a certain proportion of British and Indian officers and non-commissioned officers are allowed to take part in an attack on a position—the remainder are sent back to stay with the 2nd line transport, and are not allowed forward till ordered, the idea being to have reinforcements available to take command, in case casualties in Commanders are very heavy. Of those sent back, the C.O. or the 2nd in Command, has to be one. In this case it was the 2nd in Command—Captain Welch—110th Mahratta L.I., attached 105th L.I. Further Captain Wright—Indian Army Reserve of Officers (I.A.R.) attached 105th, Lieutenant Bland, M.C., who belongs to the Regiment, and Lieutenant Douglas, the Quartermaster.

"The following officers actually took part in the attack:

"Colonel A. Delmé Radcliffe.
Lieutenant Macalister, 105th, commanding A Company.
Lieutenant Lancaster, I.A.R., attached—commanding B Company.
Lieutenant Watson, M.C., I.A.R., attached—commanding C Company.
Lieutenant Pattinson, I.A.R. attached—commanding D Company.
Lieutenant Kenny, 116th Mahrattas, attached—Intelligence Officer.
Lieutenant Phillips, I.A.R., attached—Acting Adjutant.

"At zero hour—4.30 a.m.—the very first signs of approaching daylight were beginning to appear in the sky. It was just light enough to see about 50 yards—not more. The orders for the infantry were to advance at zero minus three minutes. All watches had been synchronised to the second beforehand, and punctually at 4.27 a.m. all platoons started moving at a good fast pace in order to get on to the forward slope of the ridge, behind which we had deployed, as quickly as possible, as many of our guns were going to shoot very close up the reverse slope 3 minutes later. We moved very silently until 4.30, when the whole sky was lit up by flashes from guns of every size and description for about 25 miles, and the din was simply indescribable. A moment later every Turkish trench was simply a line of bursting shells—absolutely overwhelming, and suppressing the occupants so that not one of them could put up his head over the parapet to fire. The barrage was perfectly wonderful.

"The position we had to attack consisted of a network of trenches of which the diagram shows the general shape of the front trenches only. The double line marked with arrows represents our advancing leading

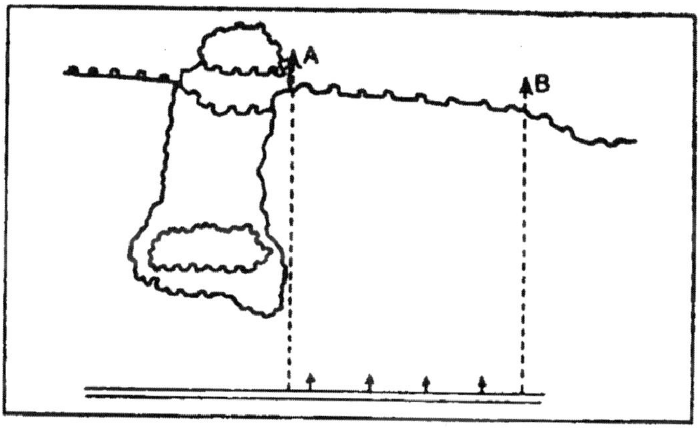

wave—the long dotted lines with arrow heads represent the flanks of the Battalion. The British Battalion on our left had to capture the peculiar excrescence of trenches shown, and while they did so, we had to move steadily on without any alteration of pace or direction to A B, about 500 yards farther on—which was A Company's objective. From its point of departure the Battalion had to go about 1,200 yards altogether before reaching the trench A B. This took about 12 minutes. The men were going fully 100 yards a minute. From the point of departure they had to go down a slope into a shallow valley about half-way to the enemy's lines, then up-hill again to the objective.

"At about zero plus five minutes the enemy's barrage came down. He put it principally in two places—i.e. on the line of departure, and right along the bottom of the shallow valley. There it caught the Battalion a bit, but it soon got out of it.

"There was a fairly strong line of barbed wire in front of the first enemy trench (about 40 yards from it). Our barrage was so perfect that A Company walked up to this wire and cut it without difficulty. Just as the men finished cutting it, our barrage lifted, and A Company rushed the trench. They killed a few of the enemy with the bayonet—the remainder very quickly put up their hands. This trench hardly delayed A Company appreciably, and they were quickly on their way to No. 2 on which our barrage was now playing. The companies behind were at this time passing through the enemy's barrage. It is difficult to understand how the Battalion's casualties from this barrage were not heavier than they were, as shells seemed to be bursting everywhere among the men for a time, and many of them were big high-explosive shells. The Battalion was soon enveloped in a fog of smoke and dust as thick as the thickest of pea-soup London fogs. Nothing could be seen; the Unit was only able to find its way by marching on compass bearings. To control the men at this stage was practically impossible. The noise was so tremendous that officers could not make themselves heard by men quite close by, though they shouted at the top of their voices. The officers simply had to trust the men to watch each other and keep their places and direction. The fog soon got so thick that Units could not see one another, consequently they could not keep their places exactly, but they kept their direction wonderfully well considering the difficulties and the result was that when the Battalion got out of the fog again, about 2½ miles farther on, Units were not far out of their places, and the formation was soon corrected. The fog was really caused by our own barrage as much as by the enemy's. Our barrage moved along in front of us as the Battalion advanced. The morning was practically dead calm. The ground over which the advance was made was sandy, consequently every shell that burst threw up a huge cloud of fine sand. As the shells were bursting in thousands, the country was covered with a thick cloud of dust which did not settle for a long time after the bombardment had passed on to the back areas. The sun was not visible till about 1½ hours after it had risen!

"Our barrage lifted off objective No. 2 just as A Company reached the wire 30 yards short of it. This wire, however, turned out to be weak and the company wasted very little time forcing a way through it, and reached the actual trench just as some of the enemy in it were beginning to recover themselves and open rifle fire. However, A Company was on to them with the bayonet before they could do much damage, and they very soon held up their hands.

"Naik Dyanu Bhosle of A Company did a neat piece of work here. Having had the position of an enemy machine gun—as revealed by an aeroplane photograph—carefully explained to him on the map before the battle, he took two men with him to search for this gun on his arrival at the work. They were suddenly fired on by several riflemen at close range, and one of them was wounded. They instantly dashed at these men and killed 3 or 4 of them with the bayonet—the remainder surrendered. It was then found that this was the very detachment with the machine gun that they were seeking. The gun had not opened fire, because the men had been crouching at the bottom of their trench during our barrage. When the barrage lifted, they got up, and were getting their gun into position, when Dyanu Bhosle and his party appeared at close range out of the fog, and surprised and rushed them before they could bring their gun into action. It was entirely due to Dyanu Bhosle's quick action and decision that they failed to open fire with the machine gun, which would probably have caused us a good many casualties.

"In accordance with the orders A Company now remained in the captured work, to clear all dug-outs, machine-gun emplacements, and shelters of the enemy, while the remaining Companies of the Battalion passed through them, and on to the remaining objectives in the position, followed by the Battalion supporting us, which also had orders to pass over A Company. The latter was to follow that Battalion as soon as the 'mopping up' task in the captured work was completed.

CHAPTER XXXIII

HOT FIRING AND FOG (*account of attack continued*)

"B AND C COMPANIES, having passed through A Company, were to push on to several objectives in the intricate trench system which had been allotted to the several platoons. Having established themselves in their final objective, D Company, armed with four extra Lewis guns in addition to its own normal four, were to pass through B and C, maintain touch with the enemy, consolidate, and be prepared to meet any possible counter-attack. B and C were to reorganise and get ready to meet a counter-attack on their right flank, on which side a counter-attack by the enemy was considered likely. But it never came.

"At this stage, the supporting Battalion was to pass through us and take up the pursuit.

"As soon as that Battalion was clear, we were to form up, follow it in échelon 400 yards in rear, and 400 yards to the right, so as to guard the right flank of the Brigade against any large-scale counter-attack from a number of villages and plantations covering the area away to our right. These villages—Kalkilieh, Jiljulieh, and Bir Adas—were still held by the enemy and afforded him much cover.

"What then happened was this: A Company stopped in its objective—as already explained—and the remaining Companies swept through A Company and made for their several objectives, but failed in the dense fog to recognise these when they reached them. Some platoons got to their right objectives, but having captured them, imagined they were not yet at their final positions—though they actually were—and pushed on. Others did not hit off quite the same spots in the fog, so they went on. In fact, at this stage, all knew that they were winning, nobody could see anybody else, and everybody pushed on, the enemy having been completely overwhelmed by our tremendous artillery fire.

"All the same, there were several little local instances where enemy machine gunners tried to hold out, with which our men dealt skilfully and bravely without hesitation. The following is an example of such incidents. Lance-Naik Tanu Kadam was in command of a Lewis-gun section on the flank of his Company. During the advance he came up with a Company of a Gurkha Battalion which was held up by an enemy trench containing Infantry and four or five machine guns. He quickly took his section to a flank position from whence he could enfilade the enemy's trench, making skilful use of the ground, but coming under heavy fire before he got into position he lost two of his men. However, he found a good position, and as soon as he opened fire with his two Lewis guns the enemy began running back. Their machine guns ceased firing, which enabled the Gurkhas to charge and capture many of the enemy and all their machine guns.

"Zero plus 37 minutes (i.e. 5·07 a.m.) was the time fixed for us to enter our final objective in the enemy's main trench system, so as to fit in with our artillery barrage programme. At this time, our supporting Battalion was to pass through us and become the leading Battalion. Many of our platoons however were already moving on, and it was hopeless trying to get control of more than a section or two at a time, as they could not see their officers, still less hear them. In a few minutes the whole Battalion was on the move again, going steadily forward on the same compass bearing, and expecting to come to more trenches, the Companies having failed to realise that the last trenches passed had been the final objective allotted to them. The Battalion was through the enemy's trench system. Everybody was on the move. The Brigade was pursuing the defeated enemy, so of course nobody thought of stopping. The enemy's guns were still firing and they were apparently straight ahead. The Battalion now got beyond where their own shells were falling, but we were still in dense fog because we were passing over ground where our own shells had been bursting thickly only a few minutes before. However, the atmosphere gradually got clearer, and after the Battalion had gone on about a mile, it became possible to see the landscape and the different platoons. The Companies began to see one another, and they corrected their relative positions as they moved on. The Battalion was not now under fire, and went steadily on till a ridge of low sand hills about another mile farther on, was reached. Here, a short halt was made in order to get into touch with other Battalions so as to adjust formations and make sure of the position. However one of the Companies was missing and could not be located. This was D Company, under Lieutenant Pattinson. The Regiment was soon on the move again, as the pursuit was going on and it was no time for stopping. It was certain that D Company was not left behind. It seemed that they must have gone off their line in the fog and would probably soon rejoin now that it was clear. This they did, though not quite in the way expected. This is what had happened. D Company's orders were that they were to push on ahead of the Battalion on the capture of the final objective in the trench system and consolidate beyond it, forming a covering screen with its four extra Lewis guns, to the Battalion re-forming them behind. D Company knew that their time for getting ahead was zero plus 37 minutes; and on the stroke of time, they more or less rushed through the other Companies and got ahead. Having done so, they and everybody else went on forward, and the Unit, instead of halting to re-form, was coming up behind them.

Added to which, the fog prevented their being able to distinguish a suitable ground on which to consolidate.

They could see no enemy ahead, and they were eager to get in touch with him, so pushed on. They then saw the supporting Battalion coming through, but did not realise that it was the supporting Battalion, and they had no intention of letting anybody get ahead of them, so quickened their pace almost to a run. Having done this, there was no stopping them, and they got well ahead of everybody! As they came to the ground where the fog began to get thinner, they heard guns

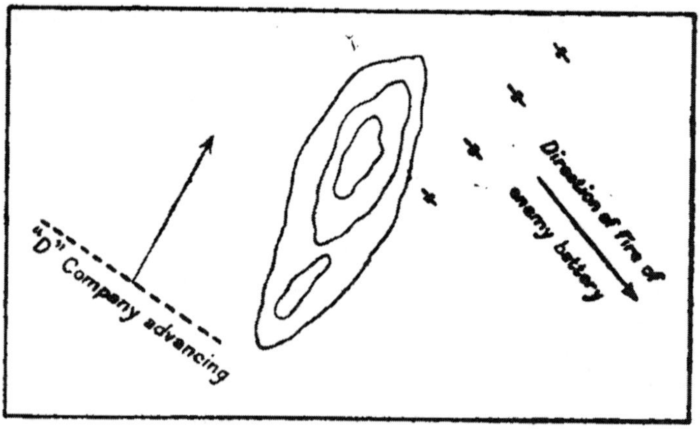

firing not far ahead, and shortly afterwards they emerged out of the smoke and dust cloud, practically on to a hostile Battery in position in some gun-pits, completely surprising and capturing it. Pattinson went into a dug-out, and there found the Adjutant of the Battery. The scared individual was surrounded by Mahrattas with their bayonets pointed at him, about an inch off his chest and throat. He was sitting by his telephone with his hands up. A look of great relief came over his face when he saw a British Officer. He spoke a little English and told Pattinson he was Adjutant of the Battery. He had been directing the fire by telephone when he suddenly heard them stop firing, and a moment later the 'wild Indians' had swarmed into his dug-out. Till Pattinson appeared, he thought his fate was sealed. He was a Turk.

"Pattinson and his Company, however, wasted no time with this Battery. They were off again looking for more quarry almost at once, and very soon located another enemy Battery in some gardens ahead, just to the right of their line of advance. This Battery was the other side of some low sand-hills, and was firing on a Brigade away to our right, so they never saw D Company advancing as indicated in diagram opposite.

"Directly D Company realised the situation, they made for the sand-hills and opened fire with Lewis guns, enfilading the Battery, which instantly ceased fire, the gun detachments running off. However, most of these were rounded up and taken prisoners by a platoon of D Company which had worked away in rear of the Battery in anticipation of this happening.

"A little farther on a third Battery was found among cactus hedges and gardens. It had just ceased firing and a few of its personnel were captured.

"The Company then went on again in hopes of finding more to capture, and having got rather off its correct line, Pattinson now directed it on to a point on the railway about one mile or a mile and a half N.W. of Kalkiliyeh, where he calculated the Battalion should cross the railway. Having reached this point, and seeing nobody, he thought it time to stop and get into touch with us again. Not very long afterwards, the remainder of the Battalion (and of the Brigade) came up, the Battalion striking the railway at the very spot where D Company were waiting.

"In accordance with the general plan, the whole Brigade now swung round to the east—(it had up to this, been advancing N.E.) and made for the hills, passing about one mile north of the village of Kalkiliyeh. The Battalion was now again in the front line, as the wheel to the east had brought us into line with the leading Battalion of the échelon. After we had gone on a farther 2½ miles or so, we came within 2,000 yards of some steep rocky hills. These were held by the enemy, who opened with long-range machine-gun fire.

"We replied with Lewis guns. It was now noon and exceptionally hot. The men had been on the move since 2 a.m. carrying weights. The going had been heavy (mostly over loose sand), and they had had no food. They were somewhat done, and not in a condition to start an attack up steep rocky hills. Also we had no guns to support an attack, as our guns had not got through the captured trench system as quickly as the Infantry had done and were still a long way behind. The Brigade therefore halted for a rest and some food before attacking. Meanwhile, the enemy suddenly withdrew into the hills farther east. When we advanced again, he had disappeared.

CHAPTER XXXIV

ENEMY PUT TO FLIGHT (*account of attack continued*)

"We followed in pursuit for another 4 or 5 miles over very bad country. Hills increasing in height and covered with huge lime-stone boulders, about as bad going as can be imagined. The final objective allotted to the Brigade for the day, had been a village called Jiyus. There was a conference of Commanding Officers at the place where we halted, and the Brigadier was a little doubtful of our being able to reach Jiyus before nightfall, but was very anxious that we should do so.

"As the Brigade went on, the pace got slower and slower. The men were evidently done, but they smiled at once when spoken to, and in spite of being very tired were full of spirits. We were fired on by snipers several times, but our Lewis guns were on to them at once and quickly silenced them. The Lewis gunners were wonderful the whole day. All had heavy weights to carry, and as the Lewis gunners have to carry their guns and magazines, they almost always drop behind before others do on a long march, or during an attack; but on this occasion, not a bit of it! In spite of the bad going, and the very trying day, they were up in the front line to the end of the day!

"We reached Jiyus just at sunset. On arriving there we surprised a few Turks, a German artillery officer, and German sergeant, in the village, and took them prisoners. The Germans were captured by the leading Company of the Battalion on our left.

"Early next morning a contact aeroplane came over, to whom our next position was signalled, and soon after, we received orders to join the Brigade on the march, following in rear as reserve Battalion, and a message from the Brigade Commander, saying that he was very pleased with the marching and work done by the Battalion on the previous day. (Not a single man, by the way, had fallen out.)

"Accordingly, on the morning of the 20th, the Brigade marched through us, and we tailed in as reserve Battalion, and started on the march, which was part of the general pursuit. At this time, we did not know what our destination was. About 5 miles, there was a halt by a spring for water, and there we heard that we were to march to a place called Kuryet Hajja, about 10 miles farther on, where it was hoped to cut off a number of the enemy who had been defeated in another part of the line, and were withdrawing north through the hills. As the men had no food at all that morning, I began to wonder how many of them would get there, as we had a big climb of 2,000 feet before us and lots of up and down work over rocky hill paths. About 14 miles over bad ground on no food at all, was going to be a pretty severe test. The country was getting somewhat like the Indian Frontier Hills; not so high, but the same kind of bare rocky hills.

"We reached Kuryet Hajja at 5 p.m. One man had fallen out and was sent to hospital, completely exhausted and ill. The leading Battalions got into touch with the enemy for about an hour before dark, and there was an exciting ten minutes when there was a race for a hill between one of our Battalions and the enemy. The British Battalion got there first and captured 140 prisoners, and an Indian Battalion captured another 100.

"That night we had to eat our emergency rations, and we furnished two Companies on Brigade outpost duty. On the following day—21st September—the Brigade marched at daybreak for five miles, and then halted, another Brigade having been detailed to carry on the pursuit.

"By this time the enemy was in disorderly flight, and

during the march we passed great quantities of war material, impedimenta, guns, stragglers, wounded men and dead. The Brigade was compelled to halt on this day to wait for its rations, which had completely run out, and we had now nothing left to eat.

"Just after the Battalion had halted, an enemy mountain battery fired half a dozen shells from somewhere behind the hills, practically doing no harm, and this was the last thing we saw in the nature of hostilities, for the time being. We shifted on the following day, to another camp, where the whole Brigade was concentrated; a move of only half a mile. On the next day we remained stationary, and the G.O.C. of the Brigade came to see the Battalion, and addressed the men as follows:

"'I wish to congratulate and thank all ranks for their splendid performances of the past few days. The operations have been completely successful—practically the whole Turkish Army and all its guns have been destroyed or captured, and in this great victory you have done your full share. There was much hard work done in the period preceding the battle, in training and preparation, and to this work all applied themselves with keenness and good spirit. Now all can see the results of their efforts, and will understand the value of such training. The Battalion is one with a fine historical record. Its discipline is of a high order. It has nobly upheld its high traditions. I am proud to have such a Battalion under my command.'

"On the 23rd, the Brigade marched to a camp at a place called Messudieh (really only a railway station close to Samaria). There we stayed for two days, waiting for further orders. When they came, they were rather disappointing, for we were to march back to a place close to our starting point on the day of the battle, and the Battalion has been there ever since, living more or less under peace conditions except for being in bivouacs.

"There were not many acts of great individual

gallantry to record. This was IN NO WAY the fault of the men or of anybody else. The fact is, that our Artillery is too magnificently powerful, overwhelming and accurate nowadays, and except here and there locally, the enemy was defeated and crushed by the time the Infantry reached him. I never saw anything so wonderful as the barrage of that day. But the men were magnificent all the same. They were simply out for blood, and were searching for the enemy, and plainly anxious to close with him whenever they could. They went through the enemy barrage in splendid order although it was heavy, and it is marvellous that the casualties were not heavier. The Battalion went into action 667 strong, and the casualties amounted to 121, and as most of them occurred within an hour, it will be clear that it was quite a warm hour. But all were as cool and as steady and as keen as could be, and every British Officer who went through with them is full of admiration for our men. They really are splendid fellows. I regret that one Indian Officer, Jemadar Daulet Bhosle, I.D.S.M., was killed. It was particularly hard luck, as he had only arrived from India the day before the battle. He already had the Indian Distinguished Service Medal for service in Mesopotamia and was due to be promoted Subadar.

"Lieutenant Watson, M.C., was wounded during the action, rather severely, but is now doing well, I hear.

"Our Medical Officer, Lieutenant Sohan Lallbhatia, did most excellent and skilful work under very heavy fire. His aid post was in a small work on to which for some reason the enemy concentrated a number of guns for nearly two hours, during which the Doctor must have had a very unpleasant time. Many big shells bursting close to you when you are trying to dress a wound, do not I imagine tend to steady the hand and nerve required for surgical work. Yet his dressings and skilled services were most highly praised by the senior Medical Officers through whose hands they afterwards passed. He was, I am glad to say, awarded an immediate Military Cross by the C.-in-C.

"Two other immediate rewards were given to the Battalion. The Indian Order of Merit 2nd Class in both cases. The recipients were:

"Naik Dyanu Bhosle, for his action described earlier in the narrative.

"Private Gopal Rao Mahamunkar, for showing great pluck and considerable skill in rapidly bringing his Lewis gun into action at close range, from a flank on an enemy machine gun which was firing on our advancing Infantry. While firing he was wounded, but continued to fire until he had silenced the machine gun."

CHAPTER XXXV

MARCHING THROUGH PALESTINE

AFTER the events just recorded, the Battalion returned to El Kefr, and carried out salvage operations. The 9th Brigade was then ordered to Damascus, and started on its thirteen days' march on November 1st, 1918. Colonel Delmé Radcliffe thus picturesquely describes part of this interesting march, over ground familiar to all readers of the New Testament:

"From Samaria, we marched across the plain of Armageddon, through Nazareth, Cana in Galilee, and Tiberias. The lake of Galilee is beautiful, as was also much of the country through which we passed. We had a day's halt on the shores of the lake and all of us most thoroughly enjoyed a swim. Officers and men alike, were badly in need of a bath at the time. A tremendous squall got up in the evening and the lake became very rough. The storm was extraordinarily sudden, as lake storms so often are. It was almost a dead calm at 3 p.m. and a regular gale at 5 o'clock. After leaving Tiberias and Capernaum, we crossed the Jordan, then through El Kuneitra, past Mount Hermon to Damascus. The latter delightful old city has beautiful surroundings. Charming gardens for many miles around, and many lovely and interesting birds, which delighted me as they are my particular hobby."

The following notes of dates and mileage, giving the distances and route traversed during the march, may be of interest to record here:

1st.	Marched to Fendakumiyeh	12	miles.
2nd.	" " Jenin	13	"
3rd.	" " El Fuleh	13	"
4th.	" " Kefrkenna	10	"
5th.	" " Tiberias	16	"
6th.	A day's rest.		
7th.	Marched to Roshpina	12	"
8th.	" " Deir Essaras	12	"
9th.	" " El Kunitra	8	"
10th.	" " Sasa	19	"
11th.	A day's rest.		
12th.	Marched to Artuz	12	"
13th.	" " Damascus	10	"

The Regiment encamped three miles south of Damascus.

In March 1919 half the Battalion was sent to Amman, the rest remaining at Damascus.

Amman is about 115 miles south of Damascus as the crow flies, and 23 miles east of the Jordan River. From the Mediterranean to the Jordan, is comparatively civilised country, but from the river eastwards, it becomes wilder and wilder, and Amman lies at an elevation of 3,000 feet, on the fringe of the Syrian desert.

Generally speaking, the object of the British troops being sent there was that they might show themselves to the Arab tribes, in order to inspire them with confidence during the rather unsettled state of affairs in the country.

The Regiment was occupied in patrolling the country whilst at Amman, these patrols being undertaken on the recommendation of the Political Officer of the district. They had the good effect of giving our troops some knowledge of the surrounding country. The feeling of the local inhabitants towards the troops was entirely friendly. The patrols were well received both by Arabs and Circassians, who did everything that they could to procure food for them, such as sheep, eggs, etc., the Headmen of the villages invariably offering hospitality to the British Officers. These patrols therefore were very popular with all ranks, and another great advantage gained from them was, that they kept the men fit, and maintained for them those marching powers for which the Regiment was renowned in the Brigade.

Colonel Delmé Radcliffe reported that the men were in splendid condition and excellent spirits, in spite of the fact that many of them were naturally longing to go to their homes.

"But they well understand," he adds, "that they must stay and hold the countries they have helped to win, until in due course they can be relieved. The men give me now the impression they have always done," he continued, "that no matter what the conditions are, they remain always a really marvellously good spirited and happy lot. The keenness with which they go about their work and really try hard to keep themselves as efficient as possible, is just as evident now as it was while the fighting was going on."

The Divisional Commander, General Hoskins, paid a surprise visit to the Regiment by aeroplane, on May 31st. He asked to see all the officers and men as he wished to speak to them. As soon as they were ready, he addressed the Regiment in these words:

"I have come to say good-bye. I have been given a command in England. I am very fond of the 105th. It is composed of very stout fellows and has done extremely well. I am very sorry to leave the Regiment, and hope I may have it under my command again some day. I wish you all very well."

The Battalion was much impressed, thinking it extremely kind of General Hoskins to fly over on purpose to tell them this, especially when very much pressed for time. The Regiment had been under his command in both Mesopotamia and Palestine, and he had won the respect and admiration of all, so that there was universal regret at his leaving.

In June Lieut.-Colonel Waller took over the command of the Regiment from Colonel Delmé Radcliffe, who was ordered to proceed to Upper Egypt to command the 29th Punjabis, temporarily.

The two Companies and Head-quarters left Amman on December 4th, moving out with highest honours amidst decorations of the streets, and an infantry escort and troop of cavalry, provided by the Arab Governor Rashid Pasha, who rode out three miles with the Regiment. Colonel Waller thus describes what must have been a very unpleasant five days' march to Jerusalem.

"In spite of a downpour of rain, the men marched splendidly, and did the first twenty-seven miles under full loads, without a single straggler, and swaggered through Es Salt singing. The next march was a very disagreeable one. Fourteen miles on a steep down grade, with a drop of over 4,000 feet into a wet bivouac, after handling and loading twenty-six tons of impedimenta. The drop into that awful crevasse of the Jordan Valley, 1,200 feet below sea-level, after having been for many months in the upland air, was very trying. We were kept a whole week at the bridgehead before getting to Jerusalem, always in rain and biting cold. Jerusalem was a horrid, muddy, windy camp, and we were glad to move on by train to Ludd—animals and carts by road. We struck bad weather again at Ludd (close to Jaffa), but the Wing from Damascus, which arrived there before us, had got our camp up and we were all together again after ten months. After a strenuous fortnight we trained to Kantara to re-equip for India. Here we had the satisfaction of hearing that our indents and books were the best that Ordnance had dealt with, and we were ready again in *days* when others had taken *weeks*, so my young men forgave me for the way in which I had been driving them. Whilst we were at Ludd, they all passed the Hindustani Colloquial test, at which I was proud, for I was their only coach. One actually managed the lower standard. On taking leave of the 3rd Division and 9th Brigade, we received very complimentary farewells. We marched to Ismailia (Egypt), and I had to foot it the whole way as all our horses were taken from us. The rheumatism I had picked up in the trenches in Mesopotamia made the way for me a road of penance. At Ismailia we made many friends, and had not a *khamseen* [1] followed by rain, ruined it, our celebration of Seedaseer day would have been a great show."

The Regiment left Ismailia on February 1st, 1920, and camped in the desert near Suez for a month, at the Indian Transit camp, pending the loading up of the heavy kit. The Regiment embarked on the R.M.S. *Dufferin*, on April 25th and sailed for India. The march out of the Suez camp to the ship was a triumphal procession; there were some 16,000 Indian troops in the area assembled to give the Unit a stirring send-off. Bombay was reached on May 6th, and the Regiment left for Belgaum the same evening. All the men who returned from service were given two months' war leave as soon as possible.

[1] Strong desert wind.

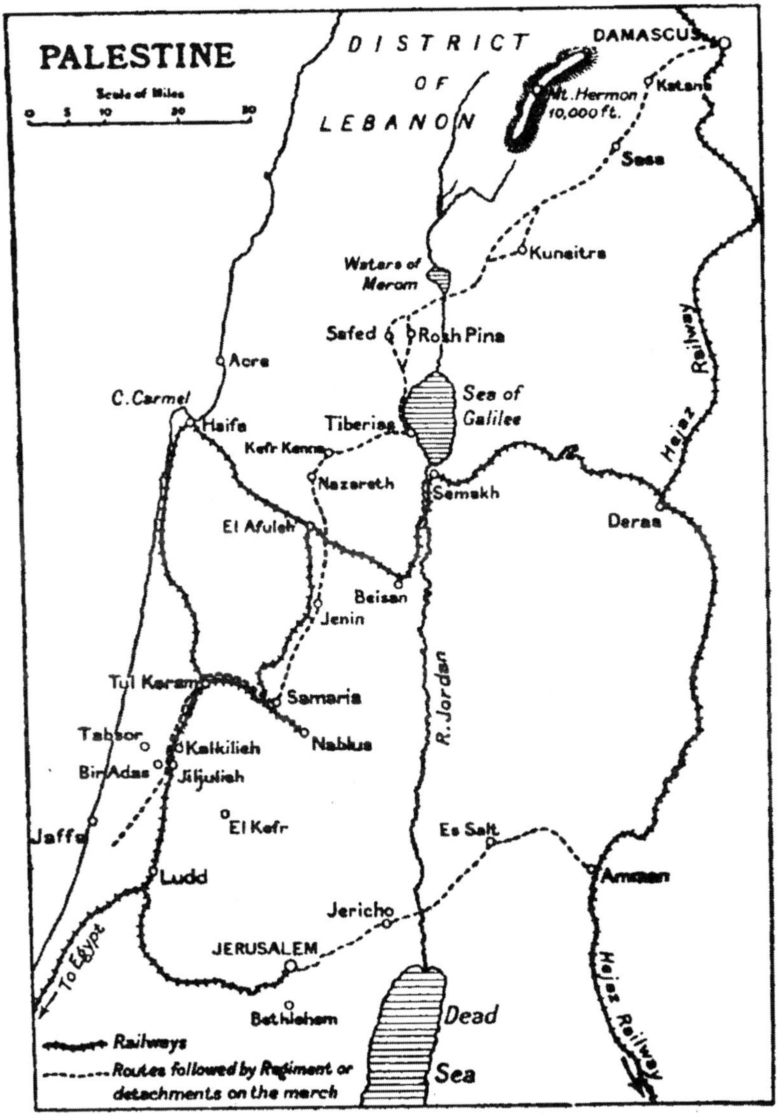
PALESTINE
Scale of Miles
0 5 10 20 30
DISTRICT
OF
LEBANON
DAMASCUS
Katana
Mt. Hermon
10,000 ft.
Sasa
Kuneitra
Waters of
Merom
Safed
Rosh Pina
Acre
C. Carmel
Haifa
Tiberias
Sea of
Galilee
Kefr Kenna
Nazareth
Semakh
Deraa
Hejaz
Railway
El Afuleh
Beisan
Jenin
Tul Keram
Samaria
Nablus
R. Jordan
Tabsor
Kalkilieh
Bir Adas
Jiljulieh
El Kefr
Jaffa
Es Salt
Amman
Ludd
Jericho
JERUSALEM
To Egypt
Bethlehem
Dead
Sea
Hejaz Railway
Railways
Routes followed by Regiment or
detachments on the march

CHAPTER XXXVI

CONCLUSION

THE organisation of the Indian Army was about this time altered to conform with that of the British Army. Each Battalion was to have four Companies and a Headquarter Company, the latter to be made up of machine guns and Administrative Units, such as Bandsmen, Transport drivers, "*Mochis*" (Saddlers).

On August 30th Colonel Waller retired from the Service, and Major Haughton was appointed officiating Commandant in his place. In a farewell order, Colonel Waller gives "his thanks to all ranks, British and Indian, for the loyal assistance they have at all times offered him during his period of command. He bears willing testimony to the sterling discipline shown by the men while in occupation of enemy territory, and during the long wait for demobilisation."

In September the Regiment had orders to move to Santa Cruz, thirteen miles north of Bombay. It arrived there in October and remained until February 1921. During this period the Regiment furnished Guards of Honour to General Sir Charles Monroe and Lord Rawlinson on their respective departure and arrival in Bombay as Commander-in-Chief of India. The G.O.C. Bombay District published an Order expressing pleasure with the turn-out of the Guard on these occasions.

In October the news was received of the death of Colonel H. C. B. Dann, who had commanded the

[*Vernon, Bombay.*

GROUP OF REGIMENTAL OFFICERS, WITH SILVER CHALLENGE SHIELD.

Regiment for four years up to 1914, and his death was greatly regretted by all who knew him. At this time there was also the sad news of the death of Subadar-Major Uttam Singh and Jemadar Krishnak Changnak. The former served for twenty-three years with the Regiment and the latter twenty-six. Both of these men showed an example during their service, of smartness, loyalty and devotion to duty. Their death was much felt by all officers serving, and many who had retired.

A party conveying the Colours of the Regiment was present at H.R.H. the Duke of Connaught's Durbar at Delhi, in January 1921. The Regiment was also represented at the Peace Celebration in England by Subadar-Major Sayed Suleiman; a Dekhani Mahratta Non-commissioned Officer; and a Private, Concani Mahratta, who were sent over to take part in the big Naval and Military Procession, which took place in London on July 19th, 1919, when representative troops from all parts of the British Empire who had fought together so patriotically in the Great War, were assembled to celebrate the Nations' signing of Peace after four and a half years of the most terrible war the world has ever experienced.

Editor's Concluding Note

The writer had thus brought this little history of the 2/5th Mahratta Light Infantry practically up to date, but in closing these records of events concerning it, the Editor would like to add, that before leaving Santa Cruz for Baluchistan, whither the Regiment had been ordered early in 1921, the Commanding Officer had a full-dress parade for the express purpose of the presentation of a silver shield that had been given by Colonel Sir Reginald Hennell in memory of his visit to the Regiment in December 1913. It was to be called " The Seedaseer Memorial Shield " in commemoration of the

Regiment's first great Battle Honour. Owing to the War, its presentation had been long delayed, but it had been sent out to Suez in 1919, c/o Messrs. Cox & Co., to await the Regiment's return from Palestine. The news of its despatch had been announced to the Unit at Amman, and it was handed over to the C.O. on the Regiment's arrival in Egypt en *route* for its return to India in April 1920. The description of the Presentation of the Shield at the parade at Santa Cruz will be found at the end of the Appendices.

This presentation of the author's last gift to his old Regiment makes a fitting conclusion to his tribute to it in the writing of its history. His final words were not written, but it is certain that they would have been of the warmest praise and encouragement to all ranks of the Regiment. In his declining years he had felt himself a sort of " Father " of the old Corps, and that this was greatly appreciated, is shown by various letters he received from different Commanding Officers. One writes :

" We all feel so grateful to you for the warm interest you show towards the Regiment. This works as a strong moral cement, and is also an inspiration. It makes us conscious that we belong to a living and enduring institution."

Another writes :

" Your constant interest is a strong leavening influence."

And Colonel Delmé Radcliffe, in one of his last letters to the author, at the close of the Palestine campaign, says :

" On each occasion of my hearing from you, I have let the men know it, and when your letters have contained a direct message, I have read it out to them. That you who left the Regiment over thirty years ago and now hold a high appointment in the King's Royal Body Guard, should still constantly send the men messages and proofs of your interest in and affection for the Regiment, has, I know, made a deep impression on them. Your letter congratulating them on their share in the recent victory in Palestine, which I read out on a Battalion parade, gave them the greatest pleasure."

The author would most assuredly have ended this Story of the Regiment with renewed expressions of his pride in its achievements in the late War, together with his tribute of proud memory and homage to those whose lives were given fighting for the defence of the British Empire in its stand for the upholding of Right and Justice.

But the labour of love, carried on through years of failing health and illness, oft-times acute and painful, could not be brought to final completion by the hand that wrought it.

On May 22nd, 1925, came the call from earthly service, and the relief from physical suffering. On May 27th were laid to rest the earthly remains of Reginald Hennell. The military honours which were his due were fully rendered, and the beautiful wreath sent by the Indian Regiment he loved so well rested on the coffin. Thus, even to the grave, the link remained with its old Commandant, whose last energies had been spent on writing the Story of the "Kali Panchwin."

APPENDIX I

BATTLE HONOURS OF THE REGIMENT

I. Mysore. 1790–2.
II. Seedaseer. 1799.
III. Seringapatam. 1799.
IV. Beni-Boo-Ali. 1821.
V. Kahun (Afghanistan). 1840.
VI. China. 1860, 1861.
VII. Afghanistan. 1879–80.
VIII. Burmah. 1886–88.
IX. Mesopotamia. Kut-el-Amara. 1915–17. Defence of Kut-el-Amara.
Bagdad.
X. Palestine. 1918. Sharon. Nablus.

APPENDIX II

LIST OF BATTLES, SIEGES, AND MINOR ACTIONS IN WHICH THE REGIMENT OR DETACHMENTS TOOK PART, BUT FOR WHICH BATTLE HONOURS WERE NOT GIVEN

1772. Reduction of Broach. Portuguese Fort. (Received prize money.)
1774. Storming and capture of Fort of Thana.
1775. Battle of Arras, in Gujerat. Defeat of Mahrattas.

1780. Capture of Fort Mullungurh and defeat of Mahrattas. Surrender of Bassein.

1781–2. Destruction of Mahratta Fort, Tellicherry, and capture of Calicut and other Malabar Forts.

1783. Storming and capture of Hydergurh, Bednore, Ananpore, Mangalore.

1790. Operations in Dharwar against Pureshram Bhao, the Peshwa, with Captain Little's Detachment.

1790. Storming and capture of Avery Redoubt in Malabar.

1791. Actions with Colonel Hartley's Brigade, Pondicherry Ghaut.

1796. Active Service in Ceylon. Capture of Colombo.

1797. Operations under Colonel Dow at Calicut, Malabar coast.

1799. Actions against Tippoo Sultan.

1800. Expeditions in and around Cundapore against Robber Chiefs. Attack on Pagoda near Karwar, etc.

1803. First Mahratta War. Battle of Alighur. Taking of Delhi. Battle Laswaree, etc.

1804. Battalion with General Lake's force. Defeat of Holkar at Deeg.

1805. Siege of Bhurtpore, when Battalion lost heavily.

1806. Battalion with General Murray's force. Attacks on Dewas, Ujjain, Indore, Kotah.

1809. Field Service in Khandeish, against Mulhar Rao Holkar.

1813. Operations against the Pindharees.

1814. Continued Operations against Pindharees and Rohilla rebels, under Colonel Lionel Smith, in vicinity of Jafferabad.

1815. War with the Peshwa pending. Operations connected with murder of Shastree.

1817. Continued operations against the Pindharees and Rohilla tribes. Second Mahratta War, and war with the Peshwa. Capture of Poona and Bijapur. Rout of the Peshwa.

1818. Capture of Sattara and battle of Gopal Ashti. Battalion with General Smith's force in pursuit of the Peshwa. Rajah of Nagpur beaten and deposed.

Nagpur captured. Mulhar Rao Holkar's army defeated at battle of Medipore.

1819. Operations in Persian Gulf, under General Sir William Keir. Siege and capture of Fort Ras-el-Khyma, and Fort Zayah.

1826. Capture of the Fort of Bohna Kathiawad.

1828. Capture of Gaekwar territories (sequestered districts) Dubhai, Bahadurpur, and Sirnoor.

1830. Capture of the Fort of Akalkot.

1839–40. First Afghan War. Escort of Convoys in Scinde. Actions with the Murrees, Brahuis, etc. Attack on Fort Khandgurh, Baluchistan. Defence of Dadar.

1856. Persia. Light Company bombardment and capture of Muhamra, under General Sir James Outram.

1857. Detachment against Eshwant Rao Kadam. Capture of the Fort of Khundaree.

1858. Operations against the Bheels with Col. Tapp's Field Force.

1859. On Field Service in Khandeish and the Nizam's Dominions.

1861–62. Operations in China. Capture of entrenched camp at Wang Kaza. Capture of entrenched town of Tseerpoo. Battle at Nazean; taking of Khading, Tsingpoo, and Nazean.

1867. Abyssinian War. Battalion ordered to Annesley Bay but found operations over on arrival, so were too late to take active part in the war.

1880–1. Second Afghan War. The Regiment took part in the relief of Kandahar with General Phayre's Division.

1886–8. The Regiment sent with the Expeditionary Force to Upper Burmah. It was engaged for two years in this strenuous campaign against the Dacoits.

1901. Four Companies of the Battalion took part in a Punitive Expedition against Turco-Arabic incursion near Aden.

1914–19. The Great War. The Regiment, as a unit, was on active service in Mesopotamia and Palestine. Some of the officers were also for a time on the French Front.

APPENDIX III

WAR MEDALS, DECORATIONS, AND MENTIONS IN DESPATCHES, WON BY OFFICERS, N.C.O.s, AND MEN OF THE REGIMENT

1799. SEEDASEER. Lord Mornington wrote to the Directors of the East India Company:

"I am confident that Your Honourable Court will be of the opinion that the conduct and success of the Army of Bombay on that day has seldom been equalled and never surpassed."

1800. SUBADAR IBRAHIM KHAN and a small Detachment were decorated for conspicuously gallant conduct in an attack on a Pagoda near Karwar.

1817. General Orders Appreciation of the successful operations in pursuit of the Pindharee Force.

1818. Letter of thanks and appreciation of the splendid work of the Battalion from the Brigadier, during the battle of Gopal Ashti, on February 20th.

1818. HAVILDAR MOHIDIN KHA recommended for promotion for his valuable assistance. Mahratta War.

1819. LANCE-NAIK BHOWANI SINGH, promoted to Havildar, for bravery and fidelity in defending the village of Sylapur.

1819. PRIVATE ESNAK SALNAK, promoted Havildar for gallant conduct at the storming of Mandangarh.

1819. General Orders thanking officers and men for the zealous way in which they performed their duties during the Siege and Capture of Fort Ras-el-Khyma, Persian Gulf.

1824. Honorary Badges, "SERINGAPATAM," "SEEDASEER," awarded to the Battalion as battle honours.

1830. Brigade Orders: appreciation of the conduct, discipline and zeal of the troops, and thanks to LIEUT.-COLONEL GIBBON for his cordial co-operation and assistance.

1839. ENSIGNS STANLEY and TAYLOR, and CAPTAIN SMEE, mentioned in despatches for gallantry during the attack on Fort Khangurh.

CAPTAIN BROWN nominated to the appointment of Brigade-Major for his meritorious conduct during the defence of Kahun.

CAPTAIN BROWN and DR. GLOSSE mentioned in despatches.

1839. SURDAR BAHADUR, SUBADAR MOHAMED KHAN, killed in action, at storming of Fort Khanghur, mentioned in despatches.

1839. ENSIGN STANLEY, ENSIGN TAYLOR, and CAPTAIN SMEE, mentioned in despatches.

1840. LIEUTENANT CLARKE, killed in action, SUBADAR BAJI JADHAO, and party met their death while returning to Kahun, in a fight at Nafusk, Afghanistan. Splendid example of bravery and devotion to duty. Acknowledgment of their fine conduct from Field Army Orders.

1840. Extract from letter through Secretary to the Government of India, Commanding His Lordship's approbation of the "eminent gallantry carried out by CAPTAIN BROWN during the defence and retirement from the Fort of Kahun. Showed great prudence and ability of leadership."

1841. General Orders. Honorary Badge "KAHUN" awarded.

1841. Regiment made "Light Infantry."

1862. LIEUTENANT W. T. BROWN, dangerously wounded in action at Talping; mentioned in despatches.

1880–1. CAPTAIN REGINALD HENNELL, mentioned in despatches and received thanks from the Government and Commander-in-Chief in India, for special services rendered during the Campaign in Afghanistan, 1879–1881.

1886. PRIVATE CHANDU SAKPAL, and RAOJI POWAR, mentioned as having displayed great dash in an attack and capture of the fortified village of Yentha, Burmah Campaign.

HAVILDAR LAKSHMAN TELI, and PRIVATE GYABUKSH, mentioned for acts of conspicuous gallantry, and PRIVATE SHAIKO MOHIDIN for great fortitude when wounded, in a severe engagement with Shans near Lamaning.

HAVILDAR BINDA SINGH, conspicuous by his coolness and dash. BUGLER DASRAJI BEDAR, and PRIVATE RAOJI POWAR, distinguished themselves by untiring pluck and dash during an attack on Boh Nyoo's dacoit gang.

1887. COLONEL POOLE, MAJOR R. HENNELL, CAPTAIN NICHOLETTS, and LIEUTENANT P. HOLLAND, were mentioned in despatches by General Sir George White, K.C.B., V.C.

MAJOR R. HENNELL received the D.S.O.

LIEUTENANT T. A. FISCHER earned the thanks of the Officer Commanding Mounted Infantry in Upper Burmah.

1888. In recognition of Services in Mysore, the Regimental Colours were inserted with "MYSORE 1790–92."

In recognition of services in Burmah, the Colours also were awarded the word "BURMAH," 1885–87, to be added to them.

SUBADAR-MAJOR RAMCHANDAR CHAWAN received the Order of British India, in recognition of excellent services rendered during a period of 31 years.

1895. LIEUT.-COLONEL R. HENNELL, D.S.O., formerly in Command of the Regiment, was appointed Adjutant and Clerk of the Cheque of H. Majesty's Royal Body Guard of the Yeomen of the Guard. Was made Lieutenant of the Royal Guard in 1901.

1902. Received the Order of Knighthood from King Edward VII on his Coronation, 1902.

1910. Appointed "Commander Royal Victorian Order" by King George V.

1919. Royal Order of the British Empire (O.B.E.) by King George V.

The Great War, 1914–19

D.S.O.

Lieut.-Colonel A. Delmé Radcliffe.
Major E. J. H. Haughton.
Major A. N. Thomas, I.M.S.

Military Cross

Captain W. B. Benton, and Bar.
Captain D. H. Powell.
Lieutenant G. H. Bland.
Captain S. Bhatia, I.M.S.

Royal Humane Society for Saving Life

Major E. J. H. Haughton.

Indian Order of Merit

Subadar Chimaji Garud.
Naik Dyanu Bhosle.
Sepoy Gopal Mahamunkar.

Indian Distinguished Service Medal

Subadar Maroti Bodke.
Subadar Bala Bhor.
Sepoy Nama Thange.
,, Ramchandar Shinde.
,, Vithoba Jagtap.

Indian Meritorious Service Medal

Havildar Rambhau Dhamne.
,, Bapujirao Shinde.
,, Peer Ali.
,, Jaswant rao Taore.
,, Sadashivrao Gujar.
Naik Kesheorao Darekar.
,, Tahinat Ali Khan.
,, Anna More.
,, Ramchandar Powar.

Naik Sarjerao Rasal.
,, Bhiku Ambekar.
,, Kesheorao Darekar.
,, Tahinat Ali Khan.
,, Dattu Shinde.
,, Dagdu Gotal.
Havildar Mahamed Yusuf.
,, Yeshwanta Mahadeshar.
,, Shaikh Nasiroddin.
,, Shaikh Mogal.
,, Krishna Powar.
,, Yeshwanta Powar.
Lance-Naik Vhithoba Chawan, 110th M.L.I.
,, Mahadeo Lad.
,, Yeswanta Salunke.
,, Sitaram Mahadik.
,, Ganpat Kadam.
,, Ganpat Jadhao.
Sepoy Anna Savant.
,, Gangaram Bhagade.
,, Sakaram Watane.
,, Shaikh Abdulla.
,, Bapu Powar.
,, Ramjirao Shinde.
,, Ramchandar Falke.
,, Babli Neeman.
Havildar Ramji Garud.
Lance-Naik Shaikh Ladle.

Sword of Honour

Subadar Chimaji Garud.
Jemadar Mohammed Samshuddin.

Mentioned in Despatches

Colonel E. R. I. Chitty (killed in action).
,, A. A. P. Waller.
,, A. Delmé Radcliffe.
Captain D. H. Powell (twice).
,, E. J. H. Haughton (twice).

Mentioned in Despatches (continued).

Captain A. N. Thomas, I.M.S.
,, W. B. Benton.
,, F. E. Thornton.
Major P. M. Heath, 110th M.L.I.
Subadar Maroti Bode.
Subadar Manajirao Palande.
Jemadar Baburao Pisal (twice).
Havildar Peer Ali.
,, Rambhau Dhamne.
,, Yesu Jagdale.
Sepoy Dada Gondli.
Naik Shankar rao Rane.
,, Krishna Powar.
,, Sawlaram Barhate.
,, Pandurang Desai.
,, Ramchandar Shinde.
,, Vithoba Jagtap.
,, Nama Thange.
Subadar Sayed Suleman.

The following are specially mentioned in the Manuscript ("Officers' Letters from Mesopotamia and Palestine," pages 180–1), but their names do not come in the list of those who received Orders and medals and were mentioned in despatches, as sent from India by Colonel Haughton, C.O. of the Regiment:

Lieutenant H. Huss.
,, A. G. Mumford.
2nd Lieutenant C. R. Glyn.
Jemadar Balkrishna Khanse.
Havildar Lakshman Jadhao.
Naik Narayan Shinde.
,, Shankar Shinde.
,, Ragnuath Godse.
Lance-Naik Bhau Bhacke.
Private Kondibawagh.
,, Lakshman Tambe.

Private Gem Powar.
,, Bauder Hazare.
,, Gaupat Khedkar.
,, Yedu Kaloar.
,, Galavrao Kalbhar.

The War Medals awarded to the Men during the Great War

The 1914–15 Star	890
The British War	3356
The Victory	3356

Indian General Service

Medal 1908, Clasp Afghanistan, 1919	216
I.G.S. Clasp Waziristan, 1919–21	75
I.G.S. Clasp Mashud, 1919–20	75

The following numbers of officers and men proceeded on Field Service during the Great War, 1914–19:

B. Officers	53
Indian	46
B. Warrant Officers	1
Indian other Ranks	3,155
Public Followers	85
Private Followers	36

Casualties during the War:

British Officers	7	killed in action.
Indian Officers	2	
Indian other Ranks	286	

Wounded in the Great War, 1914–19:

British Officers	9
Indian Officers	5
I.O. Ranks	1,223

Missing between August 1914 and January 1919:

Indian Officer	1
I.O. Ranks	101

APPENDIX IV

LIST OF OFFICERS WHO HAVE COMMANDED THE 5TH BOMBAY MAHRATTA LIGHT INFANTRY SINCE IT WAS RAISED IN 1768

It is to be noted that at the earlier portion of the Official Printed Records there are large gaps during which there is no mention of any Commanding Officers of the Battalions. The only explanation that can be given is that during the numerous wars of that period, 1786 to 1820, the Regiment was continually split up into Detachments, acting alone or with other Brigades or Divisions, and therefore it was not considered necessary to mention the names of the Commanding Officers.

1. Captain Daniel Carpenter 1780
2. Lieut.-Colonel Kenneth Macpherson . . July 1796
3. Colonel Boles (mentioned as commanding at capture of Sattara) . . . . . Jan. 1818
4. Lieut.-Colonel Stuart (commanding at Poona, 1818, and at Pali in January 1819) . . 1818
5. Major Jardine (mentioned as commanding 2/5th Kandeish) . . . . Feb. 1819
6. Lieut.-Colonel J. J. Smith (commanding in Bhaj, died September 27th, 1823. Senior Officer present Lieutenant W. J. Hewitt took command. Battalion renumbered 5th Bombay Light Infantry) . . . . . . Oct. 1822
7. Lieut.-Colonel W. Sandwith . . Dec. 22nd, 1825
8. Major James Gibbon, promoted Lieut.-Colonel, 1830 . . . . April 1829
9. *Note.*—Captain Keys Commanding Right Wing . 1834
   Lieutenant Heath Commanding Left Wing . 1834
10. Major Spiller Commanding Regiment . . 1837

11. Captain Smee, Ensign Stanley and Ensign Taylor mentioned 1839
12. In the celebrated defence of "Kahun," the only name mentioned is Captain Brown Commanding Detachment of Regiment 1840
13. Major Smee Commanding Left Wing, mentioned 1844–5
Captain Heath Commanding Right Wing and Head-quarters, mentioned 1844–5
14. Major Bayly Commanding Right Wing and Head-quarters 1848
15. Lieut.-Colonel Bayly Commanding Regiment . 1852
(Major Warden Commanding Left Wing—died 1854) 1852
16. Major T. S. Heath Commanding Regiment Bombay . . . . Nov. 1855
17. Lieut.-Colonel Heath Commanding in Poona (six Companies on Field Service in Poona) July 1857
18. Major H. Stanley Commanding in Ahmednagar July 6th (took Regiment to China) . . 1859
19. Lieut.-Colonel H. Stanley Commanding Regiment Canton, May (went on sick leave 1862), afterwards Lieut.-Colonel Taylor Commanding—Major Taylor, Lieutenant Hunt and Leacock with Regiment 1860
20. Major Taylor at Shanghai, Right Wing . . 1863
Captain A. A. Des Voeux Head-quarters and Left Wing, Hong-Kong 1863
21. Lieut.-Colonel W. W. Taylor Commanding, Regiment (the Regiment was under his command from 1864 to 1868, and in March left for Abyssinia, returning to Belgaum, and in May marched to Poona, where it was in 1877) . 1868
Arrived in Aden December 8th 1870
22. Colonel F. Roome, Commanding Regiment . 1877
Colonel Des Voeux acting Commanding Regiment 1879
23. Colonel F. Roome, Commanding Regiment at Thal-Chotiali, Afghanistan 1880
24. Colonel F. Roome, Commanding Regiment . 1880
24*a*. Colonel Carew Hunt took Command until Col. Roome returned 1881

25\. Colonel Carew Hunt Commanding Regiment to 1884

26\. (*Note.*—Colonel Roome went on sick leave in 1880 in Afghanistan and Colonel Carew Hunt acted Commander until he rejoined in 1881, and again till 1884.)

26\. Colonel Carew Hunt Commanding Regiment . 1884

27\. Lieut.-Colonel Arthur Poole Commanding Regiment. (*Note.*—Major Sandy acting on Colonel Poole's retirement—1887) . . . 1886

Colonel Poole rejoined from leave on April 29th, 1886, as officiating Commandant . . . 1887

28\. Lieut.-Colonel F. S. Leacock appointed Commandant May 1888, accidentally drowned, Lieut.-Colonel Watling acting till the arrival of Colonel R. Hennell 1888

29\. Lieut.-Colonel Reginald Hennell appointed Commandant November. (Retired in November 1889) 1888

30\. Lieut.-Colonel H. Scott appointed Commandant January 1890

31\. Major C. O. Nicholetts appointed Commandant April 24th 1891

32\. Lieut.-Colonel Anthony Beale appointed Commandant July 6th 1902

Lieut.-Colonel Anthony Beale retired July 1st . 1908

33\. Colonel Dann, at Hong-Kong, assumed command July 1st. Died after retirement . . 1913

34\. Lieut.-Colonel Chitty 1914

Killed March 1917, in action, Mesopotamia.

34*a*. Lieut.-Colonel P. M. Heath, acting April 18th, 1917. Died July 14th, 1917

35\. Lieut.-Colonel Delmé Radcliffe, D.S.O., acting 1917–18 1917

36\. Lieut.-Colonel Waller. Belgaum 1919 . . 1920

37\. Major E. J. H. Haughton, D.S.O., in Fort Sandeman. 1921

Appointed officiating commander . . 1922

38\. Lieut.-Colonel A. S. Hay, D.S.O., appointed Commandant May 8th 1923

APPENDIX V

LIST OF OFFICERS WHO HAVE SERVED IN THE REGIMENT AT DIFFERENT PERIODS AS GIVEN IN THE REGIMENTAL RECORDS, WITH THE STAFF APPOINTMENTS THEY HELD 1768–1923

1779. Captain Daniel Carpenter.
Lieutenant John Young.
,, Richardson.
,, R. Read.
,, Abraham Hammond.
,, Charles Patrick.
,, Thomas Ringrove.

1788. The following officers were in the Unit :
Captain George Facey—Commandant.
Lieutenant Roger Alden Hume.
,, Hugh Tridge.
,, Richard Budden.
,, Thomas Bee.
,, John Wright.
,, George Bailey.
,, Nathaniel Flatt.
,, M. Grant.

1796. The officers posted to the Battalion were :
Lieut.-Colonel Kenneth Macpherson.
Major Malcolm Grant.
Captain Robert Nesbitt.
,, Robert Buchanan.
,, William Brown (2nd).
Captain (Lieutenant) Joseph Boden.
Lieutenant John Skelton.
,, James Gordon.

1796. Lieutenant C. J. Mears.
,, John Harding.
,, R. Wightman (Adjutant).
,, Francis Parry.
,, David Seton.
,, H. M. Fitzgerald.
,, John Wood.
,, John Beete.
,, Benj. Sarney.
Five Ensigns vacant.
1817. Ensign Matthews.
Lieutenant Michel.
,, Spar.
Captain Deschamps.
Ensign Forster.
1830. 4th Colonel Gibbon—Commanding.
1834. Captain Keys and Lieutenant Heath.
1837. Major Spiller.
1838. Captain B. Justice, 5th B.N.I.
Lieutenant Cruikshank.
Captain B. Brown.
,, Heath.
Lieutenant Erskine.
1839. Ensign Stanley.
1840. Lieutenant Erskine.
,, Symonds.
,, Robert Dennis.
,, Walpole Clarke.
1844. Major Smee.
1848. Major Bayly.
Captain Rudd.
1852. Major Wardell.
1854. Captain and Brevet-Major Wardell (died 1854).
1855. Major J. C. Heath.
1857. Lieutenant Des Voeux.
,, Browne.
,, Fellowes.
Captain Oliver.

1857. Captain Taylor
,, Boodle.
Major Symonds.
1858. Captain Mackechnie.
Lieutenant A. G. F. Hogg.
,, Browne.
,, Ramsey.
,, Fellows.
,, Burne.
Major Keane.
,, Symons.
1859. Major Stanley.
Captain Wallace.
1860. Captain Taylor.
,, C. E. Boodle.
Lieutenant Haig.
,, Ramsay.
Ensign Stratton.
1862. Major Taylor.
Lieutenant L. G. Brown.
,, W. T. Brown.
,, R. A. C. Hunt.
,, M. R. Chambers.
Assistant Surgeon Langley.
Lieutenant Leacock } attached.
Ensign Walcott }
1865. Major R. Edgerly.
1868. Major C. James.
Captain Des Voeux.
Lieutenant Hunt.
,, Hartigan.
,, Chambers, Adjutant.
,, Madden, Quartermaster.
,, Oxley.
Surgeon Day.
Assistant Surgeon Raby.
1886. Captain C. O. Nicholetts.
Lieutenant P. Holland.
,, R. Williams.

1886. Lieutenant C. H. Macdonald. } attached.
,, W. S. Delamain.
,, W. Ayerst.
Surgeon W. H. Quicke.

Joined subsequently:

Lieut.-Colonel A. Poole.
Major R. Hennell.
Lieutenant A. Beale.
,, A. Milne.
,, T. A. Fischer.
Surgeon Ward.
Major Tandy.
Lieutenant-Colonel Leacock.
Lieutenant E. R. Houghton.
1887. Lieutenant P. T. Bell.
1890. Lieut.-Colonel Scott.
Lieut.-Colonel S A. Westcropp.
1891. 2nd Lieutenant C. E. H. Poole.
1900. 2nd Lieutenant H. R. N. Pritchard.
1901. Lieutenant A. A. Smith.
Captain G. R. Rolland.
2nd Lieutenant Morris.
1902. Major M. W. Baugh.
1903. 2nd Lieutenant Chaldecott.
Lieutenant D. H. Moore.
,, Forbes.
,, Thomson.
1904. Lieutenant G. N. Ford.
,, A. Delmé Radcliffe.
,, M. E. C. V. S. Monteith.
,, R. F. Steel, I.M.S.
,, H. F. Kilgour.
,, R. G. Shuttelworth.
,, W. B. Benton.
1905. 2nd Lieutenant G. G. Richardson.
Lieutenant D. B. Gray.
1906. 2nd Lieutenant E. G. Mackenzie.
1907. Lieutenant E. J. H. Haughton.
,, D. H. Powell.

1908. Major H. C. B. Dann, Commandant.
Lieutenant E. G. J. Byrne. } attached.
,, W. A. Balderson. } attached.
1911. 2nd Lieutenant H. R. B. H. Irwin.
1912. Captain M. W. Wadia, I.M.S.
Lieutenant G. H. Chapman, I.M.S.
Major P. P. Atal, I.M.S.
Captain A. N. Thomas, I.M.S.
1914. Major H. Ross.
Lieutenant H. J. Carrol, I.A.R.O.
,, R. R. B. Maclean, I.A.R.O.
,, R. H. Burne, I.A.R.O.
,, W. S. Halliley, I.A.R.O.
,, H. J. Cardew, I.A.R.O.
Captain F. E. Thornton, I.A.R.O.
1915. Lieutenant A. B. C. Mildmay, I.A.R.O.
,, W. I. P. Roger, I.A.R.O.
,, A. M. Robertson, I.A.R.O.
,, P. R. Leigh Bennett, I.A.R.O.
,, K. Cantlie, I.A.R.O.
,, J. A. Harrison, I.A.R.O.
,, M. C. McCombe, I.A.R.O.
,, Hobbs, I.A.R.O.
,, Hillier, I.A.R.O.
,, N. G. B. Kirwan, I.A.R.O.
,, T. Jenkins, I.A.R.O.
,, R. B. Gildea, I.A.R.O.
,, H. Tierney, I.A.R.O.
,, R. R. B. Falcon, I.A.R.O.
Captain John, I.A.R.O.
2nd Lieutenant Normand, I.A.R.O.
Lieutenant S. A. Huss, I.A.R.O.
,, J. M. Young, I.A.R.O.
,, F. Tomlinson.
,, R. G. R. Glyn.
,, J. A. Swainson, I.A.R.O.
,, G. H. Bland.
Captain J. C. De, I.M.S.
1916. Captain F. G. Greenstreet, 103rd M.L.I.

1916. Lieutenant S. B. Gothaskar, I.M.S.
,, A. G. Munford, I.A.R.O.
Captain H. R. Wilson, 114th Mahrattas.
Lieutenant G. T. Auston, I.A.R.O.
,, C. N. Harding, 88th Carnatic Infy.
,, V. J. P. Fleming, I.A.R.O.
,, A. E. R. Douglas.
,, H. Osborne, I.A.R.O.
1917. Lieutenant J. H. Phillips, I.A.R.O.
,, R. W. B. Wright, I.A.R.O.
,, H. B. Graveston, I.A.R.O.
,, J. N. Chaudhari, I.M.S.
,, V. A. Warren, I.A.R.O.
Major P. M. Heath, 110th Mahratta L.I.
Captain F. E. Welch, 110th Mahratta L.I.
Lieutenant E. J. Kenny, 116th Mahrattas.
,, E. C. Priestley, I.A.R.O.
,, S. C. Macalister.
1918. Lieutenant P. C. Watson, 98th Infantry.
,, E. Pattinson, I.A.R.O.
,, M. P. Lancaster.
,, R. L. Phillips.
,, M. A. Strudwicke.
1919. Lieutenant C. S. M. Finlayson, I.A.R.O.
,, C. K. Kay, 33rd Cavalry.
,, J. A. T. Seed, 110th M.L.I.
,, H. Armstrong.
,, E. S. Bartley.
,, R. E. Eberhardie, I.A.R.O.
,, I. Somerset.
1920. Lieutenant C. F. M. Godtschalk, 30th Lancers.
,, A. Munro.
,, E. H. Edge.
1921. Lieutenant J. B. Dedman,
,, W. Storm.
,, W. A. Hasler.
Captain H. S. Morris.
1922. Lieut.-Colonel A. S. Hay, D.S.O., Commandant.
2nd Lieutenant E. I. B. Jeffcott.

1922. Lieutenant V. C. Griffin.
Major R. C. Eberhardie.
1923. Captain M. W. Kennedy.
,, A. O. Kersey.
,, M. Henry.
Major J. A. Yates.
,, J. Turner.
Lieutenant D. R. G. Peal.
,, J. H. Trim.

APPENDIX VI

GOVERNMENT RESOLUTIONS AND PUBLICATIONS OF C.-IN-C.'S, GENERALS, AND OTHER OFFICERS, BRINGING TO NOTICE OF THE ARMY THE DISTINGUISHED SERVICES OF THE REGIMENT, OFFICERS, AND MEN, IN THE VARIOUS EXPEDITIONS AND WARS DURING WHICH IT SERVED FROM 1768–1923

1800 Of SEEDASEER, Lord Mornington, Governor-General, wrote to the directors :

"I am confident that the Honourable Court will be of opinion that the conduct and success of the Army of Bombay on that day has seldom been equalled and never surpassed."

The Bombay Government directed that a gold badge should be presented to Subadar Ibrahimkhan and a silver one to each of the Havildars of the Detachment in commemoration of their gallant conduct in the attack on a Pagoda near Karwar.

1817.

"CAMP NEAR DHOND, *April 23rd*, 1817.

"The Commanding Officer has great satisfaction in announcing to the force the successful operations of the Detachment under Major Smith of the 1st/14th M.I., which consists of two companies of the 1st/2nd Bo.I., two companies of the 1st/3rd Bo.I., and the flank companies of the 1st/14th M.I., and was detached from the reserve on the 12th inst. against a body of Horse rated at 3,000 or 4,000 strong in the service of Trimbukji Danglia ; after four successive days and nights' marching over a distance of 150 miles, this Detachment on the morning of the 17th came upon the enemy, killed and wounded 70, took several prisoners of consequence, a quantity of arms and many horses. Colonel Smith never troubles the troops with idle praise, he hopes therefore that the sincerity with which he applauds the steady perseverance, the cool judgment and military skill of Major Smith on this occasion and the conspicuous exertions of the officers and soldiers under him, may prove the more acceptable.

With equal sincerity and in the name of his superiors he requests the Major and all the officers and men of his Detachment to receive his grateful thanks.

The march of the six companies at this season of the year will become memorable and useful.

The result both in execution and success has been truly honourable, and they have all zealously upheld the character of the excellent Battalions to which they belong.

(*Signed*) H. Toney, *D.A.G.*"

The Brigadier-General on the conclusion of the operations addressed a letter to Colonel Stuart Commanding 1st/3rd, from which the following is an extract:

1818.

"Camp Sirur, *May* 21*st*, 1818.

"I desire you to assure both the European and Native Officers and rank and file, how deeply I appreciate their cheerful and most honourable exertions, and that I shall not fail to do them justice in all that depends upon me."

Extract from Divisional Orders by Brigadier-General Smith, C.B., dated Camp Sirur, January 27th, 1819:

"The Commanding Officer has also a painful occasion of recording his sentiments and his regret upon losing the services of that excellent Battalion the 1st/3rd Regiment Bombay Infantry, which has now been under his personal observation for nearly 5 years. In Lieut.-Colonel Stuart the Brigadier-General will gratefully remember that he found a Commanding Officer of a battalion on whom he could always rely to support his authority and execute his orders.

The 1st/3rd has upheld its established reputation in the Bombay Army, it is entitled to all the praise of those qualities by which a brave Infantry can run down Horse, and its exertions in that trying service for seven months have deserved the most grateful applause.

Lieut.-Colonel Stuart is requested to receive the Brigadier-General's best thanks, and to deliver them to all ranks of the Corps with the assurance that it carries with it to its new destination, his confidence and admiration together with his ardent wishes for its future fame and welfare.

(*Signed*) T. Halifax, *D.A. General.*"

(*True copy*)

Copy of the General Order published on the demolition of Rasel Khyma :

"Headquarters, Bombay, *Friday, September 22nd*, 1820.

By the Honourable, the Governor in Council.

Bombay Castle, *September 12th*, 1820.

"The Honourable the Governor in Council having received the official reports of the demolition of the town and Fort of Rasel Khyma and the removal of the troops to the Island of Ken, desires to express his acknowledgment to Captain Thompson of His Majesty's 17th Dragoons, the Officer Commanding, for the judicious manner in which these arrangements have been effected.

Captain Price of the Corps of Engineers and the whole of the officers, non-commissioned officers and privates of the detachment of Artillery 1/2nd Bo. N.I., Det. 1/3rd, Bo. N.I., Det. 1/11th Bo. N.I., Det. Pioneers, Detachment in the Persian Gulf, together with Captain Malliand, Lieutenant Macdonald and the Marine Branch of the service have equally merited the commendation of Government by their unremitted exertions and zealous co-operation in the execution of these arrangements.

The laborious duties to which the troops were continually exposed, under privations of no ordinary nature, have been performed with the utmost cheerfulness and alacrity ; and the Honourable the Governor in Council has great pleasure in recording his high sense of the exemplary conduct of the Detachment stationed at Rasel Khyma from the capture of the place up to the period of its final evacuation.

By order of the Honourable the Governor in Council.

(*Signed*) J. B. Simson, *Secretary to Government.*"

1824. June 14th.—The honorary badges "Seringapatam" were awarded to the Battalion by General Orders of May 24th, 1824, affixed to the colours this day, having been received from the Adjutant-General on June 12th.

Brigade orders by Lieut.-Colonel Robertson :

"CAMP NEAR SHOLAPUR, *July 26th*, 1830.

"Before the separation of the Brigade, Lieut.-Colonel Robertson begs to return to all ranks his warmest thanks. Short as the service has been, it has not been wanting in circumstances calculated to evince the advantages arising from discipline and zeal. In the first instance the troops moved from cantonments on a very short warning, and after performing a long night-march encountered on the following morning a degree of fatigue with a cheerfulness which nothing but their devotion to their duty could produce, and which had there been occasion for their further services must have led to most satisfactory results. During too the stay of the Brigade at Aukalkot, the calls of duty which the nature of the service required, and which led to much exposure in the worst of weather, were obeyed with a promptness and alacrity that could not be surpassed.

To Lieut.-Colonel Gibbon, Commanding the 5th Regiment Bombay Native Infantry, Captain Meldrum, Commanding a Detachment 9th Bo. N.I., and Captain Groundwater, Commanding the Royal Horse Artillery, the Commanding Officer tenders his best acknowledgments for their cordial co-operation and assistance.

(*Signed*) T. POOLE, *acting Major of Brigade.*

(*True Extract*)

(*Signed*) T. R. H. BAYLY, *Adjutant.*"

Field after orders by Brigadier Gordon, Commanding in Upper Scinde :

1839.

"CAMP, SUKKUR, *May 15th*, 1839.

"Brigadier Gordon has to perform a pleasing duty in publishing to the troops in Upper Scinde, his high sense of the exertion and gallantry of Ensigns Stanley and Taylor of the 5th Regiment Bo. N.I. in the recent successful attack on the small Fort of Khangurh with a Detachment of the

5th Regiment headed by Captain Smee, on which occasion a body of Baloochees were signally defeated, having a chieftain and 48 men killed and another chief and 46 men wounded and taken prisoners with a trifling loss to our side.

The result of this affair is very creditable to Captain Smee and the Brigadier will take an early opportunity of bringing it to the notice of His Excellency the Commander-in-Chief. The Brigadier laments the loss of Subadar Sirdar Bahadur Mahomed Khan who was shot early in the attack.

By Order,

(*Signed*) T. Clibbon, *Captain* M.B.

(*True Copy*)

(*Signed*) R. Ferris, Lieut. and Adjutant, 5th Bo. N.I."

Commander-in-Chief's letter to Captain Brown :

"Headquarters, Bombay, *November* 21*st*, 1840.

"Sir,

I am directed by the Commander-in-Chief to assure you that he has watched with deep interest your late proceedings at the outpost of Kahun.

The judgment, perseverance and skill which you displayed in keeping possession of the Fort for so long a period, under circumstances of unusual trial and difficulty, in His Excellency's opinion redound in every way to your reputation as an officer and to the infinite credit of those serving under you.

The Commander-in-Chief hastens therefore by the earliest means at his disposal to mark the high sense of your services on the occasion, by nominating you a Brigade Major upon the establishment of the force now assembled in Scinde, vacant by the promotion of Major Boscawen of Her Majesty's 40th Regiment, an appointment which, however inadequate it may be considered, as the result of your meritorious conduct will, His Excellency hopes, be viewed by you as a testimony of his approbation.

(*Signed*) W. J. MacMahon, *Captain and Military Sec.*

(*True Copy*)

(*Signed*) Lewis Brown, *Captain 5th Regiment.*

To Captain Brown, 5th Regiment."

Extract from Field Army Orders, by Major-General Brooks, Commanding in Scinde:

"CAMP SUKKUR, *December 4th*, 1840.

"Major-General Brooks has the highest gratification in publishing to the troops composing the Field Army the following extract from a letter from the Secretary to the Government of India, expressing the high approbation of the Right Honourable the Governor-General of India in Council, of the gallantry, cheerfulness and prudence, which characterised the proceedings of Captain Brown, 5th Regiment N.I., in his late defence of Kahun, as well as the admirable support afforded by his gallant companions in arms, Lieutenant Erskine of the Artillery and Doctor Glasse of the 5th Regiment composing his garrison.

The Major-General feels satisfied every individual of the Field Army will be delighted to find, that the merits of these brave men have been so honourably noticed by the highest authority in this country."

Extract (Para. No. 2) of letter No. 1133 dated November 11th, 1840. Received from T. Mattock, Esq., Secretary to the Government of India:

2nd Para.—"In the meantime his Lordship in Council will not withhold the expression of his highest approbation of the eminent gallantry, cheerfulness and prudence, which characterised the proceedings of Captain Brown in the critical position in which he was placed, and of the admirable manner in which he appears to have been supported by those who were serving under him.

He requests you will communicate this opinion to the Major-General, Commanding in Upper Scinde, who will convey it accordingly to Captain Brown and the officers and men of his Detachment.

(*True Extract*)

(*Signed*) T. DONNELLY, A.A.G., S.F.A.

(*True Copy*)

ROBERT DENNIS, *Lieutenant and Adjutant*, *5th Regiment*."

April 5th, 1841, it was notified in General Orders that the badge "Kahun" was to be worn on the colours and accoutrements of the Regiment. Six months' batta was given to the survivors and the heirs of the killed of the Kahun Detachment.

1858. The following letter from H. L. Anderson, Esq., Secretary to Government, dated July 29th, 1858 :

"SIR,

"With reference to your letter dated 19th inst., No. 428 and its enclosures detailing the operations of the Detachment under Captain Mackechnie, I am directed to state for the information of His Excellency the Commander-in-Chief that the operations appear to have been conducted with judgment and activity, and that in the opinion of the Right Honourable the Governor in Council the Detachment has performed good service.

(*Signed*) H. L. ANDERSON, *Secretary to Government.*"

Extract from G.O.C. :

"The Commander-in-Chief having been directed by the Government to nominate two Regiments of Native Infantry required for service in China, has been pleased to appoint the 3rd and 5th Regiments for this duty.

"In order to make these two Corps as complete as possible, the two Companies which were transferred to the 1st and 3rd extra Battalions respectively, by the General Orders, will be re-transferred and incorporated among the Companies of their original Regiments in such a manner as the Commanding Officers may determine."

Farewell Order. Southern Division of the Army.

"BELGAUM, *January 23rd*, 1860.

"Her Majesty's Regiment 5th Bo.N.I. being on the point of quitting this Division and embarking on foreign service in China, Major-General Farrell considers it not less a pleasure than a duty to state that the old and well-known reputation of this Regiment extending over half a century, has been fully maintained during the period that it has served in his Command. The Major-General, in thanking Major Stanley and his Officers and men, can assure them that he feels certain that all their comrades whom they are now leaving unite in wishing them all honour and success in the forthcoming campaign.

(*True Extract*)

(*Signed*) J. C. Coles, *Major*, *D.D.A.G.*, *S.D.A.*"

On the evacuation of Canton by the British troops, and consequent breaking up of the Canton Brigade, the following Divisional Farewell Order was issued by Brigadier-General Crawford, C.B., Commanding in Southern China:

"October 29th, 1861.—The troops forming the late garrison at Canton being withdrawn, and the city surrendered to the Chinese authorities, the Brigadier-General Commanding in South China desires to express his unqualified approbation of the high state of discipline and efficiency of the several Regiments and Corps comprising this Garrison.

From the Officers Commanding the R.A., R.E., Her Majesty's 99th Regiment of Foot and Her Majesty's 5th N.B.L.I., and from all Heads of Departments the Brigadier-General has at all times received the utmost support and cordial co-operation in all duties connected with their several stations. No. 4 Battery First Brigade arrived in this command with the first expeditionary force on August 18th, 1857: to this battery the Brigadier-General tenders his best thanks for their regularity and efficiency as Artillerymen, their steadiness and good conduct in the performance of all their duties.

The Brigadier-General tenders his best thanks to Lieut.-Colonel Day, Her Majesty's 99th, for their steady and zealous co-operation in carrying out all the duties of the garrison, and entertains the hope that by their continued exertions and good conduct they will maintain at Hong-Kong their high reputation.

The Brigadier-General is aware that the two Native Regiments from Bombay came to China in full expectation of participating in Active Service in the Field and were disappointed in being retained for garrison duty; they have, however, performed all duties required of them most cheerfully and efficiently, and to both these Regiments the Brigadier-General tenders his best thanks for their constant attention to their duties, their good conduct in quarters and the high state of discipline and efficiency they have maintained.

To Major Stanley is due all praise for the high sense of efficiency of the Regiment under his command and for his close attention to the comforts and welfare of his men, and the Brigadier-General will have much pleasure in bringing to the notice of the Commander of the Forces the valuable services rendered by the Regiment under his command, and the very favourable opinion of their services entertained by the distinguished Generals who have reviewed them. To the Officers of the Divisional and Personal Staff, viz. to Captain C. F. Grant, Deputy A.A.-General, Captain E. Grant, Deputy A.G.M.-General, Lieutenant J. Crawford, A.D.C., the Brigadier-General tenders his best thanks for their close attention to the duties of their respective departments and for their zealous and cordial co-operation at all times. Captain E. Grant has served in this office from the first arrival of his Regiment in China, and the Brigadier-General has always found him an active and zealous Staff Officer.

By Order,

C. F. Grant, *D.A.A. General.*

(*True Copy*)

Jas. H. Ramsay, *Lieutenant and Adjutant H.M.'s 5th Regiment N.L.I.*"

Copy of a letter No. 92, dated Mandalay, April 2nd, 1888, from Brigadier-General G. B. Wolseley, C.B., A.D.C., Commanding 1st Brigade U.B.F.F., to the Assistant Adjutant and Quartermaster-General, Upper Burmah Field Force :

" I have the honour to forward the following report upon the 5th Bo.L.I. :

I. Conduct and Discipline in the Field :

Exceedingly good. The Regiment had a lot of hard work in the Field on flying columns, etc., and has always done well.

II. Dress and Turn-out :

Exceedingly good.

III. Sanitary Condition and Efficiency :

Very satisfactory, taking into consideration the continuous Field Service on which the Regiment has been employed.

No. 74 B.C.

(*Signed*) R. C. Low, *Brigadier-General Commanding U.B. Force,* Mandalay, April 23rd, 1888."

No. $\frac{1808}{7620}$.

"Adjutant-General's Office, Poona,
July 31*st*, 1888.

Memo.

"Forwarded to the Officer Commanding 5th Bo.L.I. for information with an intimation that H.R.H. the Commander-in-Chief has expressed his satisfaction at receiving such a gratifying report on the Regiment.

By Order,

(*Signed*) C. B. Knowles, *Brigadier-Gen., Adjutant-General.*"

No. 2368.

"Military Department, Bombay Castle,
October 1*st*, 1890.

"In the opinion of H.E. the Commander-in-Chief, Lieutenant A. H. R. Milne of the 5th Bo.L.I., the Officer Commanding the Detachment, acted with much discretion under difficult circumstances, and he and his men deserve credit.

(*Signed*) B. H. Pottinger, *Major-General, Secretary to Government.*"

"The Governor-General in Council has much pleasure in announcing that Her Majesty the Queen-Empress of India has been graciously pleased to permit the Corps named below to bear upon their colours, standards, and appointments the words 'Burmah 1885–87' in commemoration of their gallant conduct during the operations resulting in the conquest of Upper Burmah.

The 5th Regiment of Bombay (Light) Infantry."

APPENDIX VII

REGIMENTAL AND COMPANY ORGANISATION AT DIFFERENT PERIODS, 1768–1922

1768. Battalion. 1,000 of all native ranks with 1 Captain, 1 Lieutenant, 1 Ensign, and 2 European Sergeants each. 1 Subadar, 2 Jemadars, 6 Havildars, 6 Naiks, 3 Tom-toms, 1 Trumpeter, 1 Waterman, and 80 Privates = 100 men.

1778. December.

Battalion establishment increased to 1 Captain, 5 Lieutenants, and 5 Ensigns.

1779. Reorganisation.

1 Captain.	11 Sergeants.
6 Lieutenants.	20 Drums and pipes.
1 Commandant (native).	2 Trumpeters.
11 Subadars.	60 Havildars.
1 Native Adjutant.	60 Naiks.
20 Jemadars.	680 Sepoys.

1784. Bombay reorganised 8 Battalions as below:

1 Bombay Grenadiers.
1 Marine Battalion.

1786. Recruits' Height:

5 ft. 3 in. for Infantry.
5 ft. 5 in. for Grenadiers.
5 ft. 2 in. for Marines.

1788. Existing 7 Battalions formed into 12, each consisting of 8 Companies. 1 Subaltern, 1 Sergeant, 1 Subadar, 1 Jemadar, 4 Havildars, 4 Naiks, 1 Drummer, 1 Fifer, 68 Privates.

1790. Battalion completed to 40 Havildars and 40 Naiks.

1791. Battalion increased to 10 Companies. Reduced, in 1792, to a peace establishment of 8 Companies.

1795. The officers of the Grenadier and Light Infantry Corps were ordered to make use of their swords instead of fusils as heretofore.

1796. The establishment of British Officers was fixed at:

1 Lieut.-Colonel.
1 Major.
4 Captains.
11 Lieutenants.
5 Ensigns.

The Battalion was formed in 10 Companies of the following strength, viz.:

1 Subadar.
1 Jemadar.
5 Havildars.
5 Naiks.
1 Drummer.
1 Fifer.
90 Privates.
1 Waterman.

The flank Companies were still called Grenadier Companies, but the left Grenadier Company was no longer composed of tall men, but of "such men as, by merit and activity of make, are deemed deserving of that distinction, and equal to the fatigues that may be required from a chosen Company."

1823. On September 27th, 1823, the Battalion was re-numbered as 5th Regiment Bombay Infantry.

1838. By General Orders of July 12th, 1838, Regiments of the Bengal and Bombay Armies were increased from 75 to 85 men per Company, and by a subsidiary order of 3rd September, 1838, they were further increased by 1 Havildar, 1 Naik, and 10 men per Company, making each Regiment 800 men.

1841. By General Orders of May 10th, 1841, the Regiment was made Light Infantry, an honour conferred for their services in Afghanistan. Under instructions from the Adjutant-General of the Army, 150 General Service Recruits were transformed to other Regiments, to enable the Regiment to enlist men better adapted for Light Infantry soldiers.

1842. By G.O. of March 11th, an additional or 10th Company, consisting of 2 Native Officers, 12 Non-commissioned Officers, 2 Buglers, 100 Privates, was added to each Native Infantry Regiment of the Bombay Presidency, and Commanding Officers were directed to adopt immediate measures for bringing their corps up to the new strength.

1843. By G.O. of February 2nd, and March 10th, the establishment of each Regular Regiment of the three Presidencies was reduced by 1 Havildar, 1 Naik, and 10 Privates per Company.

1845. By G.O. of March 26th and June 14th, the strength of each company was again raised to 2 Native Officers, 6 Havildars, 6 Naiks, 2 Buglers, 100 Privates.

1847. By G.O. dated February 15th, the establishment of each Native Infantry Corps belonging to the Bombay Presidency was reduced by 10 Havildars, 10 Naiks, and 200 Privates, leaving the strength of each Company, 1 Subadar, 1 Jemadar, 5 Havildars, 5 Naiks, 2 Buglers and 80 Privates.

1856. By G.O., No. 858, the appointment of one additional Captain and one Lieutenant, to each Regiment of Light Cavalry and Regular Native Infantry, was sanctioned.

1857. G.G.O., No. 677, of July 14th, 1857, sanctions addition of 2 complete Companies to every Regiment of Native Infantry of the Bombay Presidency, the total strength of a regiment of Infantry not to exceed 1,000 Privates.

1859. By G.O. dated June 6th, 1859, the Regiment was reduced to 700 rank and file.

1860. The establishment was increased to 1,000 prior to the embarkation of the Regiment for China.

1893. The Regiment was formed into Caste Companies as under :

A Company, Rajputs.
B ,, Dekhani Mahrattas.
C ,, Konkani Mahrattas.
D ,, Bedars.
E ,, Purdhesis.
F ,, Sikhs.
G ,, Konkani Mussulmans.
H ,, Dekhani Mussulmans.

The previous Wing Organisation was maintained. Recruits were obtained through the recruiting Officers at Satara Ahmednagar, and Rajputana.

1903. The organisation of the Regiment into 2 Wings, was abolished. At this period the Regiment consisted of:

One Double Company of Konkani Mahrattas.
Two Double Companies of Dekhani Mahrattas.
One Double Company of Dekhani Mussulmans.

1916. The Regiment was organised into 4 Companies, each commanded by a Captain or Major, with a junior Officer as 2nd in Command. Each Company consisted of 4 Platoons, each of these being commanded by an Indian Officer with a platoon Havildar as 2nd in Command. Platoons were numbered serially 1 to 16, throughout the Regiment.

Each Platoon was in turn subdivided into 4 sections, each section being commanded by a N.C.O. and numbered 1 to 16, throughout the Company.

A Company was composed of Dekhani Mahrattas.
B ,, ,, ,, ,, Konkani Mahrattas.
C ,, ,, ,, ,, Dekhani Mahrattas.
D ,, ,, ,, ,, Dekhani Mussulmans.

1921. A Headquarter Wing consisting of 4 groups composed of those details who normally are not available to the Companies in action:

No. 1 Group consisting of Signallers and Bandsmen.
No. 2 Group consisting of Machine Gun Section.
Nos. 3 and 4 Groups, Artificers and followers, etc.

1921. The Battalion in conjunction with 103rd Mahratta L.I., 110th Mahratta L.I., 114th Mahrattas, 116th Mahrattas, and 117th Royal Mahrattas, was formed into a Regimental Group, designated the 5th Mahratta L.I. The Battalion now became the 2nd Batt. 5th Mahratta L.I. The Training Battalion, 10th Batt. 5th Mahratta L.I. (late 114th Mahrattas) located at Belgaum, was responsible for training all recruits and keeping the active Battalions up to strength in drafts. In addition, the Active Battalions were relieved of the maintenance and periodical training of Reservists, by the Training Battalion. In the event of war, the Training Battalion, in addition to being the Depot of the Active Battalion, became charged with any expansion or raising of Battalions to meet war requirements. To assist the Training Battalion in its task, each Active Battalion was affiliated with a Company in the Training Battalion, and became responsible for providing the necessary training staff for that Company. This training staff was to be increased on mobilisation.

APPENDIX VIII

UNIFORM AND EQUIPMENT

THE subject of dress was taken up soon after the official forming of the Indian Army, and at this period it was ordered that the officers of the 1st Brigade should wear gold and their men yellow lace, while the 2nd Brigade officers wore silver and their men white lace.

1786. Turbans were to be bound round the edge with lace, yellow or white, according to the Brigade, with bands and tassels of similar colour. Two strips of lace were to be worn round the front of the cummerband, and the short drawers were to be edged with stripes of blue and yellow, or blue and white.

1798. Turbans and cummerbands were to be blue. Fronts of black leather were to be worn on the turbans with the number of the Battalion in yellow or white metal, in Roman characters, in the centre. The plumes authorised for the 3rd Battalion were blue, and the badge a "crescent." The 9th Battalion (now 4th Rifles) wore the same plumes and had the same badge on their appointments, being distinguished by their lace only. The Grenadier Companies wore white plumes. "These badges were given," as stated in the General Order, "as honorary marks of distinction to the old corps forming the peace establishment of the Presidency."

1789. New Arms were issued to Native Corps in the course of this year.

1798. The numbers of the Colours were altered to suit the new designation, but the old device, the "Crescent," granted in 1788, was retained.

1859. A new pattern tunic for Infantry was issued to the Regiment. Mention is made of the Regiment being allowed to wear their overcoats rolled up in the form of a valise, slung over the left shoulder by the sleeves and fastened by two small removable straps.

1875. All men were armed with the breech-loading Snider rifle.

1877. Serge frocks replaced tunics, and knickerbockers and gaiters replaced trousers. This new pattern was first supplied to the Regiment to be reported upon as to its suitability for general adoption in the Bombay Army. The Regimental Committee's report being favourable, it was issued to the whole Army.

1878. A new valise equipment was issued.

1891. The Snider rifles were withdrawn and Martini-Henry rifles, Mark IV, issued in their place.

1895. The Glengarry cap for the British officers was abolished. The Peace Manœuvre cap, authorised for the Regiment in its place, was of Austrian pattern, in dark green with red piping. The badge was a silver bugle with the numeral V, in the centre.

1896. Colour Havildars were ordered to wear cotton chevrons in khaki uniform, and the red sash of Havildars was limited to be worn only in Review Order, on Orderly duty, and when walking out.

A new pattern sword was taken into use by British Officers. Below the Crown on the hilt, the Royal and Imperial Cypher, V.R.I., was introduced. The stand-up collar of the tunic gave place to a lay-down collar. In Review Order, Officers were to wear jack-spurs and a gold sword-knot.

1903. The Regiment was armed with the Magazine Lee-Enfield Rifle, the Lee-Metford Rifle previously issued being withdrawn.

1908. The Regiment was equipped with Bandoliers of the pattern now issued to Cavalry (1926).

1913. Rifle, Short M.L.E. Mark I, taken into use.

1916. Accoutrements, pattern 1914, received and worn on Service.

1919. Webb Equipment pattern 1908 received.

APPENDIX IX

YEARLY INSPECTION REPORTS

1842. The first entry in the Regimental Records of any Official Inspection occurs in January 1842, when it is recorded that the Regiment was reviewed by Major-General Sir Charles Napier, K.C.B., Commanding the Poona Division of the Army.

Major-General MacNeil reviewed the Regiment in December of the same year.

1844. Reviewed by General Baumgarten.

1845. Reviewed by Major-General Brough.

1846. Reviewed by Lieut.-Colonel Robertson, commanding Deesa Field Brigade.

1847. Reviewed by Lieut.-Colonel Cotton, Commanding Deesa Field Brigade.

1848. Reviewed by Major-General Bare, Commanding Northern Division.

1849. Reviewed by Colonel Soppitt, Commanding Northern Division.

1850. Reviewed by Brigadier-General Capon, C.B., Commanding Northern Division. At the close of the same year it was reviewed by Brigadier-General Manson.

1853. Reviewed by Brigadier-General James, Commanding S.D.A.

1858. Reviewed by Brigadier-General Blood, who paid the Regiment a high compliment in regard to general efficiency, drill, etc.

1859. Reviewed by Major-General Sir Hugh Rose, Commanding Poona Division, vide letter No. 2341, Adjutant-General's Office, Poona. July 6th, 1859.

"The Inspection returns of the 5th Regiment, Native Light Infantry, as taken by General Sir Hugh Rose,

G.C.B., having been received subsequent to the departure of that Regiment from the Poona Division, and the Regiment being now within your Command, I am desired by the Commander-in-Chief to inform you that the Major-General has reported very favourably on the state of the Regiment, and that he considers Major Stanley conducts the duties of his command in a very satisfactory manner."

1860. The Regiment was reviewed by Major-General Farrel, Commanding Southern Division Army, vide letter No. 979, dated January 3rd, 1860.

"I have the honour to receive and submit to the Commander-in-Chief, the Inspection Report of the 5th Regiment Native Light Infantry, for 1859–60. I am now desired to convey His Excellency's gratification at receiving so favourable a report of the efficiency in every respect of this excellent regiment, and in causing this to be communicated to Major Stanley, you will add that Sir Henry Somerset feels assured that the good conduct and discipline of the 5th Regiment N.L.I. will be uniformly upheld by all ranks, and be conspicuous during its service in China, for which country they are about to embark. The C.-in-C. desires his acknowledgments to be expressed to Major Stanley, on whom, and on his officers, the present state of the Regiment reflects much credit."

1861. The Regiment was reviewed by Lieut.-General Sir Hope Grant, G.C.B., who expressed himself as being much pleased with the state of the Regiment generally, both as on parade and in barracks. Also in regard to hospital arrangements, etc.

April 16th, reviewed by Major-General Sir T. Michel, K.C.B., Commander-in-Chief in China. He desired the C.O., Major Stanley, to explain to the Regiment, after parade before marching to quarters, the sincere gratification that he had experienced from what he had just witnessed as to the efficient manner in which the Regiment had behaved, and he desired it to be interpreted to the men that he was glad further to observe that the conduct of the Regiment in quarters was as satisfactory and creditable as it had been on parade.

1861. Brigadier-General Crawford, C.B., Commanding in Southern China, added the following remarks:

"This Regiment having been reviewed in the presence of Brigadier-General Sir Hope Grant, G.C.B., and Major-General Sir T. Michel, K.C.B., both these General Officers concurred in expressing their highest praise of the steadiness and precision of drill of the 5th Regiment N.L.I., and their perfect state of discipline and efficiency, which was pronounced to be not surpassed by any Regiment in Her Majesty's Service. To Major Stanley is due all praise for the high state of efficiency of the Regiment under his Command, and for his close attention to the comfort of his men."

1862. From Major-General Sir T. Michel, K.C.B., Memorandum No. 16, Headquarters Shanghai, February 18th, 1862, to Major Stanley, Commanding 5th Regiment Bombay Native Light Infantry.

"The Major-General Commanding in China having inspected the 5th B.N.L.I., desires to express his approval of its condition. He cannot too highly applaud the state of its discipline and its appearance in Quarters, its interior economy, and lastly its great efficiency in all evolutions and movements in the Field. He has notified in his report to the Commander-in-Chief at Bombay, the sense he entertains of the zeal and judgment of Major Stanley, and his unqualified approbation of everything connected with the Corps under his Command. He desires that this Memorandum be notified to the 5th B.N.L.I., in Regimental Orders."

1863. The Regiment was inspected by Brigadier-General Adams.

1868. The Regiment was inspected and reviewed by Brigadier-General Domville, Commanding Belgaum Brigade. Decision of His Excellency the Commander-in-Chief:

"This is a highly satisfactory Report, creditable to the Commanding Officer and all Ranks."

1869. The Regiment was inspected and reviewed by His

Excellency Lord Napier of Magdala, on January 26th of this year. Extract from the Report of the same by Order of His Excellency, Commander-in-Chief of the Bombay Army:

"Lord Napier has never seen a better Regiment. The 5th B.N.L.I. have built Lines that could not be surpassed in neatness and efficiency. They are a model of good order and neatness. The men cut timber in the forests and quarried stone for the gables to face the drifting monsoon of Belgaum. The Native Officers' houses are extremely comfortable and more suitable to the improved position of these Officers than the old style of hut. Every hut has a small border of plants or a few flowers in front of it, and the whole Lines are a model of neatness and propriety, most creditable to Colonel Taylor and the Officers and Men. The 5th Regiment B.N.L.I. is the only regiment that has cultivated small gardens, and if they received any assistance in tools and seeds, they would emulate any European Regiment in gardening. The School is very good. I have never seen a Regiment more advanced in drill, discipline and efficiency."

1870. The Regiment was inspected by Brigadier-General Adams.

1872. The Regiment was inspected and reviewed by Brigadier-General Beale on January 29th of this year, and by Brigadier-General Schneider, at Aden, on December 14th. Remarks by His Excellency thereon:

"The Commander-in-Chief considers the Report on this Regiment is very satisfactory, and His Excellency is glad to notice that the Corps keeps up the high character it has borne for years."

1874. The Regiment was inspected and reviewed by Brigadier-General Adams, on January 16th of this year at Belgaum. Remarks by His Excellency the Commander-in-Chief thereon:

"His Excellency considers that the Report on this Regiment is very satisfactory. The subject of rifles is now under consideration."

1875. The Regiment was inspected and reviewed by Brigadier-General Kirby, on January 15th of this year, at Belgaum. The remark of His Excellency the Commander-in-Chief:

"The Commander-in-Chief is very glad to receive so satisfactory a report of his old friends the 5th N.L.I. Regiment."

1876. The Regiment was inspected and reviewed by Lord Mark Kerr, C.B., Commanding Poona Division, on February 15th of this year, at Poona. The remark by His Excellency the Commander-in-Chief thereon:

"The report on this Regiment is very satisfactory."

1877. It was again inspected and reviewed by Lord Mark Kerr, on February 15th, at Poona. The remark of His Excellency, the Commander-in-Chief, thereon was:

"The report on this Regiment is very satisfactory."

1878. The Regiment was inspected and reviewed on January 18th, at Poona, by Major-General Primrose, C.S.I., Commanding Poona Division of the Army. Remarks by the Commander-in-Chief thereon:

"The report on this Regiment is very satisfactory, except as regards the figure of merit for shooting."

1882. Regiment inspected this year by Major-General Wood, on February 22nd. The remark thereon by His Excellency the Commander-in-Chief was:

"Very satisfactory."

1883. The Regiment was inspected at Deesa on January 6th of this year by His Excellency General Hardinge, C.B., Commander-in-Chief. His Excellency expressed himself very much pleased with the Regiment, both as regards discipline and drill, especially complimenting it on the manner in which it performed the proposed new Double Company Formation.

1884. On March 7th this year, the Regiment was inspected and reviewed by Lieut.-General Sir Robert Phayre, K.C.B., at Mhow. The remark by His Excellency the Commander-in-Chief thereon was:

"Very satisfactory."

1885. The Regiment was again inspected and reviewed by General Sir Robert Phayre, the remark by His Excellency the Commander-in-Chief being as before, "Very satisfactory."

1886. Again inspected and reviewed by General Sir Robert Phayre, the Commander-in-Chief's remark on his report being "Very satisfactory."

1888. The Report on the Regiment after its return from the campaign in Burmah was as follows:

"I have the honour to forward the following report upon the 5th Bombay Native Light Infantry.

I. *Conduct and discipline in the Field*, exceedingly good. The Regiment had a lot of hard work in the Field, on flying columns, etc., and has always done well.

II. *Dress and turn-out*, exceedingly good.

III. *Sanitary conditions and efficiency*. Very satisfactory, taking into consideration the continuous Field Service on which the Regiment has been employed.

No. 1808. Adjutant-General's Office, Poona, July 31st, 1888."

Forwarded to the Officer Commanding 5th B.N.L.I., for information, with an intimation that His Royal Highness (the Duke of Connaught) the Commander-in-Chief has expressed his satisfaction at receiving such a gratifying report on the Regiment.

1889. On February 25th of this year the Regiment was inspected and reviewed at Baroda, by Brigadier-General W. T. Budgen, D.S.O., Commanding the Bombay District. The report thereon was as follows:

No. 1808/356-T. Adjutant-General's Office. Headquarters Mahableshwar, May 11th, 1889.

Observations by His Royal Highness the Commander-in-Chief:

"Generally satisfactory. More attention should be paid to Barrack Squad Drill."

1890. The Report this year on the Regiment was as follows:

No. 1808. Adjutant-General's Office, Poona, February 25th, 1847:

1890. "Observations by His Royal Highness the Commander-in-Chief:

"Generally very satisfactory."

1891. The Regiment was inspected on February 3rd by Brigadier-General Budgen, D.S.O., Commanding Bombay District at Baroda.

Remarks by His Excellency the Commander-in-Chief thereon as follows:

"This is a satisfactory report and the condition of the Regiment is creditable to Colonel Scott and all ranks."

1892. The Regiment was inspected at Bombay on February 15th by Brigadier-General Budgen, Commanding Bombay District.

Observations by His Excellency the Commander-in-Chief:

"A satisfactory report. The good character given to the officers was very gratifying. I trust the musketry will improve with the new rifles."

1893. The Regiment was inspected on February 4th and 8th by Brigadier-General Budgen, D.S.O., Commanding Bombay District.

Observations by His Excellency the Commander-in-Chief:

"This is a very satisfactory report and creditable to Colonel Scott, Major Nicholetts and all ranks."

1894. The following were the observations by His Excellency the Commander-in-Chief, on the inspection of the Regiment on March 7th of this year:

"The Regiment is in very good order in all respects and well commanded, which reflects credit on the C.O., Colonel Scott, and the British and Native Officers of the Regiment."

1895. The General Officer Commanding, at his Inspection of the Spinwana post, in April, expressed himself greatly pleased with the smart appearance of the men.

1896. The following remarks were made by the General Commanding the Forces, Bombay Command, on the Inspection of the Regiment:

1896. "This Regiment has suffered under the disadvantage of having many Detachments, but it has good officers, good material, and when it gets together I have no doubt that the good feeling and conduct that is shown in the Regiment, will enable the Commanding Officer to bring it fully up to the required standard."

The following remarks on the musketry progress of the Regiment were forwarded under D.A.G., A/208/386, dated July 9th, 1896:

"The high figures of merit of the Regiment attained, is a proof that Officers, British and Native, and all ranks, have worked well and with success, and that great interest has been taken in musketry."

1897–98. The following remarks were made by the Lieut.-General Commanding the Forces, Bombay Command, on the Inspection of the Regiment taken at Rajkote, on February 9th, 1898, by Major-General G. C. Hogg, C.B., Commanding Deesa District:

"The 5th Bombay N.L.I. is in a satisfactory condition and it drills well, and is very good in Musketry Training. Fit for Active Service."

The following remarks were made by His Excellency the Commander-in-Chief in India, on the Confidential Report on the Inspection of the Regiment for 1897–8:

"Has improved in drill since last year, and appears to be an efficient Regiment, for which Colonel Nicholetts is to be commended."

1899. The following remark was made by the Lieut.-General Commanding the Forces, Bombay Command, on February 20th and 21st, 1899, by Major-General Hogg, C.B., Commanding Deesa District:

"Satisfactory report on the whole."

1900. The following remarks were made by the Lieut.-General Commanding the Forces, Bombay, on the Inspection of the Regiment taken at Rajkot on December 22nd, 1899, by Brigadier-General Black. To be published in Regimental Orders:

"A very satisfactory Report, creditable to Lieut.-

Colonel Nicholetts, who takes a great interest in his Regiment."

1902. The following remarks were made by Lieut.-General Commanding the Forces, Bombay, on the Inspection of the Regiment by Brigadier-General Ventries, on January 9th of this year:

"This Report shows that improvement and more attention has been paid to fire, discipline, and practical musketry. A portion of the Regiment did well in the recent Expedition from Aden to Addareja."

1903. The following remarks were made respectively by the Lieut.-General Commanding Forces, Bombay, and the Commander-in-Chief, on the Inspection of the Regiment by Brigadier-General Sir James Willcocks, K.C.M., D.S.O.

"Satisfactory Report. The improvement noted last year is well maintained. The general musketry efficiency is now satisfactory. The Regiment is fit for service.

"Satisfactory on the whole, but more care must be exercised in recruiting, and more decentralisation of authority must be introduced before I can accept the interior economy of the Regiment as all satisfactory."

1907. The following remarks were made by the Colonel on the Staff Commanding Karachi Brigade, at his recent Inspection of the Regiment:

"A useful, hard-working Regiment. Always ready and willing to do anything required. Mechanically well trained, but war conditions not fully appreciated. Fairly good with the spade, very good at stone wall entrenchments. Fit for service. More practice in First Aid is required."

1908. The Regiment was inspected during the Karachi Manœuvres of January and February, and the following Report was made by Major-General G. H. Westmorland, Commanding Karachi Brigade:

"The Regiment, though of slight physique, has very good powers of endurance and marching. Its war training is satisfactory, and there is good feeling pervading all ranks. The Regiment is fit for service."

1909. On March 10th this year the Regiment was inspected, and the following Report made by Major-General R. G. Broadwood, Commanding Troops in South China:

"The physique of the men is poor; they have not the appearance of belonging to a fighting race. They are, however, well trained and active. The instruction was painstaking and thorough, but often showed a lack of appreciation of war conditions. Great keenness in musketry is shown by all ranks and the men shoot well. The Battalion is fit for service."

1910. On April 2nd the Regiment was inspected and reported on by Major-General Broadwood, Commanding the troops in South China, as follows:

"Marching powers very satisfactory. The activity and marching powers of the men dispose me to substitute the word 'Fair' for the 'poor' which I used last year as applicable to their physique. A good deal of good training work has been done, but there is still a great failure to appreciate the conditions of war."

1911. On February 7th of this year the Regiment was inspected, and the following Report made by Major-General Anderson, Commanding the troops in South China:

"The personnel of the Native ranks is light and of small physique, but active, alert, and exceptionally healthy. The Field Training of the Regiment shows satisfactory results. Musketry is good, and keen interest is taken in signalling by Morse Code, and Semaphore is good and the knowledge thereof very general. This is also the case as regards Roman Urdu. There is good feeling between the British and native ranks, which is well fostered by the keen participation of both in games. A little practical experience in the Field would very much improve this Regiment, which shows a good spirit and keenness at field work. I consider the Regiment fit for service."

1912. On February 9th this year the annual Inspection

Report of the General Officer Commanding Poona Brigade was as follows :

" Instruction and training satisfactory. The system of drill and physical exercises is particularly good, and much attention is paid to the important feature of setting up the recruits well, and making them active and strong. The officers are as a whole a keen and hard-working body, and the Native Officers have been well trained. The men are well set up, active, and keen. The system of improving the physical condition of the recruits is a very good one, and has been attended by excellent results. Discipline, Musketry, etc., satisfactory. The Battalion manœuvres smartly in the field and the work is done with knowledge and intelligence. Musketry is quite satisfactory, and the discipline and interior economy leave nothing to be desired. The Battalion is altogether in a good sound state, and is in every respect fit for employment on Service."

1913. The following were the remarks of the General Officer Commanding 6th (Poona) Division, on the Inspection of the Regiment for 1912-13 :

" This is a smart, well-trained Battalion. The men are wiry and active, and move quickly in the field. They are also well behaved in Cantonments.

" There is an excellent system of interior economy. I am well satisfied that this Battalion would do itself credit if it had a chance of Active Service, for which it is in all respects quite fit."

APPENDIX X

ACCOUNTS OF REGIMENTAL CEREMONIES, NEW COLOURS, ETC.

1799. On March 6th of this year the battle of Seedaseer was fought, in which the Regiment gained its first Battle Honours. The anniversary of this event is usually kept by the Regiment and celebrated by special Regimental Sports.

The first mention of Regimental Colours in the old Records of the Kali Panchwin occurs in 1798, when the numbers of the Colours were altered to suit the new designation of the Battalion.

New Colours were subsequently presented to the Kali Panchwin as follows :

1823. Per Lieut.-Colonel Mackonochie, at Bhuj.

1857. Per Brigadier-General Blood, at Ahmednagar.

1893. Per Lady Harris, wife of the Governor-General, at Bombay.

1915. The Regiment received new Colours on March 9th.

1888. On September 17th of this year the Regiment celebrated its Centenary.

1921. At the beginning of this year a silver Shield, given by Colonel Sir Reginald Hennell, in commemoration of the battle of Seedaseer, was presented to the Regiment by Major Haughton—then Acting Commandant—at a full-dress parade expressly arranged for the purpose.

For the Ceremony, the Regiment formed three sides of a square, with the Shield under a guard, facing the south side. Major Haughton first addressed the Battalion and explained the object of the parade. For the sake of newly joined men who had not had an opportunity of knowing it, he told them all about Sir

Reginald Hennell's connection with the Regiment, and explained that before the Shield left London it had been taken to Buckingham Palace that His Majesty King George might see it. Major Haughton then read out His Majesty's gracious and complimentary letter, after which he requested Colonel Delmé Radcliffe, late C.O. of the Regiment, to address the men, the latter being then with them on a farewell visit before leaving India on his retirement.

Colonel Delmé Radcliffe told the men that the battle of Seedaseer, which the Shield commemorated, was the first big action in which the Regiment had ever taken part, just after it had been raised. He recorded how greatly it had distinguished itself on that occasion, thereby making a name for itself as long ago as in 1799. From that date the Regiment had fought in many battles and had never failed to add lustre to the name it had won a hundred and twenty years ago, until finally, in the last and greatest War of all, it had upheld its highest traditions, adding yet more glory and honour to the past.

Colonel Delmé Radcliffe went on to say that Colonel Sir Reginald Hennell had served with the Regiment for many years, and had commanded it before retiring from the Indian Army thirty-seven years ago. In spite of the long time that had passed since then, he was as keenly interested in it as ever, and proud of his association with it because of its deeds in the past and its gallant fighting in the recent Great War. Through Sir Reginald Hennell, the doings of the Kali Panchwin had been brought to the notice of the King-Emperor, who, after inspecting the Shield, had sent the gracious message to the Regiment which had been read out to the Unit, first at Amman, and again to-day. This Royal Message now hangs framed in the Officers' Mess-room beside the letter sent by Queen Victoria twenty years ago. The Silver Shield presented by Colonel Sir Reginald Hennell was to remind all ranks of the glorious past of the Regiment, beginning with the battle of Seedaseer, in order that all its present and future soldiers should strive to emulate the performances of their predecessors and uphold the fair name which these had won for the Corps.

The Regiment was then photographed, and the men were allowed to inspect the Shield and study the devices carved upon it. Before the Parade was dismissed, the Regiment gave three splendid cheers for Colonel Sir Reginald Hennell, and this was followed by a Royal salute for His Majesty the King-Emperor, the Band playing "God save the King."

INDEX